THE JOURNEY MATTERS

Jonathan Glancey is a much-travelled journalist, author and broadcaster. He has worked on the staff of the *Independent*, the *Guardian* and the *Architectural Review*. His books include *Wings Over Water*, *Concorde: The Rise and Fall of the Supersonic Airliner*, *Harrier*, *Giants of Steam*, *Spitfire: The Biography*, *Lost Buildings*, *Nagaland: A Journey to India's Forgotten Frontier*, *Tornado: 21st Century Steam*, *Architecture: A Visual History* and *London: Bread and Circuses*.

'Glancey combines his passion for the era with an insight into the social and political clouds brewing over the heads of passengers... The joy really is in the minute detail... For anyone with an obsession with the Golden Age of Travel, this will be the first class ticket.' *Wanderlust*

'A thoroughgoing, eloquent corrective to complacency... The historical context is always nicely etched in, but what stands out is the experiential detail... Detailed yet dreamlike.' *Country Life*

'Jonathan Glancey's imaginative work is a reminder that it is often the journey rather than the destination that is the best part of travelling. His book cleverly brings to life various historic settings through the mechanism of transport, with entirely believable scenarios, and each time helpfully brings us up to date.' Christian Wolmar, author of *Railways and the Raj*

'Engrossing and lively... Enchanting' *Steam Railway Magazine*

By the same author

Wings Over Water
Concorde
Harrier
Giants of Steam
Spitfire: The Biography
Nagaland: A Journey to India's Forgotten Frontier
Tornado: 21st Century Steam
Architecture: A Visual History
London: Bread and Circuses

THE
JOURNEY
MATTERS

Twentieth-Century Travel in True Style

JONATHAN GLANCEY

Atlantic Books
London

First published in hardback in Great Britain in 2019 by Atlantic Books,
an imprint of Atlantic Books Ltd.

This paperback edition first published in Great Britain in 2020
by Atlantic Books.

123456789

A CIP catalogue record for this book is available from the British Library.

E-book ISBN: 978-1-78649-417-7
Paperback ISBN: 978-1-78649-418-4

Map artwork by Jeff Edwards

Printed in Denmark

Atlantic Books
An Imprint of Atlantic Books Ltd
Ormond House
26–27 Boswell Street
London
WC1N 3JZ

www.atlantic-books.co.uk

In memory,
Don Pedro

Contents

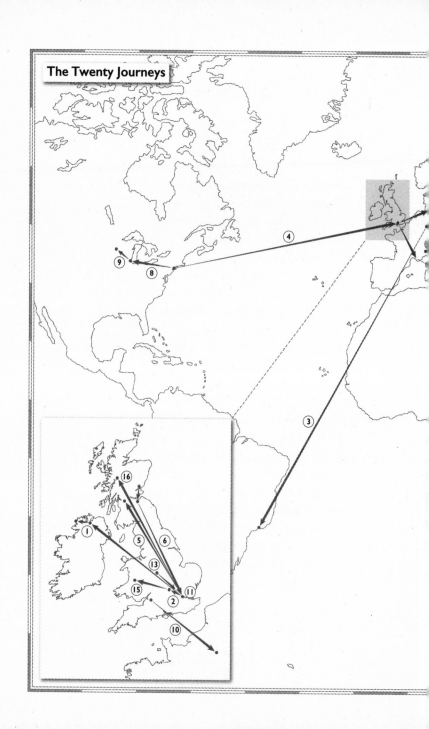

The Twenty Journeys

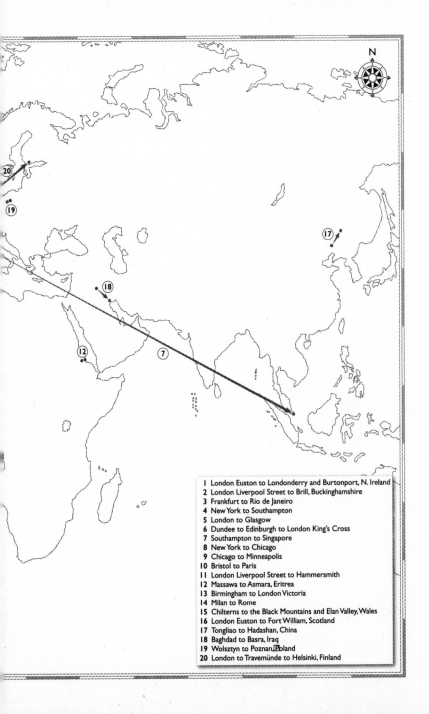

N

1 London Euston to Londonderry and Burtonport, N. Ireland
2 London Liverpool Street to Brill, Buckinghamshire
3 Frankfurt to Rio de Janeiro
4 New York to Southampton
5 London to Glasgow
6 Dundee to Edinburgh to London King's Cross
7 Southampton to Singapore
8 New York to Chicago
9 Chicago to Minneapolis
10 Bristol to Paris
11 London Liverpool Street to Hammersmith
12 Massawa to Asmara, Eritrea
13 Birmingham to London Victoria
14 Milan to Rome
15 Chilterns to the Black Mountains and Elan Valley, Wales
16 London Euston to Fort William, Scotland
17 Tongliao to Hadashan, China
18 Baghdad to Basra, Iraq
19 Wolsztyn to Poznan, Poland
20 London to Travemünde to Helsinki, Finland

Introduction

Boarded and fully booked, United Express Flight 3411 to Louisville, Kentucky, operated by Republic Airways on behalf of the United Airlines subsidiary, was at its gate ready for departure. A sky bully came on board the Embraer 170 jet and said four passengers had to give up their seats. The airline wanted these for its own staff. There were no volunteers, even when a first offer of $400 compensation was raised to $800.

In the end, four passengers were selected by computer to be bumped. Three complied, but the fourth, Dr David Dao – a 69-year-old doctor who was flying back to Kentucky to see patients the following morning – was unwilling to give up his seat. So, instead, he was wrestled from it by three baseball-capped operatives. Dragged unconscious along the aisle, his nose and two of his teeth broken, blood trickling down his face, the doctor was taken off the aircraft. Fellow passengers filmed this malevolent scene on their mobile phones. Videos would go viral on YouTube, although not before Dr Dao had managed to re-board the aircraft. This time, the wounded, concussed and evidently distraught medic was dispatched on a stretcher.

1

Airline staff took their hard-won seats. Flight 3411 departed O'Hare two hours late. A later press statement claimed that the airline had simply been 're-accommodating' passengers, and a leaked internal email said that employees had 'followed established procedures for dealing with situations like this'. Who could think of criticizing United's Oscar Munoz, the very model of a modern airline CEO, with years of experience working for AT&T, Coca-Cola and Pepsi? The previous month, *PRWeek* magazine had named him its 'Communicator of the Year'. He held an MBA degree from Pepperdine University, a devoutly Christian college near Malibu, California.

The following month, United flew more passengers than it had a year earlier. It posted significant gains in passenger miles flown, and recorded the fewest cancellations in its history. The airline's share price hit an all-time high. Warren Buffett, the veteran business magnate and a major investor in airline stocks, told *Fortune* that although United had made a 'terrible mistake' over the Dao affair, the public wanted cheap seats. This meant 'high-load factors' and, for passengers, a 'fair amount of discomfort'.

A gun barrel of online US commentators said, in no uncertain terms, that Dr Dao deserved every injury and humiliation that came his way. How dare he delay other passengers and obstruct an all-American corporation going about its lawful business? As for the assault on the doctor, one of his three assailants, the aviation security officer James Long, felt he had been unfairly dismissed as a result of attempts by United Airlines to placate those Americans, including President Donald Trump, who said its methods had been wrong.

Long took legal action against United Airlines and Chicago's Department of Aviation, claiming that he had not been trained properly in the handling of out-of-line passengers. How was he to know that violence against them was inappropriate and that, in this case, he wasn't following 'established procedures'?

'Drive,' commented one online reader in response to CNN's coverage of the story, 'and, if you cannot, then consider flying in a cramped seat with surly airline employees treating you like animal-cargo.'

When anyone complains, they are reminded – whether by Warren Buffett or fellow travellers – that they cannot expect commercial flight to be as it was in the days of silver service, adequate legroom and well-spoken, Grace Kelly–lookalike stewardesses with impeccable manners.

What has changed is the way in which, as perceived by the majority of passengers, airlines have abandoned, along with common decency, any notion of the romance or poetry of flight. For Michael O'Leary, the never-less-than-controversial CEO of the European budget airline Ryanair, passengers are in cahoots with this change: 'Most people just want to get from A to B. You don't want to pay £500 for a flight. You want to spend that money on a nice hotel, apartment or restaurant... you don't want to piss it all away at the airport or on the airline.' Of Ryanair, he says: 'Anyone who thinks [our] flights are some sort of bastion of sanctity where you can contemplate your navel is wrong. We already bombard you with as many in-flight announcements and trolleys as we can. Anyone who looks like sleeping, we wake them up to sell them things.'

For O'Leary, the romance of flight has long been in the grave, where it deserves to rot. 'Air transport,' he told BusinessWeek Online in 2002, 'is just a glorified bus operation.' As Alfred E. Kahn, the American economist who became known as the 'father of airline deregulation', had said a quarter of a century before: 'I really don't know one plane from the other. To me they are just marginal costs with wings.'

Robert L. Crandall, the president and CEO of American Airlines from 1985 to 1998 and a fierce critic of deregulation, called the airline industry 'a nasty, rotten business'. And Al Gore, back when he was vice president of the United States, stated: 'Airplane travel is nature's way of making you look like your passport photo.'

If they (or their employers) can afford it, passengers can, of course, fly in anodyne, faux-posh first class. And yet, to echo O'Leary's thinking, who – unless they are travelling on expenses – would want to fritter away thousands of pounds on a first-class ticket now that the very concept of 'first class' no longer means what it did in decades gone by?

On and off, for more than a decade, I have ridden Liverpool Street to Norwich expresses. These trains have long been busy, to the point in recent years where standard-class passengers who are paying through their noses are forced to stand for long distances. When supplementary fares were available on weekdays, I'd 'upgrade' to first class.

It wasn't so many years ago that these trains offered breakfast, dinner, lunch and tea. Paper tablecloths might have replaced linen at the beginning of the twenty-first century, and silver cutlery may have been a thing of the distant past, and yet there was still something of a half-remembered air of first-class travel in these East Anglian dining cars. By the second decade of the century, the restaurant cars had gone. And so what on earth – or in Greater Anglia – was the point of first class?

When I lived in the Scottish Highlands, I'd drive south to Inverness to take the Caledonian Sleeper to London. The sleepers were time-worn, yet clean and well maintained. The Scottish stewards were cheerful. The bar car was fun, with a varying cast over the seasons of MPs and lairds, fishermen, artists and writers, doctors, lawyers, engineers, oil riggers, architects, and American and Japanese tourists. Although not first class in a contemporary 'top celebrity VIP' manner, the *Caledonian Sleeper* had the charm and elan of a less-bullish era.

But while waiting at Euston for the staff of the return *Caledonian Sleeper* to let waifs and strays like me on board, the best option was always to perch on a luggage trolley or lean against a column on the bare concrete platform and read. Even on the coldest winter evening, that utilitarian platform was – to me at least – more first class than the Hieronymus Bosch-style 'First-Class Lounge'.

Many of the journeys I've made in Britain and around the world have been by penny-plain and matter-of-fact boats, trains, planes, taxis and hire cars. By foot and on bicycle, too. It hasn't mattered that a train or ferry has been spartan, if the scenery, people, weather or occasion itself has been special. These, though, have been very different journeys to those made by forms of transport in which passengers are synonymous with cargo, and when our sole interest appears to be to get from A to B as cheaply and as quickly as possible.

One of my favourite books since I first read it in a public library as a child – I then bought a second-hand copy in a

5

Brooklyn bookstore years later – is Charles Small's *Far Wheels*. Published in 1955, it evokes the steam railway journeys that Small made while working for the American oil industry in the Congo (the Chemins de fer du Kivu, 'a 60-mile narrow gauge streak of rust'), Madagascar, Mozambique, Fiji, Jamaica, the backwaters of Japan and blazing East Africa.

I have wanted every place I have been to – whether the Aleutian Islands or Zennor, Doncaster or Dimapur, Lecce or Llandrindod Wells, Zapopan or Arnos Grove – to be particular and special. Far too much twenty-first-century travel is homogenous in character. It is now possible to travel more or less around the world by more or less identical Boeing or Airbus jets from one more or less identical airport to another, to stay at the same chain hotels, and to ride the same high-speed trains on dedicated tracks – as travel by picturesque regional railways declines – and to eat identical food at the same chain restaurants while wearing the same clothes as pretty much everyone else.

I mentioned the East Anglian main line from Liverpool Street to Norwich. From 2019, its express services have been run not by individual class 90 electric locomotives and their trains of British Rail Mark 3 coaches, but by flavourless – if hopefully efficient – electric multiple units. What I'll lament when I use these trains is not so much the fact that, in terms of rolling stock, an old order is yielding to new – all things must pass – but a further loss of a regional identity. In recent years I have been spun down this line by trains pulled by *Sir John Betjeman* – former Poet Laureate, champion of railway heritage and once an assistant editor at the *Architectural Review* – as well as *Vice*

Admiral Lord Nelson, Royal Anglian Regiment, Colchester Castle and *Raedwald of East Anglia.*

Some time in 2016, *Raedwald of East Anglia* – named after the seventh-century Saxon king buried in the ghost of the longship excavated at Sutton Hoo in 1939 – returned from overhaul without its nameplate. When I asked passengers waiting for an express train at Ipswich station one morning if they were sorry that *Raedwald of East Anglia*'s name had gone missing, most, even if friendly, looked at me blankly. No one I spoke to had noticed. Many had no idea the locomotives had names.

The stories in this book begin in the 1930s, because it was this decade that saw transport raised from a service and engineering skill to something of an art in every which way, from the design of the machines themselves to the posters, promotional films, and associated poetry, architecture and music. The 1930s are commonly thought of as the 'Golden Age of Travel'.

But later decades offered journeys that have mattered, too. They exist today for all classes of travellers on board Japan's latest bullet trains, which get better by the decade; for those living on the outskirts of Dresden in Germany, who are served on the way to work or school by characterful narrow-gauge steam railways; and for those who ride the 1930s trams that are still very much a part of the streetscape and civic culture of fashion-conscious Milan.

Aside from its clarion call – all journeys should be special; all journeys should truly matter – this is a book for those who want to know what journeys by the great ocean liners, airships, express trains and airliners were like in decades beyond our reach. It is a book, too, for those in search of the world's most romantic transport byways, from the Atlantic coast of Donegal to the Red Sea port of Massawa. It shows, I hope – and despite insistent propaganda to the contrary – that not only is the journey far more than a way of getting from A to B, but that today, as it has been in the past, it can be a more rewarding experience than either the point of departure or arrival.

What was it really like to take the LNER's Art Deco *Coronation* streamliner from Edinburgh to King's Cross; to cross the Atlantic by SS *Normandie*; to fly with Imperial Airways from Southampton to Singapore; to steam from Manhattan to Chicago on board the New York Central's *20th Century Limited*; or to dine and sleep aboard the *Graf Zeppelin* airship? What did people eat and drink? What did they wear? How did they behave? What were their expectations? How safe were they? What did these journeys sound like? How did they smell? And what about washrooms and lavatories?

Recreating these journeys allows me to explore the history of routes taken and the events – social and political – enveloping them, and to find out what has happened to them since. This book contains the stories of the machines that made these journeys possible, of the people who shaped them, and of those passengers, too, who played key roles in modern history – like Le Corbusier, who flew to Rio on *Graf Zeppelin* to forge the transatlantic link between European and nascent Latin American Modernism.

The journeys I have written about fall within the period 1932 to 2005. I have connected them to specific dates and told their stories in the first person. The final five journeys are those I have made in real life. The 15 twentieth-century journeys are those that I have dreamed of making, and I have written them as if I had made them myself. I have often lulled myself to sleep in strange hotels, or when my mind is overactive, by imagining what it must have been like to ride the *Coronation Scot* from London to Glasgow in the late 1930s – from the bus, Underground or taxi ride to Euston and that terminus's famous Doric arch and Great Hall, to the train itself. What would the food served in the restaurant car have been like, and what about my fellow passengers? What would I have seen from the train's windows as I travelled through a countryside still farmed by horses and steam traction engines, between fleeting glimpses of smokestacks and coal yards and factories? And what of Shap Fell, free of the scourge of the M6 barging its impolite way alongside the railway; and of the arrival in pre-war Glasgow, where mighty factories built locomotives for export around the world, and shipyards, mightier still, welded and riveted the freighters – alongside opulent ocean liners – that took them there?

I cannot be sure, of course, of who exactly I would have been had I been born shortly before the outbreak of the First World War, although I have a feeling that one way or another my historic persona might well have been involved in the development of military aircraft between the wars, fought in the Second World War, and then led a busy life as the economies of the free world boomed and new technologies offered journeys to the Moon and looked to the stars.

Although certain ways of seeing the world – along with language, dress, measurements and manners – have changed since this past self rode the *Coronation Scot* and flew on *Graf*

Zeppelin from Germany to Brazil in the 1930s, his enthusiasms are very much my own. I have tried, as far as possible, to avoid hindsight, so that the narrator can only ever have an inkling of what the future might hold as he journeys through Europe, Asia and the Americas, during eras of both optimism and nagging fear.

My narrator shares journeys with characters drawn from my imagination. He also meets real people – I have tried to imagine what it might have been like for example to meet the American industrial artist Henry Dreyfuss on board the peerless *20th Century Limited*, for instance, and I have brought historical characters onto trains and planes and airships who may or may not have been on that exact trip at that precise time. They allow me to explain more fully why certain journeys mattered technically, socially, aesthetically, commercially and politically.

There are many other journeys I have dreamed of making – and, equally, many more I have taken and plan to go on. But, if told here, they would burst the finite boundaries of a book as they raced out to all points of the compass, in plumes of steam and vapour trails, the surge of spirited machines 'coming on cam', and the steady pulse of ships' engines under skies near and far.

*

NB: I use metric measurements only when an Englishman of the times would have.

ONE

Londonderry to Burtonport: Londonderry and Lough Swilly Railway

4th–6th October 1932

China has been all the vogue this year. *Shanghai Express*, starring Marlene Dietrich, set the pace in the popular imagination, while my fellow undergraduates Alec and Archie have just returned from a summer in Manchuria, which is pretty daring of them, not least because the Japs have created a puppet state there they call Manchukuo. I learn of Alec and Archie's adventure over a teatime meal in Soho at the Shanghai Restaurant on Greek Street. Over plates of crab fried rice and what the menu calls *chup suey*, washed down with a bottle of rice wine and pots of oolong tea, we wonder if any of us has been anywhere more exotic than Manchuria.

'Well, I'm off to Burtonport tonight,' I say.

'Where they brew Burton beers? Sounds very exotic,' snorts Archie.

'No. Burtonport, a fishing village on the far Atlantic coast of Donegal, the last stop on the Londonderry and Lough Swilly Railway.'

Between us, we know countries as far flung as India, Ceylon

and China, yet agree that surely nowhere could possibly be more exotic than Burtonport, and that I am to report back its wonders over Guinness and Jameson.

I walk up to Euston only just in time to board the Stranraer sleeper. By chance – or good luck – I have a third-class berth to myself, in a comfortable former London and North Western Railway 12-wheeled sleeping car. Even though we set off just before 8 p.m., I am fast asleep soon after the gently swaying train has passed Watford, and only wake up when we pull into Carlisle in the early hours of the morning. Keen to find out which locomotive has taken me this far, I slip my coat over my pyjamas and my bare feet into brogues, and walk between pools of lamplight and wafts of steam from the train's heating pipes towards the bulldog silhouette of 6122 *Royal Ulster Riflemen*. Built five years ago at the North British Locomotive Works in Glasgow, this is one of the London Midland and Scottish Railway's (LMS) powerful Royal Scot 4-6-0s. Her large boiler, crowned with the squattest of chimneys, gives her a truly massive, hunched-up appearance.

If he had been able to get his own way, Henry Fowler, chief mechanical engineer of the LMS would have built a longer – if only slightly leaner – class of four-cylinder compound Pacifics, based on the latest French practice, instead of the three-cylinder Royal Scots. Fowler's Pacific, which never got beyond the drawing board, was seen by management as being too expensive a proposition, and probably a little too exotic for the conservative tastes of Derby works. The Royal Scots were built instead, and in a rush, by North British – in association with Herbert Chambers, the chief draughtsman at

Derby. They might not be Pacifics – nor, I gather, as efficient as the latest French compounds – but the Royal Scots are potent and reliable machines.

As *Royal Ulster Rifleman* steams away to be serviced at Upperby shed, I watch a pair of smaller locomotives, coupled together, backing towards the sleeper. The train engine is 40936, a brand-new LMS 4P class compound 4-4-0 – resplendent, like *Royal Ulster Rifleman*, in gold-lined crimson lake paintwork. The compound's pilot, in the same livery, is an engine new and exotic to me: 14672, a lithe and handsome 4-6-0. Her works plate tells me she was built in 1911 by North British, for the Glasgow and South Western Railway. I have to ask her driver, amused to see me on the platform at this unsocial hour, what this elegant engine is. One of Mr James Manson's express locos, this is her last month in service. The engine is in fine shape, but the LMS is standardizing its fleet.

Unable to get back to sleep, I open the ventilator above my window to listen to the locomotives as they pound north-west from Carlisle, over the border and on through Dumfries, Castle Douglas and Newton Stewart, on the undulating line to Stranraer, 73 miles away, where we pull in at 6 a.m. The ferry across the Irish Sea to Larne is berthed right alongside us. On the platform I observe my fellow passengers. They include a sizeable contingent of what must surely be businessmen, politicians and civil servants, some hanging on to their hats and dignity as the wind scudding across Loch Ryan blows away morning cobwebs and English trilbies and bowlers. This is the shortest of the Irish Sea crossings – just 45 miles and two and a half hours – and much the favourite for those lacking sea legs.

Our ship is the handsome new *Princess Margaret* named after the younger daughter of the Duke and Duchess of York. I have details of her – the ferry, that is – in my bag. Here they are. Built by William Denny of Dumbarton for the LMS and launched last year, she weighs 2,523 tons and can carry 1,250 first- and third-class passengers, 236 cattle, 37 horses and a sizeable amount of cargo. I think the cattle must come from Ireland as I don't see any boarding here at Stranraer. No horses either. *Princess Margaret*, I read, is powered by a pair of Parsons steam turbines producing a combined 7,462 shaft horsepower at 269 rpm. Her top speed is 21½ knots.

I make my way to the cafeteria for breakfast, as members of parliament and officer ranks of the Civil Service remain tucked discreetly behind the doors of their first-class cabins. We slip anchor at 7 o'clock – sunrise – steaming smoothly from the loch. On deck, I listen to the stern hiss of water along the sides of the ship as she cuts into the Irish Sea. At her stern, I watch water churned into furious channels of foam and spray.

I find myself inwardly singing along with Bing Crosby's 'Where the Blue of the Night (Meets the Gold of the Day)', which somehow segues into Duke Ellington's 'It Don't Mean a Thing (If It Ain't Got That Swing)'. The sea certainly swings, turning decidedly choppy. I retreat to the dining room. A well-dressed, unfazed English family at the next table tucks into an ambitious breakfast. The son is engrossed, between mouthfuls of scrambled egg and bacon, by the latest copy of *The Magnet*, and its slightly incongruous stories of Billy Bunter on the one spread and exotic travels through the empire on the next. I can't help noticing that the cover features an illustration of the

Great Western Railway's *Cheltenham Flyer*, the world's fastest scheduled train.

His sister is reading *The Girl's Own Paper*, and their mother, dressed in well-cut tweeds, lights a cigarette. On the table, she has a copy of *Cold Comfort Farm* by Stella Gibbons, a novel published last month that's said to be very funny. If I hadn't fallen asleep, my own reading for the Stranraer boat train was to have been Freeman Wills Crofts' *Sir John McGill's Last Journey*, the story of a Northern Irish industrialist murdered, apparently, on the Stranraer sleeper. A part of the attraction, for me, is that Crofts is a retired civil engineer with the NCC (Northern Counties Committee, the Northern Irish division of the LMS) turned detective fiction writer.

I very much enjoy bobbing about on water, but Stranraer and our Charlie Chaplin's *Gold Rush*–style meal, our plates sliding from one side of the table to the other, are soon memories as we head into harbour at the head of Lough Larne. Out on deck, I can see gulls screaming, terns wheeling and cormorants skimming across the waters. I glimpse emerald fields over the rooftops of terraced dockside houses, as well as railway yards, cranes, warehouses and squat, glum-looking churches.

And there, on the other side of the NCC tracks for Belfast, is, to my English eyes, a wonderfully exotic sight. A purposeful 2-4-2T narrow-gauge tank engine, crimson lake liveried, is waiting at the head of a train of three corridor-connected coaches that look like the latest LMS main-line designs shrunk to fit the NCC's narrow-gauge lines. I beetle down to this train from *Princess Margaret* as quickly as I can, as do those few businessmen and civil servants not heading for Belfast, and the English family.

What a fine and unexpected train this turns out to be. Aside from its compelling engine, 104 – a two-cylinder compound designed by Bowman Malcolm, locomotive superintendent of the Belfast and Northern Counties Railway and built at York Road, Belfast in 1920 – it is very smart indeed. The four-year-old carriages boast steam heating, plush upholstery, and lavatories, too.

This is the Ballymena and Larne boat train. With three stops along the 3-foot gauge line, we're scheduled to run the 25 miles to the junction for Londonderry at Ballymena in 64 minutes. While the *Cheltenham Flyer* takes only a minute longer to run the 77 miles from Swindon to Paddington, the narrow-gauge Irish train is not slow considering the terrain. After easing our way around the harbour and then away from the stop at Larne Town, 104 gets quickly into her efficient compound stride. The first 12 miles of the trip prove to be an arduous climb through beautiful green farmland fringed with purple hills with gradients as steep as 1-in-36. We crest the ascent at Ballynashee, 600 feet above sea level.

Accelerating rapidly, we are now running at over 30 mph as we head south-west to Kells – and, from there, north at a clip to Ballymena, where we join the main line from Belfast to Londonderry. At Ballymena, our driver tells me that we're lucky to have 104 on the run today. The boat train is very often in the hands of one of the ungainly Atlantic tanks built by Kitson & Co. of Leeds in 1908. Nominally more powerful than the compounds, these are prone to slipping – making something of a misery of the long climb up from Larne in wet weather, which is commonplace here, of course. One of these 4-4-2 tanks is at work shunting a string of goods wagons while we chat. The rest of the compounds run the Ballycastle to Ballymoney line further north. 'But,' says the driver, 'we'd sure like them back on the Ballymena.'

I can't help noticing that the English children waiting on the Londonderry main-line platform are eating Mars Bars, a new tuppenny chocolate bar made in a factory in Slough passed every day, at speed, by the *Cheltenham Flyer*. But here comes our Derry flyer heading into Ballymena station, a smart seven-coach corridor train led by a brightly polished NCC 4-4-0. This is U2 class No. 74 *Dunluce Castle*, one of the 'Scotch engines' built in 1924 by North British of Glasgow. She is clearly modelled on a Midland or LMS 2P 4-4-0, although William Kelly Wallace, locomotive engineer and civil engineer of the NCC from 1922, supervised the design. Only recently, Mr Wallace introduced colour light signalling – the first in Ireland – at Belfast York Road, the terminus from which *Dunluce Castle* departed earlier this morning.

The other thing I can't help noticing is the width of the NCC track. Irish main lines adopted the 5-foot, 3-inch gauge, rather than the standard 4-foot, 8½-inch mainland gauge. I find this particularly interesting because I attended a lecture in Oxford earlier this year given by a Harvard archaeologist who has been researching the paved and grooved trackway the ancient Greeks engineered across the Isthmus of Corinth in around 600 BC. This trackway enabled ships, and perhaps even fighting triremes, to be pulled for five miles overland between the Ionian and Aegean seas, saving a great deal of time. This early form of railway was in use for 650 years, and Aristophanes refers to it in his comedy *Lysistrata*. The distance between the grooved tracks was exactly 5 feet, 3 inches. Irish railways have a classical pedigree.

The Londonderry train gets into a 60 mph stride before stopping at Ballymoney, where I lean out of the window to watch a pair of 3-foot-gauge S class compound 2-4-2Ts at work. Our next stop is Coleraine, where passengers can change for Portrush and the Giant's Causeway Tramway. I would do so if I had another week in hand, but exotic Burtonport calls, and it's still a long way off. It's midday now as we cross the River Bann, and, as if by sleight of hand, the scenery changes from the engagingly bucolic to the stirringly romantic. It's as if the poet Coleridge were in charge of the landscaping. Skirting the left bank of the Bann, we steam towards Castlerock and between the two tunnels – the longest in Ireland – passing below and through the former estate of the eighteenth-century Lord Bishop of Derry, the Suffolk-born Frederick Hervey, Earl of Bristol.

Between the tunnels, I stretch my neck up to see the Mussenden Temple, an exquisite classical rotunda overlooking the North Atlantic. I know from my interest in architecture that its design is based on Bramante's Tempietto in Rome, itself based on the Temple of Vesta at Tivoli, which I cycled to along the Via Appia only last year. The architect of Bristol's Irish *tempietto* was most probably Michael Shanahan, who accompanied the eccentric and philanthropic earl on at least one of his many visits to Italy.

The *tempietto* is, in fact, a library, commissioned in 1783 as a wedding present to Bristol's favourite cousin, Frideswide Bruce, who married Daniel Mussenden, an elderly London banker. Said to be Bristol's lover, she died in 1785. The inscription around the building, which I know – but cannot possibly see, of course, from the train at 30 mph – reads:

Suave, mari magno turbantibus aequora ventis
e terra magnum alterius spectare laborem
['Tis pleasant, safely to behold from shore
The troubled sailor, and hear tempests roar]

I know, from Latin classes at school, that this is a quote from Lucretius's *De Rerum Natura*, but what it means here on the Atlantic coast of Ulster, I have no idea.

We canter down to the white sand beaches of Benone Strand, our track right by the rolling, white-horse ocean – I see either dolphins or porpoises revelling in the swell of the sea – and with the long looming crags of Binevenagh Mountain shadowing our progress inland.

Cutting off Mulligan Point, we lope past Bellarena station and find ourselves alongside water again, crossing a bridge over the River Roe and skirting Lough Foyle. On through farmland, we rumble over a further bridge across the River Faughan, and – following the curves of the banks of the River Foyle into Londonderry – come to a stand under the glazed roof of the NCC's Waterside station, a sandstone building designed, my notebook tells me, by John Lanyon, a prolific railway architect and engineer. Dominated by a muscular Italianate clock tower, it opened in 1875.

Now my naivety shows. I have come this far, and without lunch, without knowing where the Londonderry and Lough Swilly Railway terminus is, nor the times of trains to Burtonport. I ask at the stationmaster's office. There is an afternoon train to Burtonport, I'm told, leaving at 4.45 p.m. The Swilly's Graving Dock terminus is a mile or more's walk north, on the other side of the Foyle. The timetable says it arrives in Burtonport at 9.20 p.m., but what with uncertain weather and wagons to shunt on the way, it could well be a little later. As the sun sets at 7 p.m. at this time of year, I realize this will mean at least two and a half hours in gloaming and then darkness.

'And, you should know, there's no lighting or heating on the Swilly trains.'

This sudden Home Counties accent belongs to the well-dressed mother who, with her children, has come to Londonderry on the same trains and boat as me. 'It's a rather beautiful trip in the summer, but eventful at other times of year,' she continues.

I introduce myself and ask if she and her children are off to Burtonport, too.

'No. Creeslough. We stay at the Rosapenna Hotel. It's where my husband insists on going whenever he's back from India. He fishes for salmon and plays golf there to unwind, and we all like the sandy beaches nearby. The children have permission to be out of school to see their father.'

'Army?' I ask.

'No. Architect. Working on New Delhi. Inaugurated last year, of course, but the work goes on. Anyway, I wouldn't advise the afternoon Burtonport. It could well be late. We'd arrive in the dark and it's been a long trip from Surrey for the children. The morning train leaves at 7.30, so it'd be best to stay the night here.'

If any of us was sufficiently determined, we could be in Burtonport tonight – and, all going well on the Swilly, in just a little over 24 hours from Euston.

'I've booked two rooms at the Metropole on Foyle Street on the other side of the bridge. You're welcome to have one of them. I can always share with the children.' It's a more-than-generous offer. 'If you plan to wander around town, I can take your bag on to the hotel. Why not meet us for supper at seven?'

Tucking away a cheese and pickle sandwich and a strong cup of tea in Waterside station's refreshment room, I find myself with an afternoon to spare in this busy town split in two by the dark and fast-flowing Foyle. Remembering that another of Ireland's narrow-gauge railways, the County Donegal, runs trains from the city, I ask where the station is only to find that Victoria Road is just a few minutes' walk south of Waterside. Looking out for a small red-brick station building, I spot a black main-line locomotive steaming slowly along with a rake of coaches on the other side of the river. This, I think, must be a Great Northern train from Dublin. What a railway mecca Derry is proving to be, with four terminuses – three within easy walking distance – served by four railways, two of them narrow-gauge.

Victoria Road is a modest yet well-designed and neatly built station, reached from the road through a sloping timber and glass-covered walkway. Its architect was James Barton, a long-lived engineer who was educated at Trinity College, Dublin, and devoted much time in his busy career plotting a railway tunnel under the Irish Sea between Larne and somewhere in Scotland.

Stranraer, perhaps. If he had succeeded, trains would have run directly all the way from Belfast via Glasgow and London.

Serving two tracks, the Victoria Road platform is half enclosed by an iron, glass and timber canopy adorned with decorative mouldings and revealing stirring views along the Foyle. The County Donegal timetable promises a train to Strabane, 14½ miles and just over an hour away, at 2 p.m. I book a return ticket. And here she comes now, backing into the platform – three oil wagons and one, two, three red-and-cream eight-wheeled coaches. The locomotive is a handsome black 2-6-4T, No. 20 *Raphoe*, built, says the plate on her side, by Nasmyth Wilson & Co., Patricroft, Manchester, 1907.

I ask *Raphoe*'s driver about the locomotive and train as he oils her Walschaerts valve gear.

'Raphoe. Well, it's a town in Donegal with a castle and a stone circle they say is older than Stonehenge. This is a class 5 tank. She's a darling to be sure. The oil wagons? They're for the fishing fleet at Killybegs, the biggest fishing port in all of Ireland. We drop them off at Strabane, and another Donegal train takes them on to Killybegs itself. A long way? Seventy miles and more.'

My keenness earns me a footplate ride – but not from Victoria Road, where I would be seen by a railway official. 'Come up at New Buildings. It's the first stop.'

A bustle of housewives weighed down with shopping crowds into the narrow-gauge carriages, and with the wave of a flag and the shriek of a whistle, we accelerate out of the terminus and rattle along the banks of the Foyle to New Buildings, by which time Derry has disappeared from view. At the station, I'm up from my wooden seat and on *Raphoe*'s footplate quicker than anyone can say Jack Robinson. Luckily for me, the cab is polished and as clean as a steam locomotive can be. With steam pressure at 175 pounds per square inch and her safety valves beginning to lift, *Raphoe* is off again, rocking gently as we nudge over what must be 30 mph along a track sewed neatly between rolling fields and pastures.

We whistle for Desertstone Halt ('Stops when required'), our call answered only by a brittle chorus of circling jackdaws, and trot on through countryside that appears idyllic, although I have no idea how the Depression has affected these parts. I say to the crew that Donegal is a beautiful part of the world. 'It is indeed,' replies Michael, the fireman, 'but this is Tyrone. A funny thing it is, to be sure, but Donegal's on the other side of the river. But we'll get there by and by.'

We do. All too soon, I swap the footplate of *Raphoe* at Ballymagorry for a busy carriage, all chatter and laughter. Ten minutes later we rumble over the Great Northern main line from Derry to Enniskillen, cross the River Mourne and draw into Strabane under lowering clouds. What a remarkably active station it is, with a host of red tank engines in steam and trains for distant Letterkenny, Glenties, Donegal, Killybegs and Ballyshannon. The County Donegal, I've been told, is the most extensive narrow-gauge railway in the British Isles, with, I think, lines extending to 124½ miles – 110 of them in Donegal. The county itself is across the border in the Irish Republic, just beyond Strabane station.

I'd love to explore further, for the County Donegal is evidently an extraordinary thing, a busy rail system far removed from the lonely little railways of Wales I explored last year – and, I don't doubt, very different from my holy grail, the Burtonport extension of the Londonderry and Lough Swilly. I have just 20 minutes to enjoy this narrow-gauge cornucopia, complete with a curious new diesel railcar growling out for Glenties, before *Raphoe* is whistling up passengers for the return 3.30 p.m. to Derry. Rather than oil tankers, we have four goods wagons in tow, stacked with all sorts of Donegal produce bound for Londonderry.

It's raining as I leave Victoria Road back in Londonderry and scurry across the Carlisle Bridge, an impressive iron-framed affair from the early 1860s. It has road traffic above and railway tracks below, for the transfer of wagons between the Great Northern and NCC. On the far side of the bridge is Foyle Road station, a squat brick building with arched windows and openings, and what appear to be papal emblems on the peaks of its twin towers. I stop under the entrance arch to check my architectural notes. The station was designed in 1870 by a Mr Richard Williamson, surveyor and engineer, who had teamed up some years earlier with the Glaswegian architect Thomas Turner. In April 1874, Mr Williamson went to London to give evidence to the House of Lords on the Londonderry Port and Harbour Bill. Drenched on the Steam Packet crossing to Fleetwood in Lancashire, he developed bronchitis and died that month at Euston station's Victoria Hotel.

Out on the platform, I'm rewarded with the cheering sight of two brightly polished black Great Northern locomotives. One is 198 – one of the mixed-traffic U class 4-4-0s built in 1915 by Beyer Peacock of Manchester – at the head of a stopping train for Enniskillen. The other, simmering quietly alone on the opposite platform, is a brand-new three-cylinder compound express passenger V class 4-4-0, No. 85 *Merlin*. This impressive new engine has been built for fast trains between Dublin and Belfast. Perhaps she's here on a diplomatic mission, touring the Great Northern. Officially, she's too big for the line. The crew must be taking tea. I step gingerly onto her footplate, noting the boiler pressure gauge's redline of 250 pounds per square inch, the same high figure as an LMS Royal Scot.

Both Irish locomotives are designs by Colonel George Tertius Glover, locomotive engineer of the Great Northern. I'd dearly like to see more of them, especially in a colour other than black, but it's 5 p.m. now and I must get to the Metropole and bathe before supper.

My high-ceilinged room is on the first floor of this grand classical building. A small ironwork balcony offers views up and down the teeming street. Washed and groomed, I join my friends in the dining room.

Over cutlets, I explain why I've come in search of Burtonport, and how Archie, Alec and I agreed that it must surely be a more exotic location than Manchuria. Mrs Moore, it turns out, is related – as are Archie and Alec – to Lord Lytton, the former governor of Bengal, who went out to Manchuria recently to report for the League of Nations on Japanese aggression there. So we have much to talk about, and even more when Mrs Moore proves to be related to Sir Edwin Lutyens, architect of New Delhi. I plan to go there next year after finals.

Mrs Moore is quite the exotic herself. She's taken up flying lessons and says, apropos of Derry, that only this May the American aviatrix, Amelia Earhart, landed in a field at Culmore

– just north of the city, on the banks of the Foyle – at the end of her record-breaking transatlantic solo flight at the controls of a high-winged Lockheed Vega 5B.

'She was hoping for Paris, like Lindbergh,' says Mrs Moore over a nightcap, as her children, Maude and Philip, play round after round of Snakes and Ladders. 'Must have been low on fuel. She'd certainly have got a better meal there.'

I'm keen on airplanes, too, and plan to spend time at aerodromes once free of the groves of academe. We imagine how, one day, we'll be able to cross the Atlantic in 'airliners', all cocktails and silver service, and how very slow the epic journey to Swilly will seem. We retire early, as we'll need to be up and about early for the Burtonport train.

The hotel packs us a picnic breakfast and lunch, complete with a Bakelite Thermos flask filled with hot tea. Until 1919, a horse tram ran from Foyle Road station to the Swilly's Graving Dock terminus. I choose to walk. The hotelier drives Mrs Moore, Maude and Philip there in a polished Austin 12. As I walk, I'm savouring the moment.

I've read enough about the Swilly to know that the 50-mile Burtonport extension is widely considered something of a white elephant. Opened as recently as 1903 with government help in order to provide employment in the 'congested areas' where poverty and large families have conspired against a decent life – the lack of which has prompted further emigration to America – its main goal and final destination was the fishing port at Burtonport. A railway would bring fresh fish to Londonderry, and on to London restaurants. The wild landscape, though, meant that there was never going to be an easy way for the line to reach the fishing port on the Atlantic coast. It makes its way across a largely uninhabited landscape, with stations sited miles from the villages they purport to serve. Over the past three decades, money has been tight, and the operation, it's said, is run on the proverbial shoestring.

My first sight of Graving Dock terminus, under a low-hanging and drizzly sky, appears to confirm the rumour. I almost mistook it for some rundown mechanic's workshop. Inside, its two dingy platforms are set between rough-hewn walls. Busy, though. On one platform is our train, comprising four grey compartment carriages mounted on twin bogies, with the same number of four-wheeled wagons behind them. On the other is a five-coach passenger train sitting behind a glossy black and well-proportioned 4-6-2 tank engine: No. 10, built by Kerr, Stuart & Co. of Stoke-on-Trent, the company Mr Mitchell, designer of last year's world airspeed record-breaker, the Supermarine S.6B, was apprenticed to before taking off from Stoke to Southampton, to the sea and the skies. The train is the 7.15 to Buncrana and then Carndonagh, a seaside town on the Inishowen peninsula popular in summer.

As No. 10 steams away from the claustrophobic station, which a porter tells me was built as a goods shed in the early 1880s, Mrs Moore, Maude and Philip come down the platform looking for a first-class compartment. 'We're going up in the world today,' says Mrs Moore. 'It's a long trip, and I was told that third class is wooden seats only.' We peer inside the grey coaches. Third class is indeed very basic. 'Like grooms' quarters on a Southern Railway horsebox,' she says.

First class boasts faded upholstery. It looks dusty.

As we weigh up the delights of these pallid carriages with their matchwood flanks, a second glossy black locomotive backs down to join our train. We all march up to see her, a magnificent 4-8-0 tender engine. It's No. 12, built by Hudswell, Clarke & Co. of Leeds in 1905, her side rods picked out in red. We clamber aboard the train as last-minute packages and post are shut into the vans.

'NEXT TO SAFETY', reads a slogan on the platform timetable opposite our window, 'PUNCTUAL RUNNING OF TRAINS IS MOST IMPORTANT'. On the dot of 7.15 a.m., we pull slowly away from Graving Dock and cross a road at the statutory 8 mph indicated by a trackside sign, where I catch sight of the railway's extensive Pennyburn works. Sliding down the window on its leather holding strap, I lean out to gawp at one of the Swilly's imposing 4-8-4 tank engines, said to be the most powerful locomotives at work on narrow-gauge railways in the British Isles. I must invest in a camera. I wonder how much the new 35mm Leica costs?

The driver opens up the big 4-8-0. We head across marshy country to the border post at Bridge End. We stop, but only very briefly, as if passed through with a nod and a wink. We stop again just over a mile away, to pick up post and a solitary passenger at the tiny village of Burnfoot, before threading slowly along a bank to a station set between the Skeoge and Burnfoot rivers. Inaccessible by road, this is Tooban Junction. Buncrana and Carndonagh trains heading north branch off here, while we swing south-west.

Just inland from Drongawn Lough, an Irish fjord off Lough

Swilly – all deep water, swans and greylag geese – we climb a 1-in-49 grade through a deep embankment to a stop at Carrowen. My railway map of Great Britain and Northern Ireland shows gradients along the line. Mrs Moore is amused.

Along a causeway we cross one of Lough Swilly's shallow bays before climbing again to Newtowncunningham. It's ten past eight. We've averaged just under 20 mph for this first 12 miles.

With the luxury of a five-minute stop, we investigate our hamper. The strong tea is good, as are hard-boiled egg and ham sandwiches, the soda bread generously spread with creamy butter. There's a creamery, Lagan's, at our next stop – Sallybrook, where another wagon is attached to our train. For the next 10 minutes, we writhe north then west through salt flats and mud banks along where Lough Swilly meets the River Swilly. We pick up speed down the 1-in-50 gradient towards Letterkenny, Donegal's largest town, bucking along at what must be 35 mph.

Here I watch a County Donegal train behind a red 2-6-4 tank engine impatient for Strabane. Maude and Philip prolong breakfast while No. 12's tender is is topped up with water. A party of black-clad priests and seminarians joins us as another wagon is attached to our train. I know Letterkenny most of all as the place where in 1798 the Irish Revolutionary Wolfe Tone was arrested and then died in unrecorded circumstances after his failed invasion that was supported by 3,000 of Napoleon's soldiers. The Royal Navy intercepted the French fleet at Buncrana, and that was the end of that.

I know Wolfe Tone's name from the poem 'September 1913' by W. B. Yeats, which first appeared in the *Irish Times* and was read to us at school, 15 years later, by our English master, Mr Lawrence.

'Can you still recite it?' asks Mrs Moore.

What need you, being come to sense,
But fumble in a greasy till
And add the halfpence to the pence
And prayer to shivering prayer, until
You have dried the marrow from the bone?
For men were born to pray and save:
Romantic Ireland's dead and gone —
It's with O'Leary in the grave.

And then, there's the verse, I say, with Wolfe Tone:

Was it for this the wild geese spread
The grey wing upon every tide;
For this that all that blood was shed,
For this Edward Fitzgerald died,
And Robert Emmet and Wolfe Tone,
All that delirium of the brave?
Romantic Ireland's dead and gone —
It's with O'Leary in the grave.

'But what about the Swilly?' asks Mrs Moore. 'Tell me Romantic Ireland's dead after we've passed through Barnes Gap.'

'Indeed,' says the heavily tweeded country doctor newly squeezed into our compartment. 'A most romantic land, but as poor as Croesus was rich.' He is travelling to Creeslough,

20 miles and an hour or so down the line. When I tell him I'm for Burtonport, he smiles. 'Do you know how far Burtonport is as the crow flies?' I say I'll get out my map. 'Twenty-eight miles. And how far by the Swilly? Fifty!' He snorts. 'A romantic railway indeed.'

'Why so long?' asks Philip, freed for a moment from the tyranny of his appetite.

'There are bogs, rivers, mountains in our way,' says the doctor. 'We have to go around them all. It's an *Alice in Wonderland* railway. And certainly romantic, although our fellow passengers might not agree, especially not when the thermometer falls, the wind gets up and the rain lashes across the bare countryside.'

Heading south-west from Letterkenny, we follow the south bank of the Swilly through woods and across flats flooded in earlier rain. We call, for small farms and their produce, at Newmills and Foxhall, before turning precipitately north, stopping at Churchill station – just 30 minutes' brisk walk from the village, says the doctor – and climb at 1-in-50 to Kilmacrenan, 340 feet above sea level according to my map.

'The village is at least two and a half miles away,' says the doctor. 'Day trippers come here from Derry and Letterkenny to visit the Holy Well at Doon and to climb the rock where the O'Connells were crowned kings in centuries gone by.'

The country ahead is rocky and increasingly bleak. We squeeze through Barnes Gap along a viaduct over a road and enter the valley of the Owencarrow. It's as if a door has opened into a new and strange world. This, surely, is Ireland's Wild West. We spy the towering white quartz cone of Errigal, Donegal's highest mountain, some 15 miles to our west; and, closer, the massive bulk of the flat-topped Muckish Mountain.

The track here seems lightly laid, the gradients steep, the curves tight and sudden. So very sudden, in fact, that the line turns near enough a right angle, at 10 mph, to cross the Owencarrow River over a 15-girder viaduct, the rails falling towards this lonely structure at 1-in-50. It levels out only some two-thirds of the way across the river and then climbs again. If this seems a little perilous, perhaps that's because it is. When gales blow, a common occurrence and something I need to be aware of on my return trip to Londonderry, the Owencarrow Viaduct is closed until the wind abates.

The Swilly can't be too careful. Just seven years ago, carriages of the afternoon train to Burtonport pulled by No. 14, a 4-6-2 tank engine, were lifted off the track by a westerly gale gusting at 112 mph. One six-wheeler carriage performed a somersault. Its roof gave way and passengers fell into the rocky ravine, 40 feet below. Four were killed and eight injured. The fireman, John Hannigan, ran the three miles to Creeslough as fast as he could in howling wind and driving rain to fetch doctors, priests and other helping hands.

The wind is moderate this morning. Safely over the viaduct, we pull into the curved platform at Creeslough, a passing place for up and down trains, a little less than three hours after leaving Derry. Mr Moore is at the station to meet his family. We are introduced, and before the train departs he offers to make an introduction to Sir Edwin Lutyens at his office on Queen Anne's Gate. With addresses exchanged and the whistle blowing, I steam off alone, waving goodbye to the doctor, too, as we roll away into this highland Gaeltacht, a land of pre-Celtic gods and early Christian saints who may have been one and the same local deity, then over the shorter and less daunting Faymore Viaduct and into Dunfanaghy Road, six miles from Dunfanaghy itself. We climb hard to a 474-foot summit with sweeping views across Inishbofin to Tory Island out in the Atlantic, and then on to Falcarragh station, a mere four miles from the village.

Cashelnagore, 50 minutes out of Creeslough, follows. The isolated station stands wholly surrounded by the most glorious wild landscape, at once green and rocky and ringed around by mountains. I imagine what fun it might be to be stationmaster here, as far from the madding crowd as it's possible to be in these islands, and yet with a magical railway on one's doorstep. We rumble on, braking hard for stray sheep crossing the line, downhill to Gweedore, where we stop for No. 12 to take on water. At Crolly we deliver materials to Morton's carpet factory, an enterprise that – along with providing local employment – has made hand-woven carpets using local wool for Queen Victoria and King Edward VII.

The final half-hour of this long and eventful run is southwest across the Rosses, a rocky and all-but-treeless landscape of countless lakes and small bays yielding to the Atlantic. A little after 1 p.m., and on time despite warnings to the contrary, we pull into Burtonport station, sited in the port itself and very close to the sea. It's such a small village, despite the fish sheds, that I'm half tempted to return with No. 12 on the 3.20 p.m. train. But as the rain has set in, visibility is low and the wind is picking up, I head for O'Donnell's Hotel, where I'll hole up for the night. I do, though, pop back down to the station with an umbrella to see No. 14, the 4-6-2 tank engine, roll in with the afternoon train.

No. 14 is an hour late. The rain-lashed carriages are barely lit by shadowy acetylene lamps. Passengers are wrapped up like members of Scott's last Antarctic expedition. At one point, No. 14 had been in danger of running out of water. This had to be brought to the tender from a river, courtesy of a petrol-driven pump stowed in the guard's van.

What might this trip be like in the depths of winter? Dramatic. Romantic. Wildly exotic.

*

The last trains to and from Burtonport ran on 3rd June 1940. Goods trains with a passenger carriage ran as far as Gweedore until June 1947, but the Swilly gave up the ghost completely in 1953.

There were no buyers for its well-groomed and special locomotives. No. 12 was sold for scrap in 1954, as were the giant 4-8-4 tank engines. Had the railway survived a few more years, it might well have become a focus for preservationists. Today, the ride from Londonderry to Burtonport behind No. 12 would attract enthusiasts and tourists from around the world.

The remains of the Owencarrow Viaduct can still be seen, looking like some ancient monument in a far-distant setting. O'Donnell's bar in Burtonport is no longer a hotel. Cashelnagore station has been lovingly restored and can be rented as a holiday home. The original Rosapenna Hotel, a timber building designed and made in Sweden and shipped to Donegal, burned down in 1962. Its successor remains popular with golfing folk.

The Londonderry and Lough Swilly Railway survived as a bus company until 2014. County Donegal Railways trains last ran from Derry to Strabane in 1954, its locomotives painted red since the late 1930s. The entire railway closed to passengers on 31st December 1959, and to goods the following February. No. 20 *Raphoe*, renamed *Foyle* in 1937, was scrapped in 1955. Three of her class 5 siblings have been preserved statically.

Aside from a rash of ugly new housing in towns and villages throughout the county, the Donegal landscape remains romantically wild. The county has no railways today.

Londonderry, a major allied naval base in the Second World War, was raided on 15th April 1941 by a single German bomber. There were no further attacks. The Provisional IRA and other paramilitary factions made up for this during the Troubles that detonated in 1968 and were defused for the most part 30 years later, though they continue to flare up sporadically, causing death and destruction.

Long closed, the site of the Metropole Hotel is a car park, and Foyle Street has been butchered by unsympathetic development. Three of Derry's four railway terminuses have gone. A very basic new Waterside station was opened in 1980. What survives of the Victorian Waterside station is to be redeveloped – again insensitively. Trains still run to Coleraine, Ballymena and Belfast. None stops at City of Derry Airport, despite running past it.

Trains are slower today than they were in 1938, when the North Atlantic Coast Express was booked from Belfast to Portrush – 65¼ miles – in 73 minutes. The same journey, with a change at Coleraine, takes 1 hour and 47 minutes today.

The Great Northern Railway (Ireland) V class 4-4-0 No. 85 Merlin, painted a lovely sky blue in 1934, was preserved after withdrawal from service in 1963. Today, she is a star turn on main-line special trains. The NCC U2 4-4-0 No. 74 Dunluce Castle is on display at the Ulster Folk and Transport Museum in Cultra, County Down. The Larne to Ballymena line was closed to passengers after the Ulster railway strike of 30th January to 7th April 1933. The 2-4-2T compound locomotive 104 and those fine corridor boat-train carriages were transferred to the Ballycastle branch that was closed in July 1950 by the car-crazy Ulster Transport Authority, which took over the NCC in 1949. I wish I could own and run 104, but she was scrapped in 1954.

In 1963, and on the recommendation of Dr Beeching – the chairman of British Railways remembered as the 'mad axeman' – the accountant Henry Benson proposed the closure of all Ulster Transport Authority railway lines except for the Belfast to Dublin main line and commuter service to Bangor and Larne. Services to Coleraine, Portrush and Derry were saved. For his glorious contribution to Ulster's railways, Benson was knighted in 1964 and created a life peer in 1981.

In 1961, a new car ferry between Larne and Stranraer ousted *Princess Margaret*. Sold the following year to the Shun Tak shipping company and renamed *Macau*, she plied between Macau and Hong Kong until she was damaged by Typhoon Rose in August 1971. She was broken up in Hong Kong in 1974.

Dr Beeching axed the direct line from Carlisle to Stranraer via Dumfries. It was worked by steam until it closed in 1965. The Northern Irishman sleeping car express, better known as 'The Paddy', soldiered on to Stranraer via Ayr, a much longer route, until 1990. There are no ferries from Stranraer. P&O sails car ferries to Larne from Cairnryan, six miles to the north. Today, the journey from Euston to Stranraer requires five changes of train.

My journey from London to Burtonport could be done in just a few hours today, by flying from London Stansted to Londonderry in a twin-engine Brazilian Embraer ERJ-145 jet and, after hiring a car at City of Derry Airport, driving to the Atlantic fishing port in under two hours. But what on earth would be the point of taking a direct route across Donegal and missing the beauty of the county's wild places?

TWO

The Brill Branch:
London Transport

20th–21st June 1935

My American friend Lillian glides through the late-afternoon bustle of St Mary Axe, where we meet at the top of the steps under the arcade of the Baltic Exchange. Our train leaves Liverpool Street in 15 minutes. We weave through a pavement tide of suits, hats, Mackintoshes and rolled umbrellas. Summer might well be 'icumen in', as the old song has it, and the cuckoo may be singing loudly, but in the City it has been cloudy and wet for the past few weeks. We make 'telegraphese' conversation: 'British Museum?' 'Gave it a miss.' 'Where've you been?' 'The movies. The new Hitchcock. *The 39 Steps*. You'd like the train scenes.'

Lillian is writing her doctoral thesis on something to do with the economic impact of the architecture of leisure in eighteenth- and nineteenth-century England, which is why we're on our way to Brill, a remote outpost of the London Underground – so remote, in fact, that it doesn't appear on the new pocket maps. To date, Lillian has visited the Georgian and Regency spas of Bath, Buxton, Cheltenham, Great Malvern, Harrogate,

Leamington and Llandrindod Wells. Dorton Spa in deepest rural Buckinghamshire has eluded her, as it has pretty much everyone else since its 1830s pump room and bath were, as far as I can gather, demolished in the early twenties. Brill is the nearest station, and we'll wing it from there.

It's just before 5.30 p.m., and our six-coach train is growling into the westbound Metropolitan Line platform from Aldgate. At its head is No. 17 *Florence Nightingale*, one of 20 crimson lake and gold-lined 1,200-hp electric locos built by Metropolitan-Vickers at Barrow-in-Furness some 12 years ago for the electrified section of the Met's main line. Trailing behind her is a rake of varnished-teak non-corridor compartment carriages – three of them third class and two first class, with a crimson lake Pullman car, *Mayflower*, in between.

An attendant checks our reservations and we step aboard a carpeted world utterly different from that of a regular Underground train. As Thursday's homebound City commuters crowd into standing-room-only trains, we take our seats in a rail-bound club of moveable armchairs upholstered in crimson morocco leather, glass-topped tables, red damask window blinds, veneered oak walls inlaid with Georgian decoration in wainscot oak, ormolu luggage racks, brass table lamps, deep-pile crimson carpet and plate-glass partitions.

Coats and bags stowed, the 5.30 p.m. to Aylesbury pulls smoothly away from the packed platform into tunnels blackened by soot from steam trains that ran these lines for 40 years. Brake dust, too, from trains coursing over these burnished tracks every few minutes, 20 hours a day. When new – and until 1922 – our crimson lake car had been painted umber and cream, with a white roof. Soot and dust from the tunnels had made these grubby, which is why *Mayflower*, for all her deluxe ways, looks – from the outside – a little gaunt today.

There are just ten of us in this handsome Edwardian car, seated in two saloons and a four-seat coupé. 'This is an Underground train?' asks a genuinely puzzled Lillian.

'This is *Mayflower*, ma'am', says a uniformed steward making his way along the gangway to the buffet counter at the end of the car.

'Oh, right, as in the Pilgrim Fathers?'

'No, ma'am. She's named after a yacht – the 1886 America's Cup winner.'

'For a yacht?' Lillian is none the wiser, which is understandable, but the dime drops when the steward tells her that although this car and her Metropolitan twin, *Galatea*, were built in Birmingham, England, they are both operated by the Pullman Car Company of Illinois. They were the world's first electric-drawn Pullmans.

We rumble past Aldersgate and into the open air at Farringdon, where I spot a London and North Eastern Railway (LNER) N2 0-6-2 tank huffing away with a tightly packed train formed of two sets of articulated four-car teak coaches. The train will burrow underground to King's Cross before it gains suburban Middlesex and Hertfordshire heights. Like the early steam locomotives of the Metropolitan Railway, the N2 consumes her own exhaust. Maroon and varnished-teak Metropolitan and Circle line trains on their hurried ways to and from Uxbridge, Watford, High Street Kensington and Tower Hill rattle past our window, blurring the view while *Florence Nightingale* forges on to King's Cross St Pancras.

The sight of that N2 steaming out from Farringdon brings to mind last Saturday's crash on the LNER main line at Welwyn Garden City. Fourteen people died and 29, I think, were injured. An inexperienced signalman allowed the 10.58 p.m. fast parcels train to Leeds, which was carrying passengers, too, to crash at 65 mph into the back of the 10.53 p.m. Newcastle express, which had slowed for signals. Because nearly all the coaches of both trains were of the latest design, fewer people were killed or hurt than might have been expected in such a terrible crash.

'And the guard of the Newcastle train and his dog were killed too?' Lillian looks aghast and says we need a drink. A press of an electric bell in the marquetry panelling by my chair brings the steward. We order a dry sherry and a gin and vermouth, and study the menu card. We plump for mixed grills and claret. Our train squeals over the points into Baker Street, where we stop under the towering cliffs of Chiltern Court. This is the mountainous block of 180 service flats built by the Met a few years ago. It was designed by the railway's architect, Charles Clark, I tell Lillian – assuming she might be interested in a fully serviced apartment block built to American standards, in a Beaux Arts style. A bit of Manhattan in foggy old London, with central heating, refrigerators, an internal telephone system, guest and maids' quarters, and a grand restaurant for famous residents. 'Like who?' she asks.

'Well, there's H. G. Wells, author of *The Time Machine*. He's also written *The Shape of Things to Come*. Published in '33. Predicts there'll be a world war in 1940.'

As a nicotine waft of businessmen board during our five-minute stop at Baker Street, and schoolboys press their noses against our Pullman window and laugh before being chased off by a platform inspector of military bearing, Lillian tells me that, apparently, Wells is writing a script for United Artists based on *The Shape of Things to Come*. Lillian is well connected in Hollywood circles through her friendship with Van Nest Polglase, who runs RKO's 150-strong design studio. Mr Polglase, from Brooklyn, had also studied architecture, and was with Berg and Orchard in Manhattan before going to Havana, where he worked on the new Presidential Palace with its Tiffany interior. He's designed the soon-to-be-released musical *Top Hat*, starring Fred Astaire and Ginger Rogers. Lillian has seen the sets, and says they make *Mayflower* look positively seventeenth century.

'But,' I say, 'you haven't seen the countryside beyond Aylesbury yet.'

Doors slam along the length of the train. *Florence Nightingale*'s air whistle shrills and – our car now full – we draw out of Baker Street, climbing through tunnels and along past the platforms of St John's Wood, Marlborough Road and Swiss Cottage stations up to Finchley Road, where we rumble out into sunshine, just as the Met Office – meteorological that is, not Metropolitan – promised.

'Things are looking up,' I say.

'They certainly are,' says one of the businessmen who joined us at Baker Street, from across the gangway. 'Mr Baldwin is back in office, and the Reds under MacDonald are out. Has to be good news.' He puffs on a cheroot as the steward goes to unlock the lavatory, which is worth visiting not simply for its obvious convenience but also to see its oval stained-glass window. It is one of just two lavatories to be found on London Transport trains. The other, of course, belongs to *Galatea*.

Drinks are served. To our right, a Nottingham or Manchester express from St Pancras – behind a Midland Compound 4-4-0, now in the stable of the London, Midland and Scottish – canters by, just as a 'Jersey Lily' Atlantic catches us up with a rival Great Central express to Manchester. I can remember when, as a small boy, I watched these singularly graceful locomotives steaming in and out of Marylebone, the last of London's main-line termini, opened in 1899 and as quiet in the early afternoon as nearby St Cyprian's Church, Clarence Gate. How dashing these famously fast 4-4-2s seemed, in their elaborate lined-out livery of dark green and crimson lake. They were nicknamed (though misspelled) after Lillie Langtry, the curvaceous actress who, born in Jersey, took the West End and Broadway by storm and became the best-known mistress of the then Prince of Wales, the King's extravagant father.

Now, under the yoke of the London and North Eastern Railway, which took over the Great Central in 1923, the Jersey Lily is dressed in funereal black. Still, she's clearly on form and races *Florence Nightingale*, who has now picked up her 650-volt skirts, accelerating flat out towards the Victorian suburb of Kilburn, with its cathedral-like Victorian Gothic church by John Loughborough Pearson, and on downhill to Neasden and Wembley Park.

Now we're moving, the Pullman car skimming over the rhythmic rail joints as we touch what must be all of 65 mph, as the Jersey Lily – or C4 class 4-4-2 – and its dining car express inch past us. We race past the site of Watkin's Folly, London's rival to the Eiffel Tower that never was. Sir Edward Watkin, the railway magnate and one-time chairman of the Met, had dreamed of linking Manchester to Paris via the Great Central, the Met, the South Eastern and Chatham, and a tunnel under the Channel. His Wembley tower, marking the way, was to have been taller than the one built by Eiffel in Paris.

We level out and climb up to Harrow-on-the-Hill. I spy a coal train trundling behind one of the Met's powerful K class 2-6-4 tank locomotives, its side emblazoned with the London Transport logo in Johnston capitals underlined in graphic gold. It's a lovely evening now, yet the landscape from here is all dust, mud, brick and tiles, the new and half-built semi-detached suburbs appearing to surround and grasp the railway lines like the tentacles of some enormous and unthinking man-made octopus.

At Harrow, a stopping train to Marylebone barks out from the station paced by a Baker Street–bound electric. The Jersey Lily is ahead of us as we pass through Harrow and enter Metro-land.

'Metro-land? Why that's a name I know from Evelyn Waugh. Margot Beste-Chetwynde, the smart dame who knocks down her ancient country house for a comic Bauhaus-style job and marries Lord Metroland. Was that in *Decline and Fall*, or *Vile Bodies*? I forget which...'

So do I, yet Metro-land itself is real enough, a swathe of outer Middlesex and Bucks turned into a *rus in urbe* commuters' playground. Posh suburbia.

When the Met came this way, it retained the land around its tracks, and through its Metropolitan Railway Country Estates company it developed housing for City commuters, with its residents beholden to the railway by way of season tickets to Baker Street and the City. What started as plush Arts and Crafts–style villas to the north of Harrow have become the thousands of new semi-detached houses we've been seeing since Wembley. It's as if one day this suburbia will continue to expand in all directions, until Middlesex and much of Bucks, Herts, Essex and Surrey have been filled with brick boxes, paved roads, coal yards, mock Tudor pubs and estate agents.

We stop at Moor Park, where three of our company leave with polite *good evenings*. The ambitious house remodelled by Giacomo Leoni in the 1720s for Benjamin Styles, the South Sea Company speculator, is a now a golf club owned, I think, by Lord Leverhulme. At Rickmansworth, the next stop, our 'Growler' – as *Florence Nightingale* and her siblings are known – is uncoupled from the train. I nip out to watch as she rumbles into a siding and a handsome Met Railway H class 4-4-4 tank loco, 109 – all crimson lake with black on gold lining, and the new London Transport lettering on her sides – takes her place.

109 is one of eight much-loved express tank engines designed by Mr Charles Jones, the Metropolitan Railway's chief locomotive and electrical engineer, and built 15 years ago by Kerr, Stuart & Co., Stoke-on-Trent. The Met was taken over by the efficient new London Passenger Transport Board (LPTB) two years ago. Of course, some miss the word 'Metropolitan' on the tanks of these engines, but I like the crisp Johnston script, at once up to date and yet clearly based on the Roman lettering of Trajan's Column.

The guard blows his whistle and 109 responds. I reboard *Mayflower*. Lillian sighs at my fondness for steam and, with a slight slip of the locomotive's driving wheels, we ease around the tortuous station curve and then climb in earnest towards the Chilterns. To Wendover, where a head-scarfed mother and daughter are unloading a pair of bays from a horse van in the siding alongside our platform.

Here, a party of ramblers and another of Girl Guides leave the train, no doubt to climb tomorrow up through ancient beech woods to the crest of Coombe Hill, with its wide-open views of unspoilt rural England – and, more soberly, its memorial to soldiers from Buckinghamshire who fell in the Boer War.

Down towards Aylesbury, at the best part of 70 mph, past fields, farms and meadows that look as they have done, I imagine, for the past 200 years. 'Some Underground train,' says Lillian. Aylesbury welcomes us at 7.01 p.m. on the dot in nascent summer sunshine, which is just as well as we have over an hour to wait for the Verney Junction train. Tonight we'll stay at the Verney Arms Hotel, with a day in front of us for Brill and whatever remains of Dorton Spa.

Lillian sits on a bench reading F. Scott Fitzgerald's *Tender is the Night*. I watch an ex-Great Central 'Pom-Pom' 0-6-0 shunting, the arrival and departure of a Manchester to Marylebone express behind a 'Director' 4-4-0, and a Met departure for Baker Street. The variety of locomotives and trains here is quite remarkable. If I had time, I would very much like to walk over to the engine shed where Great Western, LNER and Met locos meet. My thought is interrupted by the 7.38 p.m. arrival of the push-pull railmotor from Verney Junction.

Lillian looks up from her book. 'Is that a toy train?' It certainly looks it, a tiny ex-Great Eastern 'Crystal Palace' 2-4-2 tank loco

47

attached to a long carriage with what appear to be dozens of windows and a single central door. There are very few through trains to the end of the line from the City and Baker Street these days. The railmotor serves as a shuttle between Aylesbury, the end of the line for most Met trains, and Verney Junction.

The railmotor is a fascinating thing. The locomotive 8307 – one of just a dozen built in 1909 to run on lightly laid East Anglian branch lines – boasts a tall and airy cab with exceptionally big windows (hence its nickname), while its 30-year-old 12-wheeler saloon is a leftover from what was once a trio of Great Central railmotors, in which even tinier locomotives were hidden from view inside the single carriages. At the opposite end of the train from the tank engine is a driver's cab connected to 8307 through a system of cables, push rods and mechanical pulleys. There is no need to turn the train. Inside, along with a luggage compartment, are two open saloons for 16 first-class and 48 third-class passengers.

The crew are happy to give me these details. I tell them I think we're travelling on the railmotor from Verney Junction tomorrow morning. 'What time?'

'8.50 a.m.'

'That won't be us. Should be a two- or three-coach job with the F1.'

Just then, our train to Verney Junction rolls in behind Met 4-4-4T 103. Departure, scheduled for 8.12 p.m., is not immediate. The imperious tank engine runs to the back of its train and takes three of its six coaches away. It returns to the front of the truncated train. This is very much a sign of the times. The stations beyond Aylesbury, where Metro-land meets the buffers, generate precious little revenue. I have yet to ride this final stretch of the Met, but once we're under way it is easy to see why the LPTB bosses in St James's Park have plans to close both the Verney Junction line and the Brill branch. The LPTB's New Works Programme for 1935 to 1940 envisages the further electrification of the Met from Rickmansworth to Amersham. Beyond this, as far as I can make out, there is little hope for Brill and Verney.

So, best to enjoy the line while we can. Our first-class Met carriage is certainly comfortable. Its six plush seats are covered with William Morris–style floral-patterned moquette. Armrests are leather-capped. Above the fabric beading on top of the seats there are mirrors, maps of the line, luggage racks, and framed photographs of Metro-land beauty spots. The Met's advertising slogan 'Live in Metro-land' is embossed in the door locks – although to remind us of new ownership, 'No Smoking' signs on the windows are incorporated into red and blue London Transport bullseye motifs.

Stations on the way to Verney Junction are as well kept as any on the Underground, yet as their names suggest – Quainton Road, Granborough Road and Winslow Road – these are sited quite some way from the villages they purport to serve. Window slid down, we hear skylarks and crickets intermingled with the beat of our tank engine. Verney Junction is in the middle of nowhere, too, although it does allow passengers to change for the Oxford to Cambridge line and the Buckingham and Banbury branch.

Unhurried, we draw into the station at 8.32 p.m. Very few passengers have come this far. Those who have are swept discreetly out of the station yard in a small fleet of polished cars, including a venerable chauffeur-driven Daimler. We are fifty miles and a world away from London.

Our hotel, a modest two-storey red-brick affair opened in 1896, offers simple rooms. We join the few locals in the bar for sandwiches and drinks. 'Saw you coming off the London train,' says one tweed-capped fellow, a hard-worked collie asleep at his feet. 'Thought you must be for the big house.'

He means Claydon, two miles away. I don't know the Verneys who own the house, a legend in architectural circles for its eighteenth-century *chinoiserie* Rococo plasterwork, yet I do know that Sir Harry Verney, 2nd Baronet, was much involved in the building of these local railways, and his grandson, Sir Harry Verney, 4th Baronet, has been a director of the Metropolitan Railway and owns much of the land around the stations between here and Quainton Road.

'I used to see Miss Nightingale up at the house,' says an old fellow, pint in one hand, pipe in the other. 'Used to be a gardener there. Don't think she ever came on the train. Sir Harry, you see, wanted to wed her. Turned him down. Married her older sister. Now what was her name?'

'Parthenope,' says Lillian, who has been reading up on the area. We chatter on until it finally gets dark enough for us to want to sleep. Tomorrow is the longest day of the year, and we want to make the most of it.

The hotel has made us a picnic lunch. I tuck this, along with a bottle of red Chassagne-Montrachet and travel glasses I've brought from town, into a canvas rucksack folded into my bag. We plan to leave our luggage, light as it is, at Quainton Road.

The 8.50 a.m. train is worked today by a former Great Eastern F1 class 2-4-2 tank pulling a pair of varnished-teak LNER compartment coaches. At Quainton, we leave our bags and cross over to the Brill platform. Lillian knows full well that, much as I am keen on finding her spa, the Brill branch has been the stuff of childhood dreams for me. I don't know why I haven't been this way before. Still, here we are watching a ghost from the Metropolitan's past steaming towards us. This is Met No. 23, a Beyer Peacock A class 4-4-0 tank engine built in 1869 to pull the trains of the world's first underground railway. Sixty-six years old this year, she sports a coat of smartly turned-out crimson lake emblazoned with the legend 'London Transport' in Johnston lettering on her sides. No. 23 is one of three surviving A class locos based at Neasden that are dispatched to Brill, where they work the branch for a week each. They have survived because no other London Transport locomotive is light enough to operate the line. They are also impressive engines in every way. Only last year, No. 41 took over an 11-coach Leicester to Marylebone express from a failed Gresley A3 Pacific at Aylesbury.

No. 23 comes to a halt with the 9.22 from Aylesbury at the head of a single and ancient eight-wheel fixed-axle coach. Built by the Ashbury Carriage and Iron Company three years before the A class tank engine and re-bodied in 1896, it's a brake third. No first on the Brill branch. What makes it truly first class for me, though, is the fairy-tale, history-book character of our train and the promise of a run – well, a 25 mph canter at most – along the most unlikely Underground line of all. If there are no passengers, crews are said to stop the trains to go rabbiting in the woods, while coal from the engines' bunkers is swapped at unscheduled stops by wayside farms for eggs, milk and game.

We clamber into a compartment, its horsehair-stuffed seats puffing dust as we sit. Flag, whistle, a toot from No. 23 and off we go, curving sharply west and swaying out like some old-world stagecoach between hedges along a quiet straight road across open fields. Our first stop, Waddesdon Road, comprises a single platform of rough-hewn timber planks and a small wooden waiting room. Ahead of our track, the gates protecting the Bicester–Aylesbury road are closed. A lady walks a terrier; a horseman in a bowler rides by.

The station was built to serve Waddesdon Manor, the imposing Loire Valley–style château commissioned by Ferdinand de Rothschild in 1874 from the euphoniously named architect Gabriel-Hippolyte Destailleur, as a weekend retreat. Completed in 1889, its construction had consumed up to 25,000 bricks a week, ferried by train from the brickworks at Brill. Bricks and Corsham stone were hauled up to the site by steam winch, from a siding hidden under brambles and willowherb.

Crossing the road, we buck slowly for what can't be more than a mile to the next Lilliputian station and set of closed gates. This is Westcott, and, quite remarkably, it actually serves the village. Ladies with shopping baskets are waiting on the platform for Brill. I wouldn't mind getting off here to see the parish church by the Victorian architect G. E. Street, but as the next train onwards to Brill is at about ten past one, I stay on board, leaning out of the window, and trying my best to take in the sights and sounds of what must be one of the most idiosyncratically rural and antiquated of all British branch lines.

We steam between aisles of trees and fields of cows, and under a bridge carrying the Great Central main line. A walking-pace curve guides us in to Wotton. The station is like an illustration from a children's story. If Pooh Bear, Eeyore and Piglet were to travel by train, this surely would be their destination. To add to the fun, there are now two Wotton stations. The Great Central's is up by the bridge, and a single stationmaster works for both. All we need now is for Will Hay to take the job.

'Will who?' asks Lillian.

'As in, *Oh, Mr Porter!*'

'Featuring trains, no doubt?'

How did she guess?

The station is close to Wotton House, a lovely Baroque affair built in the style of Buckingham House for Richard Grenville and rebuilt after a fire in 1820 for a later Richard Grenville, 1st Earl Temple, by John Soane, architect of the Bank of England – one of London's great buildings, which is being butchered today by Sir Herbert Baker, who seems hell-bent on turning Soane's masterpiece into a grandiloquent office block that he would never have got away with when working with Lutyens in New Delhi.

The Grenvilles became the dukes of Buckingham and Chandos and it was the 3rd Duke, a former chairman of the London and North Western, who in 1871 built the Brill branch, a horse-drawn tramway, as far as Wotton. It was meant for estate workers and stockmen, and it fetched and carried milk, chalk, hay, manure, coal and those thousands of bricks for Waddesdon. But there was a local demand for passenger services and an extension to Brill. The duke ordered a pair of steam engines that I can't help thinking set the tone for this charmingly wayward railway. They were not conventional railway locos, but single-cylinder Aveling and Porter 10-ton chain-driven traction engines mounted on flanged wheels. They had a top speed of 4 mph.

The Met took on the lease of the line in 1894, and by 1910 had upgraded it with new stations and with trains that could run at 25 mph. But before that, the 3rd Duke and Sir Harry Verney, with initial financial backing from the Rothschilds, won Royal Assent for an extension of the line – as a proper railway – from Brill to Oxford. It would have steamed through Boarstall, Stanton St John and Headington. The Oxford terminus was to have been at the back of St Clement's High Street, a couple of minutes' walk from Magdalen Bridge. Imagine the luck of varsity undergrads strolling out of the porter's lodge at Magdalen, ambling over the Cherwell and catching a train to Baker Street and the City.

It didn't happen. Even the Rothschilds balked at the cost of tunnelling 1,650 yards under nearby Muswell Hill, which you can see at the end of an avenue from the library at Wotton House. A cheaper tramway option made little sense. It would have been far too slow. The proposal for an electrified line in the 1890s was altogether too far-fetched.

After the 3rd Duke's death in 1889, Wotton House was let to tenants. Major Michael Beaumont, the right-wing Conservative MP for Aylesbury, bought it six years ago and has, I hear, employed the architect A. S. G. Butler to conceal its Soane interiors with Neo-Georgian designs in the style of Lutyens.

Wood Siding, our next stop – also built to serve the Wotton estate – is remarkable, its setting sylvan and bucolic. But in 1910 the Great Western cut its new line to Birmingham, avoiding Oxford directly below this tiny Brill branch station; so, rather unexpectedly, modern express trains thunder at 90 mph just yards beneath us. As we stop, a piercing whistle from the deep cutting has me out of our Victorian coach in an instant. I can read the number plate of the magnificent Great Western King class 4-6-0 thundering towards us below at great speed. This is 6022 *King Edward III* hurrying a chocolate-and-cream-liveried two-hour Birmingham express to Paddington. I wonder if any of her passengers know of the Brill line's existence. When the Great Western express vanishes from sight and out of earshot, we're left with the sound of sparrows, a woodpecker, wood pigeons and No. 23 simmering, a wisp of steam escaping from her safety valves.

We put on a turn of speed for Brill, rollicking along at a full 25 mph, along past Spa Wood and braking at the bottom of Brill Hill, close by the Duke of Buckingham's brickworks, which is now a timber yard. The terminus, 12 miles east of Oxford, is a matter-of-fact little station – equipped, though, with the full set of booking office, waiting room, lavatories, engine shed and sidings, their points set by trackside levers.

With thanks to our crew, Lillian and I hike past what was the Dorton Spa Rural Hotel and is now a girls' school, then out to the Warrens. This is the elm-lined path leading in an arrow-straight line to Spa Wood. The Bucks countryside here is wide, rolling and wholly enticing. England *in excelsis*. Lillian knows the background to the Regency venture that was to have made Brill, a truly lovely spot, as fashionable as Tunbridge or Leamington. Charles Spencer Ricketts RN, who it seems served under Nelson, owned Dorton House, a venerable Elizabethan affair. Since the seventeenth century, there were records of horses drinking local spring water and being cured of mange, while the fumes from cowpats burned in cottage hearths were said to be effective in cases of – among other conditions – scrofula, psoriasis, leprosy, hysteria and, of course, ague, though perhaps not housemaid's knee.

What Captain Ricketts had on his land was one of the strongest chalybeate, or iron-rich, springs in Europe. With this fortifying news strongly in mind, in the late 1820s he commissioned the architect James Hakewill, author of *Plans, Sections and Elevations of the Abattoirs in Paris, with considerations for their adoption in London*. Hakewill produced a stately Grecian pleasure dome set by a serpentine lake in 12 acres of romantic parkland. A domed semi-circular Corinthian portico led into a high, barrel-vaulted pump room. Aside from 12 spring baths, those taking the waters could also relax by playing billiards, posing like Keats in the reading room, or thrilling to a quadrille, reel or newly acceptable waltz in one or perhaps both of the spa's ballrooms. Or, at least, Lillian thinks they could. No one appears to recall quite how much of Hakewill's ambitious proposal was actually built.

The venture failed early on. There was nothing much to do in Brill itself, unlike Leamington, Tunbridge and Bath, and village and spa were difficult to reach. Nor did Queen Victoria come this way, except late in life to spend some days with the Rothschilds at Waddesdon Manor. But has anything remained?

We reach the spa woods to find them surrounded by railings. A gamekeeper leans over and says, 'S'pose you'll be looking for the spring?' We say we are. He decides to let us in to this now-secret dell. This really is like being in a fairy tale.

The gamekeeper explains that we're a bit late to see the pump room, as Hakewill's building was pulled down some twelve years ago. And, indeed, there is little to see here beyond a solitary broken column rising from overgrown foundations. I am bemused, though, to see *Acanthus mollis* blooming here. Acanthus leaves were, of course, the inspiration for the fronds of the capitals of Corinthian columns.

The gamekeeper walks us on further into the wood, to a small brick and timber building. He opens the door. Inside is a well of sulphurous water. 'Got a mug, then?'

I dig into my rucksack, pull out a small leather case, unclip it and hand over an eighteenth-century claret glass. 'Needs must,' says the gamekeeper, dipping the delicate glass below a crust of salts into the brew below. 'Try this.'

Lillian appoints me taster-in-chief. Honeydew this is not. In fact, it tastes perfectly disgusting. No wonder the spa failed. I say it's rather good, hits the spot and recommend the vintage to Lillian. She manages not to spit it out. 'Put hairs on your chest,' says the gamekeeper, chuckling.

'Thanks so much,' says Lillian. It's time to open the Chassagne-Montrachet. We drink a toast to Captain Ricketts and Mr Hakewill – 'That's a nice drop of whatever it is,' says the gamekeeper – and make our exit.

We sit down in the sun, eat our picnic, drink the rest of the wine and snooze. The spa might have gone, yet this is truly a perfect spot. In the early afternoon, we amble back to Brill, an English version of a remote Tuscan hill town, drink tea at the Sun Hotel, take in the commanding view, and trot back down the hill to catch the 5.30 p.m. to Quainton Road. No. 23 eases us away from the station and back through a glowing first-day-of-summer countryside – innocent of our modern 1930s world – under vaults and parasols of sun-flecked trees, past crossing gates and along by lonely lanes to the main-line junction, where a big, four-cylinder Great Central locomotive thunders through with an express for Marylebone.

H. G. Wells, who lives at Chiltern Court, wrote that famous book *The Time Machine*. No. 23 and her train have been exactly that. The Brill branch, though, has no future. Mr Pick, the formidably effective chief executive of the LPTB, says closure will save £2,000 a year, or a fifth of his well-deserved salary. But it's not just a case of money. Neither spa nor Metro-land have taken root here. There are no commuters, nor are there likely to be for many decades to come. It seems an odd thought, yet Brill was probably at its most fashionable 900 years ago when Edward the Confessor had a hunting lodge here and the parish church was a royal chapel.

Waving goodbye to No. 23 and her carriage and crew, we steam away from Quainton on the 6.08 p.m. LNER Brackley to Marylebone semi-fast, formed of six varnished-teak non-corridor compartment carriages and a hunched and muscular A5 class 4-6-2 tank, 9807, a Great Central design by John Robinson dating from 1911. Today she'll stop at Wendover, Amersham, Rickmansworth and Harrow-on-the-Hill only. Lillian makes notes on Brill and Dorton Spa. I stare out of the window as frequent steam and electric trains rock by in the other direction, and as rural England – the England of the poets – yields to swathes of suburbia and then, through smoky tunnels, into red-brick and terracotta Marylebone. 'Did we dream today?' asks Lillian.

*

The Brill branch closed on 30th November 1935, and its effects were auctioned for a pittance the following April. Its track bed can be followed on foot in parts, and seen quite clearly in satellite images of the area. Geographically, Brill remains happily isolated, although its streets are full of cars today. The Vale of Aylesbury is largely unspoilt, but not for long. The proposed HS2 railway designed to ferry people hungry for London from northern cities and the Midlands at inordinate speeds looks set to slash its gormless way through this beautiful farming and walking country.

From 6th July 1936 there were no more passenger trains from Quainton Road to Verney Junction. The Verney Arms Hotel became a pub, and in recent years an Italian bistro. The building was empty in 2019. When John Betjeman made his delightful film *Metro-Land*, directed by Edward Mirzoeff in 1973, he looked over a fence at Shipton Lee, south of Verney Junction, saying, 'Grass triumphs. And I must say I'm rather glad.' But, again, perhaps not for long. There are threats of a new 'garden village' (for which read 'unthinking suburban sprawl') here – in fact, one of five, the spawn of an unholy marriage between developers and politicians plotting a future in which Oxford and Cambridge are strung together on the revived Varsity Line by clumps of horrid new suburban housing, dim business parks, dull supermarkets and shiny car dealerships. A painstakingly restored Quainton Road station is the headquarters of the Buckinghamshire Railway Centre, where you can watch preserved engines in steam while standing on the platform for Brill. 4-4-0T Met No. 23 ran in London Transport service until 1948, and is now on display in the London Transport Museum, Covent Garden.

In 1936, the Met handed over operations north of Rickmansworth to the LNER, which standardized its locomotive fleet, sending Charles Jones's H class 4-4-4Ts to Colwick and Annesley sheds, Nottingham, where they ran passenger trains to Lincoln, Derby, Mansfield, and Chesterfield with its crooked church spire. They wore coats of plain black instead of lined-out crimson lake, their chimneys were shortened and they suffered from mechanical neglect. Six survived as BR locomotives in 1948, but were scrapped soon afterwards at Stratford. No. 17 *Florence Nightingale* was scrapped after an accident in 1943, but her sister Growler, No. 12 *Sarah Siddons*, can still be seen at the head of special trains on the Metropolitan Line.

Flats in Chiltern Court became very expensive indeed, although the restaurant is currently 'The Metropolitan Bar', a branch of Wetherspoons. London Transport electric trains have run to Amersham only since 1961, when steam services north of Rickmansworth came to an end. Since 1957, Waddesdon Manor has been owned by the National Trust and managed by the Rothschild Foundation. Under threat of demolition, Wotton House and its gardens were saved from being turned into a housing estate in 1957 by Elaine Brunner, daughter of George V's valet, who paid Buckinghamshire County Council £6,000 for the privilege in six annual instalments. She rang up her husband, Wing Commander Patrick Brunner, and said, 'Darling, I have bought a house, and I just know you are going to love it.' Divided into handsome flats, Wotton was restored in the style of Sir John Soane by the architect Donald Insall, and again in 2015 by Ptolemy Dean, Surveyor of the Fabric of Westminster

Abbey. Tony Blair, the former prime minister, lives in Wotton's former coach house. What had been Brill Spa Hotel was damaged by the nearby explosion of a V-1 flying bomb overshooting London, and demolished.

THREE

Frankfurt to Rio de Janeiro: *Graf Zeppelin*

9th–14th July 1936

The Berlin Olympics open next month, and the Germans are on their best behaviour. It's certainly a pleasure this afternoon to amble through Frankfurt's medieval city centre, said to be the biggest of its kind, its half-timbered buildings decorated with flower boxes and, of course, swastika flags. I sit outside a venerable café on the corner of Gallusstrasse, where a taxi is due to pick me up at 3.30.

During my stay I've been reading a history of the city and have been fascinated to learn that if he had got his way, Johann Georg Christian Hess, a former bricklayer who studied at the Académie Royale de l'Architecture in Paris and went on to become Frankfurt's city architect in 1785, would have demolished much of this fairy-tale labyrinth. Hess thought medieval towns and cities were barbaric and unhygienic. He failed to get rid of the old Nikolaikirche, which he had hoped to replace with a Grecian exhibition hall, only because money was scarce. And if the Comte d'Hédouville, ambassador of the French occupying forces at the time, hadn't kicked up a fuss, Hess would've knocked down the medieval Eschenheimer Tower, a treasured landmark on the city's skyline. Thank God those days are long past. It's hard to imagine anyone wanting to harm old Frankfurt today. It all seems so very peaceful, and even what the Germans call *gemütlich*.

Pleasant and cheerful or not, in March, Herr Hitler marched his goose-stepping troops into the Rhineland in defiance of the Versailles treaty. Air Marshal Dowding – who, some time this week, will be appointed head of the new Fighter Command – has already addressed the Auxiliary Air Force in confidence. Like Sir Robert Vansittart of the Foreign Office, the air marshal believes Hitler wants war and that we should be prepared for it. Sir Robert told a group of us early last year that he'd be happy for Westminster to free Germany from the weight of Versailles, but only after Herr Hitler is out of office. Given the support the Führer commands here, it's hard to see that happening any time soon.

My taxi glides to a halt alongside the café. It's a brand-new and parade ground–smart Mercedes-Benz 260D, a six-seat diesel saloon launched in Berlin in the spring. The driver stows my bags, and off we go through the medieval streets accompanied by peels of church bells, tram bells and bicycle bells, over the River Main and out towards the airport. I have to say that this taxi makes our London cabs seem positively antique.

We do have to watch out that we don't fall behind the Hun. In May, the Deutsche Reichsbahn took the world speed record for steam locomotives. A streamlined 4-6-4, 05 002, designed by Adolf Wolff at Borsig, reached 200.4 km/h, or 124½ mph. On a run over the 70 miles from Wittenberge to a signal stop at Berlin-Spandau, the same loco has averaged an electric 86.6 mph, start to stop. Whether it's trains, planes, ships, racing cars or even the latest taxi cab, the Germans are certainly out to impress.

And it's hard not to be impressed. One of my tasks on this trip has been to visit scientists and engineers at IG Farben. Here in Frankfurt they've developed a new form of synthetic rubber with the promise of highly effective self-sealing fuel tanks. Our backroom boys have been working on much the same thing on behalf of the British aircraft industry, the Air Ministry and the RAF. IG Farben, one of the world's biggest companies, is a chemical giant. So big, in fact, that it occupies – this side of the airship hangars at Cardington – one of the biggest buildings I've ever seen. It is an enormous great thing designed by the architect Hans Poelzig on land that once belonged to the Rothschilds: all lofty ceilings, projecting office wings, polished marble, paternoster lifts, airy labs and improbably long corridors. In one of these, I passed a party of Americans in animated discussion with IG Farben managers. It all makes you wonder what they'll get up to here next. With IG Farben, I'd say anything goes.

While there's been a degree of cooperation between Germany and Britain as far as industry and the military is concerned, it can and should, I think, go only so far. As we cruise comfortably along towards the brand-new Rhein-Main airfield and airship port, I think of the fascinating story Tom Campbell Black told at the Royal Aero Club not so long after his record-breaking flight with Flight Lieutenant Scott from London to Sydney in the streamlined de Havilland Comet. In '31, Black had flown into Juba in the Sudan. The Shell agent there told him that a German crew had taken off from Juba earlier, but had failed to reach their destination. Black stowed fresh water and supplies aboard his craft, and flew over the desert in the hope of spotting the Germans.

Well, there they were, hopefully alive, lying under a tarpaulin in the midday sun next to their wrecked machine, being watched from a distance by unfriendly natives. Black landed and found one of the Huns rather the worse for wear, but the other in pretty good shape, all things considered. He got them back to Juba. The German able to do the talking proved to be none less than the Luftwaffe ace Ernst Udet. Flew with von Richthofen's Flying Circus and, after the Red Baron was shot down and killed, under Göring. Udet's Great War score was 62 kills. He's in charge today of the Reich Air Ministry's development wing.

Funnily enough, thinking of Tom Black leads me on to another assignment: a visit to the Instituto de Pesquisas Tecnológicas in São Paulo. Black and Scott's Comet was designed by de Havilland's Arthur Hagg. Mr Hagg is currently working to Air Ministry specification 36/35 on the construction of a four-engine transatlantic mail plane. The DH.91 Albatross is being made from a ply-balsa-ply sandwich. In confidence, de Havilland have told us that this form of lightweight and low-cost construction could prove to be ideal for military aircraft. So, any gen regarding who else is developing wooden aircraft, and how they're doing so, could come in handy.

Mr Hagg is aware of what the Brazilians are up to and, because I have a ticket for today's *Graf Zeppelin* flight to Rio, here's the opportunity to visit Signor Frederico Brotero and

Mr Orton Hoover, who are leading research into wooden aircraft in São Paulo. I've also been told that any direct diplomatic contact with Brazil is a good thing, given that at the moment the country appears to be in thrall to Messrs Hitler and Mussolini.

This opportunity has presented itself because I've been asked by one of the nationals to write up the first transatlantic Zeppelin flight from the new Frankfurt airport. They want a pilot's view. I said yes in a shot. Well, who wouldn't? My thoughts, however, fragment as we drive into the airport and immediate impressions take over. The fields around us stretch away in the early-summer evening haze. There are sheep here and – what's this? – a sea of potato flowers as far as the eye can see. Farming and flight, aviation and agriculture, in twentieth-century embrace.

And, look, here's the airport building, brand-new and, to my surprise, all very Bauhaus. I thought Herr Hitler had no time for Modern design, but, evidently, I'm wrong. The German chancellor is certainly here in spirit, though. An Oompah band is playing at an open-air café set behind geometric ponds flecked by fountains. An earnest troop of Hitler Youth marches past a stone pylon crowned with a bronze eagle, its wings outspread. Swastika flags flap the length of the terminal building.

On the field itself, a pair of silver Junkers Ju 52s glisten. I spot another of the Junker trimotors coming in to land. Most probably it's the flight from Berlin connecting with the imminent departure of *Graf Zeppelin*. We have all got used to the sight of these distinctive aircraft with their low, cantilevered wings and corrugated duralumin fuselages. Who hasn't seen a newsreel of Herr Hitler flying from German pillar to Third Reich post aboard his personal 'Aunty Ju'?

Business people and civil servants by the looks of them, the Berlin contingent steps from the plane and into a brightly polished bus – a Mercedes-Benz O 2600, I think, sporting a modestly streamlined body. I follow the Germans with a loose-knit party of stragglers. Creative types. Here is a flamboyant Brazilian with two glamorous young women in tow. There are two men who might be commercial artists, and a curious, abstracted, quizzical-looking fellow, in his late forties, I'd guess, hair brushed back from his scalp, dicky bow around his neck and a pair of thick-framed and defiantly round specs. This, I'm sure, is Monsieur Le Corbusier, the real-life Otto Silenus, who believes the house is a 'machine for living in'. I have his latest book *Aircraft: The New Vision*, published last year by *The Studio*.

The bus takes us along one side of the airfield before dropping us by the gaping entrance of the colossal airship hangar. We must look like some lost tribe of trilby-hatted pygmies as we trek into this veritable cathedral of transatlantic aviation. I do my level best to look nonchalant, although LZ 127 *Graf Zeppelin* is a truly awe-inspiring sight. She's at least as long as an ocean liner.

The purser and white-jacketed stewards welcome us aboard the gondola snug under the nose of the airship. Inside, we are guided through the dining lounge and along a rather festive striped corridor with cabins on either side. Luckily, I have one to myself. This is my den for the next four nights. It's a little bigger than a berth on a sleeper, with a sofa bed under which I can stow my bags, a desk below the window, and a folding stool.

The walls are lined in a bold and bright modern fabric patterned with summer and autumn leaves. A note on the bed issued by Deutsche Zeppelin states that the airship is heated and 'regular' apparel can be worn.

I was told by someone who made a trip by *Graf Zeppelin* five years ago that, as no heater was fitted at the time, leather coats, furs and woollen jumpers were de rigueur when dining at altitude, and especially in colder months. They also told me that for all its innovative structure and technology, the decor of the airship was ponderous and even Edwardian. Whether this was to emulate contemporary liners or to reassure nervous passengers I do not know. But, when I walk back into the dining lounge for a flight briefing, the new-look decor is more *Flying down to Rio* or Pierre Frey than RMS *Carinthia* or medieval Frankfurt.

The eighteen of us on board today – the ship can take 20 – gather around as the captain takes centre stage. In a moment, he says, we will be pulled out of the hangar, and once the engines have fired up, the ropes will be released and we'll take off. We'll be flying over France and Spain before heading out across the Atlantic to Brazil. Flying conditions are good. The 40-strong crew is here to look after our needs. They will answer any questions regarding the flight. As the skipper, who looks like an old sea dog, walks towards the bridge, the gentleman sitting next to me says, 'Do you know who the captain is?'

'I'm afraid not,' I reply.

'He's Dr Eckener, commodore of the Zeppelin fleet. And the fellow who was standing next to him with the goatee beard is Herr Ludwig Dürr, designer of the *Graf Zeppelin*.'

The man then introduces himself as Karl von Wiegand. He has certainly piqued my interest. For now, though, all is sensation rather than conversation. The airship is towed effortlessly from the hangar by a team of men. Once away from the shed, the engines – almost if not entirely silent from our roost in the gondola, even though some of the windows are open – start up. When the riggers let go, this lighter-than-air craft does exactly what a big balloon filled with God-knows-how-many hundreds of thousands of cubic feet of hydrogen will do. She rises effortlessly, and as she does we steer slowly south-west, away from the airfield, towards the Rhine. The views are glorious. I see that M. Le Corbusier is busy filming from a window with a new Siemens B 16mm cine-camera. I'm happy with my new Leica IIIa rangefinder, tucked into my coat pocket, but I must say a cine-camera would be a fine thing to have on a trip like this.

Although it's hard not to be glued to the windows, especially on a long summer evening like this, by the time we are over the Vosges, our complement is seated for dinner. I join Herr von Wiegand – 'Mr,' he corrects me – who has brought Herr Dürr to join us, together with Herr Claude Dornier, the aircraft designer. What I gather fairly quickly over glasses of Sekt, and through a slightly veiled conversation, is that none of these gentlemen are particularly keen on Herr Hitler. Neither Herr Dürr nor Herr Dornier are members of the Nazi party. They know each other well, they tell me, from the days they worked together with Count von Zeppelin. Now, though, they have competing views over the long-term future of transatlantic flight. Herr Dürr goes along with Dr Eckener's view that 'the aeroplane is tragically unsuited for ocean service'. Herr Dornier admits that his ambitious 12-engine Do X flying boat, the nearest thing yet to an 'airliner', was not a success, but he has great hopes. Herr Dürr nods and, very kindly, offers me a tour of the airship after dinner. When, though, I ask Herr Dornier about his new high-speed mail plane, the Do 17, he demurs. 'We are making good progress,' is all he will say.

Mr von Wiegand is certainly not a Nazi. He is, he tells me, an American journalist for Hearst Newspapers. Born in Hesse in Germany, he has lived and worked in New York for many years. He reported the story of Dr Eckener and *Graf Zeppelin*'s around-the-world and North Pole flights for the American press, working with his colleague Lady Drummond-Hay, of whom he speaks very fondly. The lively Lady Drummond-Hay is well known to Zeppelin staff and crews.

Mr von Wiegand explains that he had seen me this morning at IG Farben. 'Really?'

'Yes, I'm working on a story about leading American businesses working with the Third Reich.' He says this in a matter-of-fact manner. 'And, when I asked about you – I couldn't mistake your English accent – I was told you're working in aviation.'

As I've nothing to hide, I'm able to explain that my mission is to find the best form of self-sealing fuel tanks. Herr Dornier's eyes light up. This is, he says, exactly what he has fitted to the Do 17 high-speed mail plane.

We look at the fixed-choice menu. Caviar. Foie gras. Cold chicken with asparagus vinaigrette and potato salad. 'Herr Dornier must choose the wine,' says Herr Dürr. 'It's something he knows well.'

'My father,' explains Herr Dornier, 'was born in France. He settled in Bavaria, where he married my mother, a German. His business was importing French wine to Germany – but, alas, there is only one unassuming Burgundy on the list. Let's see. I think with the chicken we might do well with an Ürziger Würzgarten, a decent Riesling.'

The meal is simple, yet graciously served in the summer-bright and cheerfully decorated dining lounge. Napery, silver cutlery by – I can't help looking – Gebrüder Hepp of Pforzheim, and chinaware are all of the highest quality. It's rather funny to think that this grand hotel-style dining room is sailing 1,500 feet above ground, between walls and floors not of marble and oak but of lightweight duralumin and waterproof cotton.

As Herr Dornier and Herr Dürr pursue the debate over airships versus aeroplanes, Mr von Wiegand, while probing to see if I know anything about the Americans at IG Farben – I don't – tells me something about the passengers diagonally opposite us. 'The German gentleman is Herr Karl Ritter, envoy to the legation in Rio and tipped to be the next ambassador to Brazil. He's keen on helping to develop new industry there that will be to Germany's benefit. With him are two of the Americans you saw at IG Farben. One's from Standard Oil, the other from Ford. Both companies get on well with the Nazi government. I imagine they're planning something together in Brazil. Henry Ford did try to set up an industrial town in the country a few years ago. Wasn't too keen on Britain having a monopoly on the rubber he needed for automobile production. So Fordlândia was built as a rubber plantation, with nine per cent of the profits going to the Brazilian government. It was a failure. Abandoned in '34.'

'The Brazilian government likes Hitler?' I ask.

'More or less. There's been a branch of the Nazi party in Brazil since '28. The president, Getúlio Dornelles Vargas, is a populist keen on social welfare and workers' rights. But he's long admired Mussolini, and now, I think, he's feeling much the same way about Hitler.'

There's laughter from the table next to ours, where M. Le Corbusier is entertaining, or being entertained by, the two young Brazilian women and their male companion. 'And M. Le Corbusier?' I say quietly.

'Brazil is modernizing. He's probably pursuing a building project there. If so, you might want to talk to the young man at the American table. He's an architect, too, from Albert Speer's studio in Berlin. Worked on the design, he told me at the airfield, of the *Zeppelinfeld*, the Nazi rally ground in Nuremberg.'

'What's Zeppelin got to do with that?'

'It's called the Zeppelin field simply because von Zeppelin landed there in one of the early airships. I doubt if you'll get much on Zeppelin's relationship with the government from our captain. The Nazis don't like him and the antagonism is mutual. Dr Eckener considered standing against Hitler in the '32 election, and he's refused Hitler the use of the Frankfurt airship hangar for a party rally. But he's a popular German hero and, although officially a *persona non grata*, he's been left alone.'

M. Le Corbusier's Brazilian friends have discovered a record player, and we are now entertained with samba music. The young women sing along with Carmen Miranda's 'Alô, Alô Carnaval' and a jaunty song by Francisco Alves. Herr Dürr asks if I'd like to walk around the ship with him. Of course. He shuts the door of the newly established samba club behind us, and we enter a functional world of drilled alloy struts, dials, levers, wheels, map tables, wireless sets and other modern apparatus.

To starboard is the galley, a machine for cooking in, which M. Le Corbusier is sure to be impressed by. On our port side is the radio room and, ahead, a spacious map room. The bridge, with its enormous windows, is up front, of course. I'm introduced to Dr Eckener who, dressed like a sea captain, sports a fine pair of Zeiss binoculars. We stand staring from the windows as the airship casts its long shadow over summer fields. At this height, 1,200 feet, we can see villagers wave as we pass over them.

I ask Dr Eckener how low we can fly. 'A centimetre above the ground if it was as level as one of your English cricket fields. Herr Dürr will give you the technical specifications.'

He does. *Graf Zeppelin* made her maiden flight in September 1928. Her first four years were taken up by test and publicity sorties. She went into regular service between Friedrichshafen and Rio de Janeiro in '32. Today is her first flight from Frankfurt.

Inside the alloy frame, I learn, are 29 gas cells, 17 filled with hydrogen for lift and 12 with Blau gas – propane, essentially – for the five Maybach VL-2 12-cylinder 550-hp engines. These are located in streamlined nacelles set well behind the gondola. At maximum power, *Graf Zeppelin* has a top speed of 128 km/h or 80 mph. We cruise at 73 mph. The payload is 15,000 kilograms, or around 15 tons. Today, we are carrying hundreds of letters and as many postcards, along with cargo bound for Brazil. 'The original idea,' says Herr Dürr, 'had been for a mail airship operated by the Spanish between Seville and Rio de

Janeiro. So, the number of passengers we carry is limited to twenty. In future designs we aim to provide cabins for up to seventy.'

We look back into the radio room. 'We have three wireless operators. We can communicate with ships and ground stations. We have a radio telephone and we can also send and receive private telegrams.' It is, I tell Herr Dürr, all very impressive. But where, I can't help wondering, is the rest of the crew? I think it's 40 strong and yet, including stewards and cooks, I've seen about 15. 'In the corner there, you see a ladder. Tomorrow morning, I'll show you upstairs.'

I thank Herr Dürr and return to the samba lounge. M. Le Corbusier is now wearing a party hat made from a folded napkin. The young German architect is playing an accordion and the young women are crooning. Their bronzed colleague, head on a table, is fast asleep. The Americans and Herr Ritter are in deep conversation over whiskies. I bid them all goodnight and make my way along the corridor to my cabin. I hear a typewriter rattling and tinging, and assume my new friend, the informative Hearst correspondent, is busy at work. The washroom is vacant, so I brush my teeth, then, back in my cabin, I slip under the covers of the sofa bed. Rocked gently by the sway of the air, I fall soundly asleep.

At seven, a steward brings tea. I'm up, washed, shaved and dressed in minutes. The only other person in the dining lounge as I order breakfast – coffee, ham and eggs, and toast and butter – is M. Le Corbusier, who is making notes and rapid sketches. I decide to brave it and join him as we fly over parched Spanish plains. I think M. Le Corbusier is pleased we can converse in French, and even more pleased because I say I have his *Aircraft* book at home. I steer a careful path, yet mention that I've been staying in Frankfurt's Altstadt and have been fascinated to learn that Johann Hess, the early-nineteenth-century city architect, would have liked to demolish it. 'Of course,' says M. Le Corbusier. 'I can show you other cities we'll pass over that are just as wrong for our era as Frankfurt's Altstadt. What did I write? *The airplane eye looks with alarm at the places where we live, the cities where it is our lot to be. And the spectacle is frightening, overwhelming. The airplane eye reveals a spectacle of collapse. We need new cities from the ashes of these outmoded and disgraceful places.*'

I feel like saying, perhaps we could bomb them to pieces from the air and then rebuild them in the modern manner – all elevated roads, tall buildings and *machines à habiter* – but I don't. The idea is as absurd as it is uncouth, and yet M. Le Corbusier is clearly a man of conviction. We can agree, though, on the beauty and economy of aircraft design and engineering. When I ask him why in *Vers une Architecture* he says that the aircraft is designed in the same spirit as the Parthenon, he is about to begin a second lecture just as Herr Dürr asks if I'd like the tour he'd promised me 'upstairs'. I suggest M. Le Corbusier accompany us, which he is keen to do. *Allons-y!*

Up the ladder from the radio room, and we find ourselves in an extraordinary space – a voluminous lightweight alloy frame filled with huge flexible gas containers, and a skin that appears to breathe. Up here we can hear the wind, yet barely feel it. A metal gangway leads forwards and backwards along the length of the craft, disappearing into the distance.

I ask what the cells are made of. Rubber? No. 'Goldbeater's skin.' In other words, beaten cattle intestines that are flattened, treated and bonded. We really are in the belly of this magnificent beast. In between the cells and off the sides of the gangway are the crew's quarters, much like those found for ratings on warships. Hammocks. Bunks. Canvas covers. A small area for eating and resting. A lavatory. Boxes of tools. All tackle trim, though; immaculately clean and in its proper place. Further along, as we weave between members of the crew, we are shown the water supply – 2,000 litres, or about 450 gallons – employed as trim ballast, as well as for cooking, drinking and washing. We stop to admire a pair of fuel-powered electricity generators.

'The electricity supply,' says Herr Dürr, 'is supplemented by rammed air turbines.' Evidently, the workings of the airship are well planned and thorough. M. Le Corbusier wants to know what material her covering is made from. 'Cotton fabric,' replies Herr Dürr. 'Painted, varnished and treated with aluminium powder. This gives the airship its silver colour. It also reflects sunlight to protect the gas cells from heat and ultraviolet light. And now, the engines.'

This is very exciting. Herr Dürr opens a hatch, and there below us, in a roar of wind, exhaust and spinning airscrews, is Andalusia and a steel ladder leading down to one of the engine nacelles. 'Would you like to inspect an engine?'

'Of course.'

M. Le Corbusier takes a photograph, but decides, perhaps wisely, to return to the safety of the map room and the comforts of the dining lounge.

Down below, a mechanic has opened a hatch in the alloy nacelle. Taking a firm hold of the handrails, Herr Dürr steps decisively into what for a moment seems like nothing more than thin air. I follow suit, rather enjoying the sight of sunny Spain far below, but perfectly aware of the strength of the slipstream. A pair of hands reaches up to ensure I'm safely inside. The mechanic tends to his charge that, says Herr Dürr above the roar, is one of *Graf Zeppelin*'s five Maybach engines. Displacement: 33¼ litres. Maximum power: 550 hp at 1,600 rpm. This mighty machine, made in Friedrichshafen, is – I'd guess – about 6 feet long, 3 feet wide and 3 feet high.

To slow and stop *Graf Zeppelin*, a mechanism operated through levers by the mechanic inside the nacelle reverses the direction of the crankshaft. 'The Maybach VL-2s are very reliable,' Herr Dürr tells me. 'We replaced the original engines after six years and more than one million kilometres.'

I'd like to know more about Herr Dürr's work, and he agrees to talk over lunch. We make our way carefully out of the nacelle and up towards the gleaming fuselage. Just as he is about to climb into the belly of the airship, Herr Dürr suggests I lean out for a moment and look directly above. What a sight. Three riggers harnessed to a spider's web of ropes or wires are climbing up and around the outside of the airship. They are checking for a tear in the fabric. They can make repairs while the machine is in flight. What extraordinary 'extras' these 'spiders' – as fellow members of the crew know them – would have made in the production of *Flying Down to Rio*.

Back in the dining lounge, I look for M. Le Corbusier. He may have gone to wash his hands. On the table, his notebook lies open. I know I really shouldn't, yet I can't resist taking a quick peep at his sketches. And what's this he's written? 'I just had a look at the enchanting interior skeleton of the air vessel. What are its laws? Precise, dramatic, rigorous: economy.' I suppose you can't say fairer than that.

When M. Le Corbusier returns, he congratulates me on my bravery in climbing down to the engine nacelle. I take the opportunity to ask him what takes him to Brazil. He has been once before, he says, in 1929. That time, he sailed to Montevideo and Buenos Aires and was flown on to São Paulo and Rio de Janeiro. One of his pilots was the pioneer French aviator Antoine de Saint-Exupéry, a director of Aeroposta Argentina. I know the count's novel *Night Flight*, and have seen the film of the book with John Barrymore, Helen Hayes and Clark Gable.

This time, says M. Le Corbusier, he has been invited by Minister Gustavo Capanema on behalf of the committee of architects charged with the design and construction of the new Ministry of National Education and Public Health, to supervise the project. This is to be a Modern building, 15 storeys high, and a symbol of the new Brazil. M. Le Corbusier draws a quick sketch of the new ministry, which might easily be one of his own designs. He shows me a letter written to him by the architects involved. The names are unfamiliar to me. Lúcio Costa. Affonso Eduardo Reidy. Ernâni Vasconcellos. Carlos Leão. Jorge Machado Moreira. Roberto Burle Marx. And Oscar Niemeyer ('intern').

M. Le Corbusier will also give a number of lectures in Rio and promote his plan for the rebuilding of the Brazilian capital city – complete, *naturellement*, with elevated roads and skyscraper housing. Now, though, it's time for some reading before lunch.

When the dining lounge is back in swing again, Herr Dürr ushers me to a table on the port side of the room. He tells me, over bowls of delicious *Kalbsragout* – stewed veal and vegetables – and glasses of mineral water, that he joined Count von Zeppelin at Friedrichshafen in 1899. He worked on the very first Zeppelin, LZ 1, and has been in charge of the design and construction of every Zeppelin since. Much of the work has been a case of trial and error, although he has employed exceptional talents – among them Karl Arnstein, who specializes in stress analysis, and the Hungarian aerodynamicist Paul Jaray. 'Mr Jaray conducted wind-tunnel tests at the University of Göttingen. The results gave us a new way of designing airships with a streamlined profile, and the gondola integrated into the main structure rather than being suspended from it. In fact, the *Graf Zeppelin* owes its profile to the LZ 120 *Bodensee* of 1919. This was very much Mr Jaray's work.'

'He's still with you?'

'No, no. He left for Switzerland in 1923 to establish his own studio. He's been doing fine work for Tatra cars in Czechoslovakia, but has many clients – especially in the automobile industry.'

'And Herr Arnstein?'

'In 1924 we set up a partnership with Goodyear in the United States. Herr Arnstein went there to design two more or less identical ships: the USS *Akron* that launched in 1931, and USS *Macon* in '33. He made some radical changes to the alloy structure and was able to use helium, an inert gas produced mainly in Kansas and Texas. These were good machines, bigger than *Graf Zeppelin*, but great demands were placed on them by the US Navy.'

'Yes, I remember. They were aircraft carriers, weren't they, and flew – let me think – Curtiss Sparrowhawks.'

'You remember well. Anyhow, the *Akron* crashed in '33 and the *Macon* in '35. This was not Herr Arnstein's fault, of course, but the loss of both airships put an end to the US military airship programme. Herr Arnstein continues to work on designs for civil airships. He believes these are the future of transatlantic and Pacific travel, and has even written an article in the *New York Times* on the subject.'

I ask Herr Dürr, over cheese and fruit, what the long-term future might hold. 'Perhaps you should ask Mr von Wiegand. He interviewed Herr Hitler a year before the Munich Putsch. He saw him as a potentially great leader... anyway, to answer your question, I should direct you to two articles in *Flug*, published last summer and early this year by Dr Eugen Sänger, in which he discussed rocket-powered aircraft. The Reich government has taken him seriously and has built him a secret research institute. I don't know much about this, and perhaps you shouldn't talk about it while you're in Germany.'

'I'm not in Germany now,' I say. 'In fact, judging from what I can see, we're not all that far from Cádiz.'

In the afternoon, I catch up with work and take a siesta, something I very rarely do, and yet the sunlight and the motion of our ship – and perhaps having taken in so much that is new – has made me tired. By the time I wake, we're over the Atlantic. Inviting me back onto the bridge, Dr Eckener shows me the 'sights'. Gibraltar and Morocco are to our port side, the North Atlantic to starboard. The weather? Good.

We chat about Dr Eckener's around-the-world adventures in less-forgiving weather, and stare out to sea. We spot ships, mostly freighters, but here and there Mediterranean and Atlantic liners. And a small plane hugging the African coast. Dr Eckener tells me of how in 1928, after nearly 112 hours and almost 10,000 kilometres airborne, he landed *Graf Zeppelin* at Lakehurst, New Jersey, to a tumultuous reception – followed by a ticker-tape parade in open cars through Manhattan and dinner at the White House. *Graf Zeppelin*'s had been the first commercial passenger air crossing of the Atlantic.

As no one seems to be bothered by my being here, I stay on the bridge, mesmerized by the views and workings of the ship, until six, when it's time for a cocktail. The glamorous young women and their bronzed companion are sitting down. They flash smiles, and before M. Le Corbusier arrives, I introduce myself and take a seat at their table. The women, Andressa and Canciana, are indeed showgirls. They've been singing and dancing in German theatres to publicize *Alô, Alô Carnaval* and future productions from Cinédia, the Rio studio that made the popular samba film. Their companion is Adhemar Gonzaga – actor, screenwriter, producer, director, and founder of Cinédia – who tells me that there must be a million Germans living in Brazil. The connection between the two countries is close.

We talk happily over Oriental salad, consommé Célestine and Riesling. Canciana and Andressa promise to sing again later in the evening. We get up and watch our Zeppelin's shadow pass over the rugged Moroccan landscape. Herr Ritter joins us, and, as he does, he and I fall into conversation. He's pleased I'm travelling to Rio by a German aircraft. He orders schnapps and we drink toasts. *'Heil Hitler.'* 'God save the King.' *'Prost!'* 'Mud in your eye.'

Herr Ritter describes Brazil as the sleeping giant of the Americas. He sees it in coming years as a part of a German 'extended economic space', for which I'm sure there's a very long German word. Currently, Brazil exports mostly coffee and cacao, but with German help the country will soon be producing cotton while developing its technical sector. 'We are working well,' he says, 'with the Americans. And, of course, we have many friends in your country at the highest levels.'

I have a feeling that Herr Ritter might be looking to recruit a foreign agent, so I make a polite exit and head to my cabin to read and to drift off, even though the night is young.

I wake to the sound of rain pattering on the skin of the ship. From the window I see that we're flying low under brooding nimbus clouds. There is no point in the captain trying to fly above the clouds in search of clear skies. To do so, we'd have to climb too high for anyone's comfort. Better to scurry through the rain. The storm keeps passengers late in their cabins but it doesn't last long, and on gaining steadier air we emerge for light breakfasts.

The largely dull Atlantic weather and the prospect of a long haul over the sea make this an ideal working day. I have a report to prepare as well as my notes of this trip to write up. I set up my typewriter, an Underwood Noiseless Portable, and set to work. I keep this up until midday, when thoughts of lunch usurp those of productive work. I sit at a starboard table with M. Le Corbusier and the young German architect from Herr Speer's office in Berlin. This should be interesting. Sadly, once he has translated *Rührei mit Spargelspitzen*, which doesn't sound too appetizing, into French and English, he is met by M. Le Corbusier's best impression of an Easter Island statue.

The Swiss-French architect has decided not to engage but to withdraw into himself. I had been hoping for a lively debate on the relative virtues of Modern and Neo-Classical architecture, but it doesn't get off the ground. I end up talking to Herr Speer's architect about a walking trip I made into the Bavarian Alps as a student, and we chat about favourite Bavarian Baroque and Rococo churches, and beautiful, all-but-unchanging cities like Dresden. Nuremberg, I say, will surely never be quite the same as it was, now that the Nazi party rally grounds occupy more space than the old city centre. 'We must build for the new tomorrow,' says the young architect.

I make an early-afternoon visit to the bridge and map room. It's exciting to chart our progress. And to sneak a pot of tea from the kitchen. I had been planning to get back to my typewriter, but I find M. Le Corbusier in the dining lounge. He almost apologizes for his silence over lunch, adding that because of cultural differences he is unable to work for the Nazis. I can't shake off the feeling, though, that as an architect he would be happy to take the Third Reich's money if only the Germans would agree to a white concrete stadium raised on pilotis.

I have heard that M. Le Corbusier's German acquaintance, Herr Ludwig Mies van der Rohe, an equally celebrated Modern architect, was busy only two years ago with competition designs for the Third Reich's national pavilion for the Brussels International Exposition. Even with swastikas on his drawings, he didn't win. Not so long ago, Mr Mies was a Spartacist. Or masqueraded as one.

I return to my typewriter and work until six. It's that time again, and although there is no yardarm as far as I can see and the sun is high in the Atlantic skies, I order a dry martini and watch the waves roll and sparkle beneath us. Mr von Wiegand joins me. 'We are making smooth progress,' he says.

'Indeed.'

'We couldn't be in better hands than those of Dr Eckener.'

'I suppose not. Perhaps he should have been president, then Germany might have been in safer hands today. I hear that you cottoned on to Hitler years ago.'

'You mean I had the measure of him? Not exactly. I could see he was a firebrand and could stir crowds. I thought he had the makings of a powerful leader, but I had no idea he would revolutionize Germany in the way he has; abandon democracy and pass his Nuremberg Laws. I pity the Jews. What's the latest in Britain?'

'We're building up our forces, although a bit too slowly for comfort. But we have our appeasers and our Hitler supporters.'

But the sound of samba is back again, putting an abrupt end to these maudlin thoughts. In any case, and despite the two-storey-high swastika on one side of *Graf Zeppelin*'s tail, we are for the next 36 hours as free as birds. The captain joins us for dinner and we work our way through a consommé followed by trout, cheese and a *Bombe Kleingebäck*. The mood is cheerful. No one speaks of politics, and even the earnest American businessmen appear to join in. In fact, by ten o'clock I'm sure they're more than half-cut.

In the morning we are far out to sea. A rack of lamb at lunch tides us over until dinner. I pay a visit to the map room and bridge. And there, still some way away, a dark green line like a long low hedge, is the Brazilian coast. The temptation is to stand and watch it all afternoon. 'We'll be at Recife at 1700 hours,' says Dr Eckener. And we are.

All aboard, it seems, are pressed to *Graf Zeppelin*'s windows as we nose gently towards a fringe of sandy beaches, across the confluence of the Beberibe and Capibaribe rivers. With the city stretched around us, I can see we are heading to what appears to be a large park, with, yes, a tall red-and-white mooring mast. We circle this very slowly and, with an army of riggers waiting, come to a standstill, the airship floating just above the ground.

Once secured to the mast, we are ready to disembark. When I do, my legs have that feeling they get when walking downstairs after a long boat trip or cycle ride. Here we have a choice. We can dine on board or go into town. At any rate, we must promise to be back early tomorrow morning, ready for the onward flight to Rio. After some handshaking and thanks, a tug on my arm introduces me to my Recife contact, Alex, from the British embassy. Alex is spending the summer – I mean, winter – here in the north-east of the country.

We spin out from the city in Alex's Fiat 1500 – a lovely six-cylinder car, its svelte coachwork shaped through wind-tunnel tests, he tells me – and out to the ocean. We eat grilled cheese, beef stew with cassava, and fruits I have never seen before, much less tasted, outside a venerable *bodega* on an 80 degrees Fahrenheit street of pastel-coloured seventeenth- or eighteenth-century colonial houses in the heart of Olinda. The patron brings a special pudding for the Englishmen, a 'Top Hat Cake', made from baked bananas, soft cheese, sugar and cinnamon. We stroll by the sea and, thanks to Alex's Catholic connections, stay the night in spacious cells in the deep-eaved cloister of the Baroque convent of São Francisco.

I drift towards sleep accompanied by the muffled sound of Atlantic rollers, the electric bleeps of tree frogs, and tropical rain pattering on pantiles. I have enjoyed life aboard *Graf Zeppelin*, yet after so many days in the air, it feels good to be grounded for a night.

The morning sees us purring along the coast and cutting back into Recife, the shadow of LZ 127 and her ostentatious swastika lording it over gently swaying palm trees. Alex will drive south to Rio when the rains stop. This will take him a little longer than *Graf Zeppelin*. Cruising at 60 to 70 mph, we'll fly the 1,400 or so miles within the next 24 hours.

There has been more than enough time for whatever work passengers needed to have done on board, and so, today, we fly like a cruise ship along Brazil's luxuriant coast, a day spent eating, chatting and reading. There are card games to be played, songs to be sung, although there is a general agreement that this is no time or place for the young German architect to pick up the accordion and sing, as he promises to do, the 'Horst-Wessel-Lied'. A little encouragement and a drink or three sees him changing his tune. We all enjoy his 'Lili Marleen', as he does his handsome best to stand in for Marlene Dietrich. Andressa and Canciana, his honorary German chorus, croon 'Bei der Laterne wollen wir stehen / Wie einst Lili Marleen.'

M. Le Corbusier is busy filming. The Americans drink beer. Mr von Wiegand retreats to his cabin and typewriter. For these few aerial hours at least, and with a supply of fresh Brazilian food in the kitchen, Europe and its tensions seem far away. We are buffeted by a brief, if tense, tropical squall, yet our progress is stately. A samba evening ends the day. Fourth night aboard. I pack my bags and roll into my bunk, ready for sleep.

Awake now, and the weather is not quite so friendly as it has been. Invited to the bridge to watch our approach, I see low rainclouds and feel the force of the wind. Below us, though, is the marvellous sight of Rio de Janeiro. Guanabara Bay. Sugar Loaf Mountain. And, there, the 100-foot-high statue of Christ the Redeemer, arms outstretched from the peak of Mount Corcovado. Fighting the wind, we make a rather awkward docking at Campo dos Afonsos, some 25 miles north-west of Ipanema and Copacabana beaches. I gather that a new airport, complete with a Zeppelin hangar, is under construction somewhere else in Rio. But, we're down at last. While I'm making my farewells, M. Le Corbusier is already out of the ship, the first to do so. A huddle of fellow architects greets him, as if he were a sky god descending on some lost tribe.

While I wait for my bags, I can't help thinking of the story of Alberto Santos-Dumont, the Brazilian aviation pioneer who designed, built and flew both lighter- and heavier-than-air machines. He made his mark in Paris, where many believed he was the first man to fly a heavier-than-air-machine in 1905

– either not having heard of the Wright Brothers or unable to believe that Americans had beaten the French. Depressed by the thought of his beloved aircraft being used for warfare – especially during the Constitutionalist Revolution of 1932, when Vargas's loyalist air force bombed women and children in villages around São Paolo – he hanged himself.

On this rather morbid thought – and while I wait for my connecting flight operated by Syndicato Condor, a subsidiary of Lufthansa operating Junkers Ju 52s – I look long and hard at *Graf Zeppelin*. I hope the Germans will continue to behave themselves.

*

The transatlantic Zeppelin service from Germany to Brazil was short-lived. On 6th May 1937, LZ 129 *Hindenburg* burst into flames while trying to dock at Lakehurst, New Jersey, at the end of a flight from Germany. Twenty-two passengers, thirteen crew and one member of the ground crew died. Pathé, Hearst, Paramount and Movietone captured the event on newsreels that shook public confidence in airships. *Graf Zeppelin*, having departed Recife on a flight to Frankfurt on 4th May, received the news by radio. Diverted to Ludwigshafen, she made just one more flight from there to Frankfurt before being taken out of service. The exact cause of the fire that destroyed *Hindenburg* is not known, but because her fuel cells were filled with hydrogen rather than inert helium, the airship lit up like a torch. Ludwig Dürr had designed this later and much bigger Zeppelin with helium in mind, but a US embargo on helium sales to Germany ensured she flew courtesy of hydrogen.

The 803-foot-long *Hindenburg* carried up to 70 passengers inside its structure. Accommodation included two promenade decks, a restaurant, a lounge and cocktail bar complete with an aluminium Blüthner grand piano, and a sealed and pressurized smoking room. Lightweight furniture and design were Bauhaus in style although the decor was playful, with walls lined in silk painted with scenes of historic voyages, the round-the-world ventures of *Graf Zeppelin* and capriccios of exotic holiday settings. The designer, Fritz August Breuhaus de Groot, specialized in holiday homes for German film stars and the interiors of ocean liners.

A sister airship, LZ 130 *Graf Zeppelin II*, was launched in September 1938 but never went into regular passenger service. She was scrapped along with *Graf Zeppelin* in March 1940, on the orders of Hermann Göring. Along with repatriated duralumin scrap metal from *Hindenburg*, metal components of LZ 127 and LZ 130 were used in the manufacture of military aircraft for the Luftwaffe, a case of ploughshares into swords.

Graf Zeppelin herself, despite using hydrogen, is still considered the most successful airship ever built. In nine years of operation, she made 590 flights – including 64 to and from Brazil – clocked up 17,177 flight hours and over a million miles, and carried 34,000 passengers and 30 tons of cargo (including a car and two light aircraft) without accident. The mast she last flew from in Recife was restored in 2012–13 with public funds, under the supervision of the Brazilian sculptor Jobson Figueiredo. It was to have been the focal point of a new science and culture park, with the bonus of a Zeppelin museum. Money, though, has been tight in Brazil, and the project is in abeyance. A short walk from Mangueira metro station, the mast can be visited – although with some caution, as this is a rundown area and the site is in the grounds of a military base.

Rio's Bartolomeu de Gusmão Airport was inaugurated by President Vargas in December 1936. Its impressive Zeppelin hangar, made as a kit of parts in Germany and shipped to Rio, survives. Today, it is home to fixed-wing military jets. The hangar and attendant buildings demanded a labour force 5,500 strong, and took 23 months to erect. Appropriated from the Germans in 1942 when Brazil, under Vargas, sided with the Allies, the airport was renamed Santa Cruz Air Force Base. *Graf Zeppelin* and *Hindenburg* had used the hangar just nine times between them.

In 1937, Karl Ritter was appointed German ambassador to Brazil. That April, during the Spanish Civil War, the Luftwaffe's Condor Legion – under the command of Oberstleutnant Wolfram von Richthofen, a cousin of the 'Red Baron' of First World War fame – carpet-bombed civilians in Guernica, a market town in the Basque country. Among the bombers were 18 Junker Ju52s and a Dornier Do 17, no longer the fast mail plane its designer might have planned.

Ford, Standard Oil and General Motors continued their association with Third Reich industry throughout the 1930s. Among chemicals developed by IG Farben was Zyklon B, a hydrogen cyanide–based pesticide still available under various trade names today. The samba craze endured. Released in 1943, *Samba in Berlin*, directed by Luiz de Barros, made fun of Nazi Germany.

Le Corbusier spent five weeks in Brazil, returning to Europe by ship, a voyage that took 13 days. By this time, he was one of the world's most famous and influential architects. Hugo Eckener was sidelined by the Nazi regime he despised. In 1945, French authorities in Berlin tried unsuccessfully to charge him with pro-Nazi affiliations. He wrote a fascinating and enjoyable book, *My Zeppelins*, published in 1958. Ludwig Dürr retired when the Zeppelin company folded in 1945. Ernst Udet became the Luftwaffe's Director-General of Equipment. He committed suicide in November 1941, believing that Operation Barbarossa, Hitler's invasion of the Soviet Union, had doomed Germany.

Research into lightweight plywood aircraft led to the highly effective de Havilland Mosquito, the 'Wooden Wonder', a multi-role twin-engine RAF combat aircraft of which 7,781 were built between 1940 and 1950. It had a top speed of 415 mph and a ceiling of 37,000 feet. Arthur Hagg had left de Havilland in 1937 to build yachts, but was soon involved in an attempt to break the world airspeed record. Financed by Lord Nuffield, founder of Morris Motors, Hagg's Napier-Heston Racer made its maiden flight in June 1940. Made almost entirely of wood, it was powered by a top-secret Napier Sabre H-24 engine. Its top speed was estimated to be 480 mph, sufficient to take the world record from the Messerschmitt Me 209 flown by Fritz Wendel in April 1939 at 469.2 mph. The first Napier-Heston crash-landed on its maiden flight and, with a war on, the second was cancelled. Subsequent records were to be made, from 1941, by rocket-powered and jet planes in Germany and Britain.

Dr Eugen Sänger's Silbervogel rocket plane – designed with his wife, the mathematician and physicist Dr Irene Bredt, in a secret research centre at Braunschweig, Lower Saxony, from 1936 – was to have flown in a series of sub-orbital hops across the Atlantic at a speed of 22,100 km/h (13,732 mph) and at a maximum altitude of 145 kilometres (90 miles). It would have unleashed its single 8,000-pound bomb over New York before flying across the Pacific to land in Japan. The project was cancelled in 1942.

Sänger's wartime and post-war work on ramjets remains important, as does his research into propulsion systems for future interstellar rockets. His work influenced the design of the North American X-15 rocket plane – its speed of Mach 6.72 or 4,520 mph reached in October 1967 is still the world record for a manned, powered aircraft – and NASA's Space Shuttle. At the time of his death in 1964, aged just 58, Dr Sänger was professor of Space Flight Technology at the Technical

University of Berlin. Among the university's most famous – or infamous – graduates were Werner von Braun and Albert Speer.

As for speed by steam traction, LNER Pacific 4468 *Mallard*, designed under the direction of Sir Nigel Gresley, set an, as yet, unbeaten record of 126 mph in July 1938. Airships were never a fast way to travel in absolute terms, but in 1936, when there was no competition from heavier-than-air machines, *Graf Zeppelin* was more than twice as fast as an ocean liner. The Zeppelin company was resurrected at Ludwigshafen in 1993. The first Zeppelin NT ('New Technology'), a 75-metre (246-foot) semi-dirigible, made its maiden flight four years later. Seating a maximum of 12 passengers, Zeppelin NTs operate tourist, media, advertising and research flights.

In 1999, I made a television documentary, *Great Exhibitions*, for Channel 4, commissioned by Waldemar Januszczak and produced by Mike Lerner, broadcast on Boxing Day shortly before the Queen opened Tony Blair's £1-billion folly, the Millennium Dome. We hired an Airship Industries Skyship 500 to film the sites of great British exhibitions since 1851, the airship doubling up as a time machine of sorts as it flew slowly back into a smoke-and-mirrors past. We set off from the imperious airship hangar at Cardington, Bedfordshire, and I thought the trip the stuff of aerial sorcery.

Airship Industries has since morphed into Cardington's Hybrid Air Vehicles. The company's Airlander 10 – a semi-dirigible with the unmistakable and slightly bizarre profile of a pair of human buttocks (its nickname is the 'Flying Bum') first flown in 2012 – was developed with Northrup Grumman as a surveillance aircraft for the US Army. Its maiden flight was from the US Navy base at Lakehurst, New Jersey. But the US Army said no, so the airship was ferried back to England, where it was relaunched as the prototype of a luxury aerial cruise ship at the

2018 Farnborough Airshow. Although inelegant, the Airlander 10 – the world's biggest aircraft – was shown with a CEO/celebrity/footballer-style interior, featuring en-suite bedrooms, cocktail bar, observation saloon and tattoo parlour (not really), with glass floors. It could well succeed. Stephen McGlennan, CEO of Hybrid Air Vehicles, said, 'Air travel has become very much about getting from A to B as quickly as possible. What we're offering is a way of making the journey a joy' – which, in itself, is a pleasure to hear.

How much might a new technology airship flight to Rio cost today? It's hard to say, but the fare from Frankfurt to Rio de Janeiro by *Graf Zeppelin* in 1936 was 1,500 Reichsmarks, or about £9,000 in 2018 money. A first-class Lufthansa ticket from Frankfurt to Rio de Janeiro is approximately £7,000. If airships were to fly once more from Frankfurt to Rio, one thing that would be notably different from the journey made in 1936 would be the views of Frankfurt itself. On the nights of 18th and 23rd March 1943, two enormous flotillas of RAF bombers, led to their target by de Havilland Mosquitoes, obliterated much of Frankfurt – including almost the entire half-timbered medieval Altstadt. One building that survives there is the Alte Nikolaikirche. Neither Johann Hess nor Air Marshal 'Bomber' Harris were able to destroy it.

FOUR

New York to Southampton:
SS Normandie

5th–9th August 1936

Declan O'Donnell stands four-square in bespoke linen at
the centre of the first-class balcony of SS *Normandie*. He
commands views of both the mountainous Manhattan
skyline and of tourist and third-class passengers thronged on
the balconies below. Standing alongside him, I say nothing. The
Irishman appears transfixed. Whistles and hooters blow as our
gigantic ship is eased from Pier 88, facing West 48th Street and
the Rockefeller Center's RCA Building, by pilot and tug boats.

There's the Empire State Building, and that's the Chrysler
Building, as tall as *Normandie* is long. But, as we're nursed
into the Hudson between busy ferries and our own armada of
attendant boats, I can see that Mr O'Donnell is staring intently
at one particular skyscraper.

'When I came out here from Donegal in 1913,' he says, 'we
were squeezed into steerage like – what can I tell you – pressed
ham. That was the *Celtic*. I tell you she carried three hundred
first-class passengers and, I swear, three thousand of us below
decks looking for a crust of bread in America. Well, when I heard

someone call "Land ahoy!" I was on the foredeck quicker than an odds-on favourite at the Curragh. "There's the Statue of Liberty," a young officer told me. But I saw something else. Do you want to know what?'

'Yes.'

'Look there. The Woolworth Building. It was brand-new. Tallest building in the world. I'd been told plenty enough rags-to-riches stories on the crossing from Liverpool, but Frank Woolworth's took the cake. Started as a shop boy sweeping up and cleaning the windows, and 30 years later built that, 13½ million dollars of his own money! He thought big, did Frank Woolworth, and this, for sure, was the place where any of us might have a chance, too.'

Mr O'Donnell has certainly made the best of his chance. Not yet 50, he is a construction-industry millionaire. Today, he's making a business trip to France on board the world's biggest and – from what I've read, and now see with my own eyes – most glamorous ocean liner. Rather than in steerage aboard the White Star Line's RMS *Celtic,* which ran aground off Cobh in County Cork a few years ago and was abandoned, Mr O'Donnell is sailing to Southampton in one of *Normandie's grand luxe* suites, with its four bedrooms, private dining room, reception room, high ceilings, ocean terrace, works of art, servants' quarters, Art Deco finery – the lot.

A chance business meeting with Mr O'Donnell in Manhattan has got me on board *Normandie.* One of his directors, who was to have sailed with him, fell ill. The long and short of it, and what with Mr O'Donnell refusing to back down on his more-than-generous offer, is that I have a deluxe first-class cabin on this, the world's greatest ship, although I expect some heady debate over the next few days now that Cunard-White Star has put *Queen Mary* into service.

I'm more than grateful to Mr O'Donnell, as my travels in Brazil were rather more ambitious than I'd planned for, and getting back to London p.d.q. without breaking the bank was never going to be a piece of cake. I had to splash out a fair bit on the five-day Pan Am flight from Rio to Miami and the overnight train from there to New York, so this has been a stroke of very good luck indeed.

Actually, I did have a plan to take out a loan somehow and fly back to Frankfurt on *Hindenburg*, but then I'd still have to get back to London from there – and, anyway, who could resist *Normandie*? As we put out to sea, when even Manhattan seems Lilliputian, we agree to retire and meet for dinner with the O'Donnell clan. I can't help lingering, though. *Normandie*'s wake stretches out almost flat, as if, now that she's accelerating hard, this great ship is barely skimming the water. Uncanny.

Walking down one flight of stairs, I find my cabin. A steward is unpacking my bags. He gathers my laundry and, promising to return before the cocktail hour, vanishes. I slip off my jacket, unlace my shoes and lie on one of my twin beds. What with the summer sun, the warm breeze from the open door of my terrace and the sway of the sea, I might easily fall fast asleep.

My cabin is certainly special. Concealed ceiling lighting, lacquered walls, chaise longue, dressing table. I fight sleep and run a bath. Then, waiting for my clothes to reappear, I sit at the table on the terrace and stare out to sea. I've taken a pale green brochure from the cabin. It's a colour production showing plans of the ship, illustrations of her public spaces and, yes, details of her construction, design, decor and engines. Just what I need to keep awake. Oh, and this is fun: 'Your safety and comfort will be assured by over 1,300 hand picked men bred in the iron discipline of Breton and Norman seamanship.'

More interesting than fun is the fact that the 1,345-strong crew serve a maximum complement of 1,972 passengers, of whom 848 are first class, 670 tourist class and, tucked into the stern, just 454 third class. This is very much the opposite way around to Mr O'Donnell's crossing by RMS *Celtic* a year before the war. Liners like *Normandie*, *Queen Mary* and Norddeutscher Lloyd's *Europa* have been aimed fairly and squarely at wealthy passengers – business moguls, senior politicians, film stars – and, cocooned in this lap of luxury, it can be hard to believe that Wall Street crashed seven years ago and that we're not out of the mire yet.

Anyway, *Normandie*, it says here, was laid down at the Ateliers et Chantiers de Penhoë shipyard at Saint-Nazaire in '31 for the Compagnie Générale Transatlantique (CGT), launched to the accompaniment of a crowd 200,000 strong in '32, and made her maiden voyage from Le Havre to New York last May when, of course, she took the Blue Riband – from the Italian Line's *Rex* – covering the course in four days, three hours and fourteen minutes, at an average speed of very slightly under 30 knots, which is certainly going some. Refitted over the winter – because of the threat of *Queen Mary* – she weighs a whopping 83,423 tons. From her top speed of 32 knots, *Normandie* can stop in just over a mile. I wonder what an emergency stop in the middle of the Atlantic must feel like?

A gallery of France's top designers is responsible for her decor. Emile-Jacques Ruhlmann, Georges Saupique, Raymond Subes, Georges Remon (my cabin, and the captain's, too), Luc Lanel, Louis Sue. All of it up-to-the minute Art Deco, and no sign of run-of-the-mill French hotel 'Louis Who-ey' styling. I have to confess I have no idea who these chaps are, although one name does ring a bell. Jean Dupas. *Jean Dupas?* Of course. He's the artist whose posters you see on the Underground or advertising Green Line coaches. That'll be Mr Pick at the LPTB, always on the ball when it comes to contemporary design.

Turning the pages of the brochure, I find, to my delight, a meticulously wrought cross-section illustration of *Normandie*. Here's my cabin. How tiny it seems in this city on the sea. And look at all these rooms. A huge first-class dining room takes centre stage. There are further dining rooms and several kitchens. Indoor and outdoor swimming pools. A garage for a hundred cars. Dog kennels at the base of the third (fake) funnel. A nightclub, a hospital, a winter garden, a 380-seat theatre, a Bon Marché promenade of shops, steam baths, a Punch and Judy theatre – that's the way to do it! – a chapel, a shooting range...

This bit's about the engines. *Normandie* is steam turbo-electric powered. Twenty-nine oil-fired boilers fitted with mechanical spray burners provide steam for four 46,530 hp turbines connected to four electric motors. Sounds complex, yet this makes good sense, and is one reason why *Normandie* is so smooth and quiet. Turning back a page, I see I'd missed the massage salon, the tailor's, hairdresser's and art gallery. And the hull, to ensure we do not repeat *Titanic*'s fate, is constructed from no less than 54 watertight sections.

A knock on the cabin door. The steward has returned with my clothes immaculately pressed. He hangs them in the lacquered wardrobe and shuts the cabin door silently as he leaves. Time to put on the ritz. Shirt, studs, cufflinks, black tie. And, at seven, as agreed, I make my way one floor up to the grill room bar, with its view over the stern of the ship. Mr O'Donnell, looking every inch the plutocrat, introduces me to his wife, Bernadette, three daughters, Mary, Isolde and Róisín, and son, Conner. Champagne pops and pours.

Mary is an artist. Her three-year-old daughter, Aileen, is in the nursery. 'It has a dining room of its own,' says Mary, 'decorated by the *Babar the Elephant* man.'

'Jean de Brunhoff,' says Róisín, who's 15 and at school in New York.

Isolde works for RKO Pictures as a junior producer, and travels often between Los Angeles and New York. 'How?' I ask her.

'Santa Fe to Chicago, and the *20th Century Limited* to Grand Central.'

'I hear the new DC-3 airliners will make the journey in fifteen hours with just three refuelling stops,' I say. 'Tempted?'

'I'm not sure. I mean, Daddy could fly to Europe on the *Hindenburg*, and maybe there'll be airplanes that can cross the Atlantic daily in the future, but would you swap the Santa Fe's *Chief* for a cramped airliner? And I guess the *Hindenburg* might be fun once, but I bet it doesn't have a theatre or a dance floor.'

'Or the sea,' says Mrs O'Donnell. 'We love the sea.'

Which is just as well, as 20 minutes later we sail into an electric storm – short-lived, but enough to rock *Normandie* and, perhaps, to put a few off the thought of dinner. But not the O'Donnells. Nor me. Told our table awaits us, we rise and, arms in various arms, go in.

Some going in. The dining room is gained through a pair of 20-foot doors adorned with bronze medallions depicting French castles and cathedrals, and down a flight of Busby Berkeley-style stairs. Perhaps we should be announced. The room itself, all softly lit Lalique glass walls, columns and ceiling, appears to shimmer into infinite space.

'One hundred and fifty settings,' confides Mr O'Donnell, who I discovered over cocktails has been buying New York hotels and restaurants with the idea of making them the best in the world. 'I tell you, this room is bigger than the Hall of Mirrors at Versailles.'

'He's been there,' says Conner, 'although he hasn't actually measured it.'

'You must ask Conner for the exact details,' says Mr O'Donnell. 'Him being an engineer and all. A great engineer, too.'

'Thanks, Dad. They can seat seven hundred for dinner when the ship's full. I do happen to know the measurements. Been studying form. I think Dad wants to open a glass restaurant even bigger than this one. It's 305 feet long, 46 feet wide and 28 feet high. The Hall of Mirrors at Versailles is 240 feet long and—'

'Boring,' says Róisín.

'I bet the Germans will build an even bigger one,' I say.

We all laugh and sit down to a dinner that seems grand even by the standards of the best Parisian restaurants. Mr O'Donnell insists on ordering equally grand wines – Margaux and d'Yquem – but then he can afford to; and, as he tells me, the only wine he knew before he made it big in New York was altar wine, so sweet it should have put him off for life. But, once he had ten bucks spare, he wanted to drink the finest wines in America. And then he discovered France. He's been a Francophile and oenophile ever since.

Róisín shows me her new black pleated-leather clutch bag. 'Hermès,' she says proudly. It's shaped like the profile of *Normandie*, with three silver funnels serving as catches. There's a silver anchor on one side, too.

'They give them to all the ladies in first class,' whispers Isolde. 'We've got some rather special scents on our dressing tables, too.'

'They think of everything,' I say.

'But,' says Conner, 'they don't think about Mr Vladimir Yourkevitch.'

'Your Russian friend?' asks Mary.

'Not a friend, but I did meet him with Dad last year at a CGT reception at the Rockefeller Center. He's the one person they never seem to talk about in public. Is he mentioned in that colour brochure in your cabin? No.'

Conner gives me the gen on Mr Yourkevitch as we tackle an ambitious display of *fruits de mers* placed in the centre of our table. Mr Yourkevitch, it appears, is the Russian émigré design engineer of *Normandie*'s streamlined hull. He was an engineer with the Imperial Russian Navy and was assisting in the design of a radical new class of battleship at the time of the October Revolution. Russia pulled out of the war, the battleships never left the drawing board, and Lieutenant Yourkevitch fought in the White Army against the Reds during the ensuing civil war.

He escaped to Turkey, where he worked in a car repair shop, before emigrating to France and getting a job as a mechanic with Renault. From there he took a position as a draughtsman with Penhoët, and worked on the design of *Normandie*. My beefsteak arrives. *À point*. With a Château Talbot. I'm too engrossed in Conner's story to note the vintage. Wholly independently, our Russian engineer designed the ship's revolutionary hull, building a model to prove its superiority over conventional designs to the chiefs at Penhoët. 'The model was put on trial with twenty-four rival designs at the Hamburg Testing Basin,' says Conner, 'with the famous Dr Kempf in charge.'

'I've never heard of him,' says Róisín.

'Anyway, guess which design won?'

'So, why don't we hear more about Mr Yourkevitch?' I ask.

'I think it's this,' says Conner. '*Normandie* is the pride of France. French-built, French decor, French cuisine. So, it'd be an embarrassment for the French to admit in public that the genius behind *Normandie* is a Russian.'

'Napoleon beat them,' says Róisín. 'We learned that last year in European history.'

Not that the engineering world has heard the last of this ingenious Russian who has triumphed against the odds and is thus a good thing in the O'Donnell family. Apparently he has his own engineering design studio in France, and we should expect more surprises from him in the near future.

A very nice surprise is a pretty pudding recommended by Isolde. A glass of Château d'Yquem with a ripe peach and a slither of Roquefort.

'*Shall I part my hair behind?*' I say. '*Do I dare to eat a peach? I shall wear white flannel trousers, and walk upon the beach...*'

'Mr J. Alfred Prufrock, I presume,' says Isolde. 'Would you like me to be a mermaid and sing to you?'

Mr Eliot's fame as a poet has certainly spread, but despite visions of the streamlined Yourkevitch hull, I can't think of anything more I'd like. 'Would you care to dance after dinner?'

'Delighted.'

To borrow from M. Le Corbusier, *Normandie* is a machine for romancing. That's the French for you.

The next morning is spent touring the ship, from the engine rooms and kitchens to the bridge. Our visit has been timed with naval precision. 'If you would like to borrow my binoculars,' says Captain Pugnet to Isolde, 'and look slightly to your left, what do you see?'

'Another huge black and white and red liner.'

'Exactly so,' says Captain Pugnet. 'That is the *Queen Mary*, westbound to New York from Southampton. How does she compare to our *Normandie*?'

Isolde keeps *Queen Mary* in her sights. 'Impressive, but perhaps not so...'

'Artistic,' I suggest.

'... not quite so chic?'

The captain smiles. 'Well, of course, an artist was involved in the superstructure of *Normandie*.'

'Typical French,' I say.

'What's that?' asks the captain. 'Anyway, she also had a chief architect, M. Roger-Henri Expert, to organize the decor. Myself,

I have not had the pleasure yet of seeing on board *Queen Mary*, but I've heard she's – how you say – a little old-fashioned... More for English tastes.'

I'm sure this is true. There's no doubt as I look down from the bridge to *Normandie*'s wholly uncluttered and aerodynamic prow that she's the more modern ship of the two, although the proof of the pudding is in the eating, and it would be fun to be able to compare the two point by point.

Captain Pugnet invites us to a small pre-prandial cocktail reception in his cabin. If this sounds a rather cosy arrangement, the captain's cabin – located immediately behind the bridge – proves to be a grand suite with its own dining room, complete with baby grand. 'Your Mr Coward sung us some amusing songs here on our last voyage,' he says. '*Has anyone seen our ship... the HMS Peculiar!*'

'Oh, yes,' says Isolde. 'Noël Coward. He's been playing Broadway with Gertrude Lawrence. They're quite a pair, and great fun. There's a jazz evening tonight in the ship's theatre. That sounds fun, too.'

'Except for any Germans on board,' I say.

'No, they love jazz,' says an officer.

'I'm only joking, but Herr Hitler hates jazz apparently.'

'And Jews,' adds Isolde. 'Although I can see they're welcome on board *Normandie*. Remember the kosher kitchen we saw this morning?'

'Well, we came over in May on the *Queen Mary*,' says a radiant older woman in an equally fetching gown. 'She has her own synagogue.'

With *Normandie*, it seems, France reaches out to the world, and all's well with it. Especially in first class. It does all seem like a dream, with time and America vanishing to the accompaniment of jazz and swing and delicious food and fine wines in saloons and cabins and bars and dining rooms that – apologies to Isolde – even RKO can't better with its dazzling musicals. The liner is a glamorous world of its own. It is certainly seductive.

'You know my husband's trying to rope you into his business,' says Mrs O'Donnell at breakfast on our fourth day at sea.

'I guessed,' I say. 'It's a terrific compliment, but my heart's in aviation, I'm afraid. I've been flying for some while and expect to do a lot more of that in the future. I'm keen on the development of aircraft.'

'And ships?'

'I love the sea and have been learning to sail, but…'

'No, I don't think heavy-duty construction is for you,' says Mrs O'Donnell. 'But we'll always be happy to welcome you on board.'

We make our farewells as *Normandie* cruises serenely past the Needles, a line of jagged chalk outcrops rising from the sea, and the picturesque lighthouse designed by the Scottish engineer James Walker, who was haggis-keen on heavy construction. I tell Isolde that, as a child, I used to dream of being the lighthouse keeper there.

'What would it be like to live there?' she asks, as *Normandie* blasts her horns to let anyone daring to cross her path know we are steaming towards the narrows of the Solent and Southampton. I paint a picture of Sir Lancelot: '*A red-cross knight for ever kneeled / To a lady in his shield.*'

'She was standing in his shield?'

'Figuratively, I suppose.'

'Tennyson?'

'Yes. He lived nearby... *Where, far from noise and smoke of town / I watch the twilight falling brown / All round a careless-ordered garden / Close to the ridge of a noble down.*'

'So, he wouldn't have liked Manhattan?'

'I doubt it.'

*

Normandie's end was as inglorious as the French liner was sublime. She was to have sailed from New York to Le Havre via Southampton in August 1939, but the threat of war meant she was held back at Pier 88. She never sailed again. Impounded by the US government after the country entered the Second World War in December 1941, the immediate plan was to convert the liner into an aircraft carrier. This was overly ambitious. Instead, *Normandie* was to be turned into USS *Lafayette*, a troop carrier fitted with 10,000 plain metal bunks. Even if the plan had worked out, it is hard to imagine the US Navy coping with the intricacies of *Normandie*'s highly sophisticated power plant in wartime conditions. She was the very opposite of a warship. But we'll never know how well she would have performed as a troop carrier. On 9th February 1942, a worker's blowtorch started a fire that devastated the ship. What was so very sad is that American workers were charged with ripping out and destroying *Normandie*'s magnificent interiors at a time when the ship's sophisticated fire detection and prevention mechanism had been deactivated. Perhaps even sadder is the fact that Vladimir Yourkevitch was in Manhattan at the time. He had a realistic plan in mind of how to save the ship, but was refused entry to the port.

What happened next is a mixture of tragedy, farce, obstinacy on the part of US authorities, and sheer incompetence. Finally, the great ship keeled over. She sat there like some grim industrial fossil until she was cut up for scrap in 1946.

Furniture, decor, Hermès clutch bags, menus, ashtrays, cutlery and even keys to cabins continue to appear for sale in auctions and on eBay. They command high prices. The 20-foot bronze dining-room doors were sold at auction in 1945 to Father Mansour Stephen of the Maronite Cathedral of Our Lady of Lebanon, Brooklyn. They are still there, on the outside of the Neo-Norman church in Brooklyn Heights designed by the English-born architect Richard Upjohn.

Vladimir Yourkevitch returned to the USA, and his career as a ship-design engineer blossomed both during and after the Second World War. Greatly respected, he worked right up until his death in New York in 1964.

Unlike SS *Normandie*, RMS *Queen Mary* was profitable. A troop carrier in the Second World War, she returned to service in the guise of the glamorous liner she had been before 1939. Retired in 1967 – liners were unable to compete with airliners – she is now an unmoving tourist attraction and hotel in Long Beach, California.

Ateliers et Chantiers de Penhoët closed in 1955. The largest passenger ship at sea to date is Royal Caribbean International's MS *Symphony of the Seas*, built at Chantiers de l'Atlantique, Saint Nazaire. Entering service in 2018, the cruise ship weighs 228,081 tons and carries a maximum of 6,680 passengers served by a 2,200-strong crew. Her cruising speed is 22 knots. Passenger ships no longer even try to race across oceans. The transatlantic Blue Riband is the stuff of distant history.

Accommodation on board MS *Symphony of the Seas* is slightly different to SS *Normandie*. It features a zip line, a surfing simulator, the tallest waterslide at sea, climbing walls, games arcades, robotic bartenders, and an aqua park with water cannons. Cabins boast flat-screen TVs directly in front of beds, while restaurant menus 'are offered each night for a splurge, and include a whole Maine lobster for $29.95; filet mignon from Chops Grille for $16.95; and a surf and turf for $34.95. Dessert hits all the highlights from a cheesecake with strawberry topping or a baked Alaska, to ice cream, creme brulée and a slice of chocolate cake so large it could feed a family.'

Those who sailed on the *Normandie* are long gone. Their spiritual successors are more likely to be found in the economy section of transatlantic airliners than on board a floating holiday resort.

FIVE

London to Glasgow:
Coronation Scot

17th December 1937

The hotel windows are patterned with frost this morning. By all accounts December has been an exceptionally cold month, with widespread fog and snow. On Monday, or so the boy bringing poached eggs, toast and tea tells me, 'they' – the Met Office – recorded minus 7 degrees Fahrenheit at Braemar. Newspapers piled up on my eiderdown speak of roads blocked as far south as the New Forest, and six-foot snowdrifts along the A6 over Shap Fell.

Last Friday, a London and North Eastern express – the 4.03 p.m. Edinburgh Waverley to Glasgow Queen Street – ploughed into the back of the late-running 2 p.m. from Dundee, which was being held incorrectly at signals in a whiteout at Castlecary. Thirty-five people died and 179 were injured, many severely. The Edinburgh locomotive 2744 *Grand Parade*, a 96-ton Gresley A3 Pacific, had been galloping through driving snow along the same track at 70 mph. Telescoped into the carriages of the Dundee train, and derailed, she was damaged beyond repair.

Not quite the best time, perhaps, to think of heading north on an express train from London to Scotland, but back last night from a fact-finding trip to Germany, I have appointments with, among others, the North British Locomotive Company in Glasgow, and the shipbuilder John Brown & Co. on the Upper Clyde.

At 1.30 p.m. today, the *Coronation Scot*, making a single stop at Carlisle to set down passengers, promises to speed me from Euston to Glasgow over snow-blanketed Shap Fell, and then through the threat of blizzards over Beattock and the Scottish hills – 401.4 miles in six and a half hours, at an average speed of a little over a mile a minute. Euston does not expect the train to be delayed. Since it began regular service on 5th September, the timekeeping of the *Coronation Scot* has been impeccable. Pride of the LMS – the London, Midland and Scottish Railway – the Caledonian blue and silver-streaked streamliner is one of Britain's most striking and impressive trains. The public certainly knows about it. On its press run in June, the train's brand-new locomotive 6220 *Coronation*, designed under the direction of Mr William Stanier, the railway's chief mechanical engineer, set a new British record for steam – 114 mph – two miles south of Crewe. Braking from that great speed, driver Clarke met the first 20-mph curves into the platforms at 57 mph. Well-aligned track and the locomotive's equally well-engineered suspension ensured the 275-ton train stopped safely, although glasses and crockery flew from shelves of the well-attended bar as well-oiled journalists were flung into one another's notebooks, suits and cameras.

Cecil J. Allen, the LNER civil engineer and train-timer whose monthly column 'British Locomotive Practice and Performance' in *The Railway Magazine* I have read surreptitiously on train journeys, hidden behind the *Morning Post* or *Manchester Guardian*, was on board. He reported a wry speech made by Mr Ernest Lemon, a vice president of the LMS, to the press corps at lunch at the Crewe Arms after the high-speed run: 'Of course, gentlemen, you will realize that we shan't need to do this kind of thing on every trip of the *Coronation Scot*; we were coming in a little faster than we shall have to do in the ordinary course.'

Over whisky and cigarettes, journalists may have chortled ''Ell of a Mess' – the popular nickname for Britain's biggest railway – yet even they had been impressed. The *Daily Sketch* devoted the front page of its 30th June edition to the story under the headline '114 M.P.H. BY RAIL!', with a photograph of the train thundering towards Watford Tunnel at 70 mph and another of the top-hatted Crewe stationmaster shaking hands with driver Tom Clarke and fireman John Lewis, 'the two heroes of the day'. In Berlin for work, I missed the cinema newsreels, but hope yet to see footage of the *Coronation Scot* overtaking the aircraft filming it.

More impressive, though, was the train's return to Euston that afternoon. It ran the 158 miles from Crewe in 119 minutes at an average speed of 79.7 mph, cruising comfortably and wherever possible along this busy line at speeds between 90 and 100 mph. If this level of performance could be achieved every day, the *Coronation Scot* might easily make the run from Euston to Glasgow in six hours flat, or even less.

Last November, the LMS ran a special test train – with one of Mr Stanier's earlier Princess Royal Pacifics, 6201 *Princess*

Elizabeth, in charge – non-stop from Euston to Glasgow Central and back the following day. Driver Clarke had the down train into Glasgow in a little less than 5 hours and 54 minutes, and the up train into Euston in just over 5 hours and 44 minutes, at an average speed of 70 mph.

When I mentioned this to LMS officials earlier this year, they replied, quite rightly, to the effect that although the new Princess Coronation class Pacifics could indeed better these impressive shows, what mattered most for timetabling purposes was the provision of an express that will run to time in all weathers, and recover time when – as happens all too frequently on the busy line south of Preston – passenger trains are at the mercy of the railway's numerous goods trains. In fact, the reason why the *Coronation Scot* is scheduled to leave both Euston and Glasgow at 1.30 p.m. rather than 4 p.m. or 5 p.m. – either of which would be more convenient times for business passengers – is to give it the best possible chance of clear runs north and south.

The rival LNER streamliner, the *Coronation*, which shares the same name as our LMS loco and went into service between London King's Cross and Edinburgh Waverley and vice versa on the same day as the *Coronation Scot*, is a faster train – six hours either way for the 393 miles – and yet even with its impressive long-distance sprint south from York to London – 188 miles in 157 minutes, at 71.9 mph – the streamlined trains of the Deutsche Reichsbahn are faster. The *Daily Sketch* noted the world record for steam: 119.8 mph, held by the Germans. In fact, they went quite a bit faster than this last year. In early May, a red, submarine-like streamlined 4-6-4, 05 002, designed by Herr Adolf

Wolff of the Borsig Locomotiv-Werke, Hennigsdorf, reached 124½ mph on level track between Vietnitz and Paulinenaue on the Berlin to Hamburg line. On 18th May, Mr Stanier, chief mechanical engineer of the LMS, rode the footplate of 05 002 at 118 mph on the occasion of a visit to Germany by members of the Institution of Locomotive Engineers.

Many of us are aware of the importance of this rivalry with Germany. Under Herr Hitler, Germany has been rearming at an alarming rate and, although I cannot fault the hospitality of my German hosts over the past month, only yesterday the German government announced restrictions on passports for Jewish citizens. The RAF takes delivery of its first front-line Hawker Hurricane eight-gun monoplane fighters some time this month, while Supermarine's lighter, faster Spitfire is on the way next year. Whatever reassurances we are being given by the new prime minister, Mr Chamberlain, of Herr Hitler's peaceful intentions, British armaments production is accelerating.

I wipe a clear circle on a frosty and now slightly steamy bedroom window and turn to a story about the mass murders and rapes being committed by the Japs in Nanking. I watch one dark-blue Austin taxi after another passing through and under the hotel – which is supported over the road by four rows of cast-iron Doric columns – as these decidedly old-fashioned landaulette-style cabs whine their way to and from soot-encrusted Euston station. While in Germany, I was taken on a tour of pristine *Autobahnen* in a two-seater supercharged Mercedes-Benz 540K Spezial at speeds of 100 mph and more. Six new stretches of *Autobahnen* are due to open today.

As I run my late-morning bath, I think of how behind the times we must seem to the Germans. This is certainly something that has been going through the capacious mind of Sir Josiah Stamp, chairman of the LMS, who is mustard-keen on building a brand-new Euston. Along with Mr Geoffrey Dawson, editor of *The Times*, the German ambassador Herr Joachim von Ribbentrop, the young Conservative MP Duncan Sandys and the Duke of Wellington, Sir Josiah is a member of the Anglo-German Fellowship formed two years ago. His interest in German business affairs dates back to 1924, as far as I can tell, when he served on the Dawes Reparation Commission's Committee on German Currency and Finance.

One reliable way of ensuring war reparation payments were made was through the revenues of the Deutsche Reichsbahn (DR). The commission saw to it that the German railways were reconstituted as a nominally private railway company, 100 per cent owned by the state. At the same time, money – principally from America – was pumped into the German economy. In fact, capital available to German industry shifted the burden of reparations from the government and industry to American bond investors, creating a close tie between German industry and American investment banks.

It was a state of affairs that worked well up until the DR was relieved of war reparation payments five years ago. Freed of this burden, the DR appears to have supercharged its affairs. In fact, it was in '33 that it launched its *Fliegender Hamburger* (or *Flying Hamburger*), the two-coach streamlined diesel express that runs the 178 miles from Berlin to Hamburg in 138 minutes, an average speed of 77 mph. This is the service that has prompted the design and construction of today's streamlined expresses on the LMS and LNER.

Impressive as it is, the schedule of the *Flying Hamburger* can be equalled, as I discovered on my way back to England via Hamburg (steamer from there to Harwich, and an LNER boat train from Parkeston Quay to Liverpool Street) by Herr Wolff's class 05 Baltics. Due, I think, to the intense cold, the diesel train was replaced by a six-coach train with the record-breaking 05 002 at its head. We were in Hamburg on time.

For all the sheer speed of the new Deutsche Reichsbahn trains, I have to admit to being excited by the promise of today's ride up to Glasgow by the *Coronation Scot*. I have yet to see the train, so know it only from black-and-white press photographs and technical drawings, but in those it does look striking. And, unlike its German counterparts, it promises a very decent lunch.

Even better, a sudden and surprising wave of high pressure has lifted the clouds over much of England this morning, and we should see sunshine for the next 48 hours before the weather closes in again.

Settling my bill, I ask the receptionist what will happen to the hotel when the new Euston station is built. He is unsure, but saddened to think that this, London's very first railway hotel, might vanish in the next few years. In fact, there were originally two hotels, both designed by Philip Hardwick and built on land bought from Lord Southampton in 1839. On the west of the roadway was the Euston Hotel, a first-class affair complete with grand dining room; and on the east, the Victoria Hotel, providing sleeping accommodation and a coffee house for second- and third-class passengers. The two were joined together in 1881 by the grand, 'French-style' block I slept in – designed by J. B. Stansby, the London and North Western Railway's architect, with help from one J. McLaren. Two years ago, someone in charge at Euston decided to panel over the pairs of Doric columns that marched imperiously around the interior of the dining room, so the hotel has lost some of its grandeur – as, of course, did the nearby Midland Grand Hotel at St Pancras, which closed that same year – for lack of modern amenities – and has been used as railway offices ever since.

Now, the Euston Hotel, the Midland Grand, and Euston and St Pancras stations are all threatened with demolition, and this could well be my last time to take a good look around Euston before the vast new station planned here takes all their places. Some critics have described the new design by the Percy Thomas Partnership as looking like an American department store, but it is much bigger and more ambitious than that. I have to say that, having been shown a glimpse of the ambitious designs planned for new Third Reich buildings in Berlin by Herr Albert Speer, the newly appointed Inspector General of Buildings, the new Euston might well meet the approval of Herr Hitler's favourite architect. Although plans for a massive rebuilding of Berlin to be shown to the public at the end of next month are largely secret, Herr Speer says a grand avenue, nearly four and a half miles long, will link ambitious new north and south railway stations.

If not Berlin, the new Euston would certainly suit an American city like Detroit or Chicago. Looking up across Drummond Street at Philip Hardwick's massive Greek propylaeum, known to one and all as the Euston Arch, I think Messrs Hitler and Speer would be impressed by the architecture we built for our railways a century ago. Although blackened by soot, the Arch – with its mighty 44-foot Doric columns – remains a wonderful conceit: a suggestion that the steam railway, when it first made its way down Camden Bank to the New Road, was the harbinger of a new Golden Age that the Greeks under Pericles, and certainly the Romans, might well have admired.

I cross the courtyard beyond the arch and take a seat under the mighty coffered ceiling of the station's Great Hall. I noted last night an article on Euston in the latest issue of *The Railway Magazine*, which the hotel had kindly sought out and sent up to my room. Here it is, part two of a piece on the history of the station by D. S. Barrie:

> Dark, many-cornered, and inscrutable in its personality, Euston faces at long last an utter immolation that will wipe clean the slate of its piecemeal development. Its rambling buildings may go, even its great Doric arch may come down, but its traditions and its ghosts... yet may cling to its site, where a new and greater Euston is soon to take shape, a Euston worthy to rank with the finest railway termini in the world.

The Great Hall is looking tired and all too grey. It would have been colourful when it opened, to Hardwick's designs, in 1849. And, yet, with its grand stairs, imposing screen of Ionic columns, lofty ceiling and the sunlight shining down from clerestory windows, it retains an imposing air. On either side of the Great Hall is Euston's web of platforms: departures to the left; arrivals on the right. The platforms are huddled under surprisingly low roofs. After the drama of the Arch and the Great Hall, Euston's penny-plain platforms are very much an anticlimax. This, though, cannot be said of the *Coronation Scot*, its blue and silver coaches standing out prominently from long lines of crimson lake LMS trains and black and crimson lake locomotives. Here are trains from Scotland, from North Wales, from Liverpool, Manchester, Birmingham and Coventry; trains that have cantered up to London behind Patriots and Royal Scots, Jubilees and Claughtons, Midland Compounds, Black Fives and Princess Royals.

Porters scurry along my platform, wooden barrows piled high with well-presented luggage. Passengers in hats, coats, scarves and gloves are ushered aboard after their tickets are checked. One particularly attractive young lady, in lightweight tweeds straight out of the latest copy of *Vogue*, ushers a pair of lively Springer Spaniels into the corridor first brake at the rear of the train. A brace of high-ranking naval officers steps aboard. Businessmen. Journalists. Civil servants. A sandy-haired Highland family. A tightly pinstriped young fellow engaged with a copy of the *Anglo-German Review*. A bishop. People whose faces you half recall from stage and screen; voices that might be from the wireless.

Walking the length of the train, I watch last-minute supplies of fresh food being lifted into the two kitchen cars, and then our locomotive, 6222 *Queen Mary*, backing down the steep slope from Camden Shed. It is 1.15 p.m. and there is just time to look at the nose of this impressive machine – silver speed lines rising from a point and then curving upwards, before appearing to race down the flanks of locomotive, tender and nine-coach train. A 'good afternoon' to the crew.

'Good, but a bit nippy today, sir.'

'Good luck!'

I walk down to find my reserved seat facing the engine in the two-seat coupé of the corridor first brake. This carriage seats twenty passengers in five compartments, and two more in the discreet coupé. I've booked this so I can work quietly on my papers.

My seat is deep and comfortable. Rich wood veneer and a white Rexine ceiling offset blue upholstery. The window can be opened, although the train features an air-conditioning system. An attendant arrives with a menu – blue, of course – featuring details on its rear cover of 'Some Facts About The Coronation Scot'. While I enjoy seeing the boiler pressure (250 pounds per square inch) listed, along with the tractive effort of the locomotive (40,000 pounds) and total weight of engine and tender (164 tons 9 cwt), I do wonder how many passengers are that interested in these statistics. As for the area of the heating surface of the boiler (2,807 square feet), this is surely arcane territory for all but the dedicated railway enthusiast or professional engineer.

And there is no doubt that *Queen Mary* – and her (to date) four siblings, *Coronation*, *Queen Elizabeth*, *Princess Alice* and *Princess Alexandra* – is a newsworthy machine. Perhaps my fellow passengers might like to know what *Queen Mary* cost to build? Complete with tender carrying 10 tons of coal and 4,000 gallons of water – £13,369. To put this into some sort of engineering perspective, a friend in the Air Ministry tells me in confidence that the Supermarine Spitfires due in squadron service next year have cost about £9,500 apiece.

I'm toying with the idea of a cocktail when the compartment door slides back. 'Beg pardon, sir,' says the crisply uniformed attendant. 'I wonder if you'd be happy to share your coupé. The train's full and the young lady here would prefer to be near her dogs in the brake compartment behind rather than further up the train... Of course, if you'd rather not.' It is, though, more a case of 'rather!' than 'not'.

Seeing the work documents on my lap, she says, 'Promise I won't speak a word,' and then sits silently down, taking a brand-new book from her bag. It has a colourful cover. *The Hobbit* by J. R. R. Tolkien.

When the attendant returns to enquire 'Everything all right, sir?', a platform whistle blows. Hissing furiously up ahead, *Queen Mary* gives a deep blast on her Caledonian hooter as if she were a steamer heading seawards from the Clyde. Our carriage dances a momentary jig and then we hear the huffing of a deep exhaust as the powerful engine pulls past a throng of waving and cheering admirers – 'Happens every day, sir' – and, gliding out from under the glazed station canopy, climbs Camden Bank.

I order a half-bottle of 1928 George Goulet, Extra Dry. 'No speaking till lunch,' I say as the attendant pours the fizz. The *Coronation Scot* scythes a fast-beating four-cylinder path through confined acres of hatless, half-built semi-detached suburbs – their cinematic new churches as likely as not designed by N. F. Cachemaille-May – and a Crittall-windowed array of busy new, light-industrial factories. Should I be drinking a toast to the end of the recession?

'First sitting for lunch,' announces an attendant.

'Will you join me?'

We pass along the corridor to a pair of end seats I've reserved in the Vestibule First Diner. One was to have been for me, the other to give me space after my exhausting trip through the new Germany. Now, though, I learn about John Ronald Reuel Tolkien, an Oxford professor of Anglo-Saxon; how his family were refugees from Saxony at the time of Frederick the Great's invasion; and how *The Hobbit* is selling well. We order crème bretonne, followed by grilled turbot maitre d'hôtel, roast beef and horseradish sauce, pears Richelieu, and cheese and biscuits. We drink a Margaux as plumes of steam pulse over our carriage windows. Up ahead at a steady 80–85 mph, *Queen Mary* might be seen from a distance as some fast-moving cloud-making machine, or perhaps a mythical dragon woken from inside an English hill sparkling with frost. I reach inside my jacket for my cigarette case, but my companion doesn't smoke and I decide to join her.

Nearing Crewe at 90 mph, we return to our carriage, standing in the corridor to watch the volcanic steam railway activity at the station's enormous locomotive works. Back in the coupé, I plough back into my papers as my interesting companion switches her attention from *The Hobbit* to *The Road to Wigan Pier*, the new book by George Orwell, a journalist who has been fighting for the Republicans in Spain's brutal civil war. His book confirms that although England south of the Humber–Trent divide is indeed thriving, the North continues to suffer. Past Wigan itself – we look for the pier, of course, and chuckle – we begin to lose the light. At Preston, we pass the southbound *Coronation Scot*, the locomotives' Caledonian hooters echoing across the serried rows of terraced cottages and industrial chimneystacks.

Between Lancaster and Carnforth, I stare enchanted at a thin band of vermillion light gashed with gold over Morecambe Bay, before darkness envelops the speeding train. The sounds of bells ringing over crossings, the insistent rhythm of rail joints and the clatter of ballast swept up under the carriages – as *Queen Mary* scoops up water to assuage her marathon thirst from troughs set between the tracks – are louder and clearer now that the Lancastrian sun has given up the ghost. A bright ribbon of electric light from our train's windows shines on snow on either side of the line, as we begin our long climb up the Westmorland hills. My companion is asleep as, exhaust audible, *Queen Mary* shouts up Shap Fell, cresting the summit at 45 mph or so before galloping down to Carlisle.

A five-minute break at Citadel station gives me just enough time to walk the length of the train and back. Both first and third are opulent and as clean as new pins, including the blue and cream lavatories with their blue sinks, chromium-plated fittings and blue and white terrazzo floors. I pass sleeping passengers and passengers reading books, card players and smokers, and trenchermen still tucking into food – sandwiches, eggs on toast and hot drinks are available between meals throughout the journey – while, up ahead, *Queen Mary*'s Camden crew, ready for beer and lodgings, hand over their watch to colleagues from Carlisle's Upperby shed.

The Camden fireman has filled the tender to its 4,000-gallon brim, hosed down the footplate, trimmed the fire, and checked the operation of the steam-powered coal pusher at the back of the Pacific's tender to ensure his Upperby colleague has coal within easy reach of his shovel. This is essential, as over the remaining 105 miles from Carlisle to Glasgow, *Queen Mary* will devour close on two tons of coal. The fireman must swing his shovel with the engine at speed through a small hole, onto a searing grate measuring 10 feet by 5 feet. This takes skill, muscle, balance and sweat. Our puissant *Queen Mary* is a mobile power station on 6-foot, 9-inch steel wheels.

Back on board, a man cradling a bottle of Bass is filling in a football pools coupon, and two well-upholstered ladies furnished with gin and vermouths are knitting industriously, while a family at a table in an open third carriage seems inundated by books and comics. Agatha Christie's latest, *Death on the Nile*. Patricia Wentworth's *The Case is Closed*. The new *Dandy* from Dundee, with Korky the Cat on its front page. And Cameron McCabe's *The Face on the Cutting-Room Floor*. I make a note in my pocket diary to get the McCabe book. A Whitehall acquaintance has suggested to me, although she has no immediate proof, that McCabe is the *nom de plume* of one Ernst Bornemann, a curious young communist refugee from Germany.

Suddenly awake, my companion goes onto the platform for a necessary minute with her spaniels, returning to her seat as, at 6.15 p.m., *Queen Mary* noses out into sleet and the dark. The lamps of the Neo-Tudor station vanish in turn, each one faster than the next. 'The only time I've ever really been to Carlisle,' she says as we order cocktails – a Piccadilly and a dry martini – 'was earlier this year, to write about the Carlisle festival. I hadn't been too excited to go, but I got to hear Kathleen Ferrier sing Quilter's "To Daisies". She's a contralto, my age, and frightfully good. Said she was a GPO telephonist. They dismissed her when she married. But she did the piano and singing prizes at the festival, and I'm pretty certain she's going to go far.'

I was going to read Robert Byron's new travel book, *The Road to Oxiana*, on our gallop to Glasgow, but I chat enjoyably with my companion instead, stopping to listen to the urgent beat of our locomotive as she tackles the climb to Beattock in what looks to be a blizzard, or pretty close to it.

I find myself quoting W. H. Auden:

Pulling up Beattock, a steady climb:
The gradient's against her, but she's on time.
Past cotton-grass and moorland boulder,
Shovelling white steam over her shoulder,
Snorting noisily, she passes
Silent miles of wind-bent grasses.

My companion adds:

Down towards Glasgow she descends,
Towards the steam tugs yelping down a glade of cranes,
Towards the fields of apparatus, the furnaces
Set on the dark plain like gigantic chessmen.
All Scotland waits for her.

These, of course, are lines from the General Post Office Film Unit's *Night Mail*, a first-rate job made last year by Harry Watt and Basil Wright. They seem to be almost as well known as the lyrics of George Formby's *Leaning on a Lamp-Post*. Among correspondence in my briefcase is a card from William Coldstream, a painter who worked for John Grierson's GPO Film Unit – and with Auden and Benjamin Britten on *Night Mail* – before going back to his first love: painting. William says he has opened his own school of art in Fitzroy Street, a few minutes' walk from Euston, with Victor Pasmore, and hopes to have a show of the students' work next year.

Now, though, Scotland's great industrial city welcomes the slowing streamliner as we rumble over the Clyde and under the glass roof – said to be the world's biggest – of Glasgow Central station. Porters, whistles, hooters, streams of passengers, warm breath in cold air; we walk into the generous embrace of the station's matronly concourse centred on its famous clock, which is pointing to exactly 8 p.m. Of course we're on time.

Built in two major stages between 1879 and 1905 by the Caledonian Railway, whose locomotives shared the blue paintwork of our *Queen Mary*, the station's sandstone architecture by Robert Rowland Anderson and James Miller is bold, eclectic and noble work. It includes the opulent Central Hotel, where I am booked in for the next few days.

I say thanks to our Upperby crew and a fond goodbye to my coupé companion. I'll be meeting her for supper – although not with the spaniels, sadly – at Rogano tomorrow. And, although I'd like the *Coronation Scot* to run to a schedule that would give the Germans (as well as the LNER) a run for their Reichsmarks, the LMS has made the West Coast Main Line journey from London to Scotland a pleasure. And, who knows, if Mr Stamp and his chums can maintain a state of peace with Herr Hitler, perhaps there will be more streamliners making faster and even more special journeys in years to come.

*

The *Coronation Scot* ran impeccably until 4th September 1939, the day after Britain declared war on Germany. There had been plans to upgrade the service with new coaches in summer 1940. Built at Derby, these were shipped across the Atlantic in 1939, together with 6229 *Duchess of Hamilton* – a brand-new Princess Coronation Pacific posing as 6220 *Coronation* – for a tour of East Coast American railroads. At that year's New York World's Fair, they received two million visitors.

The locomotive returned to Cardiff Docks in February 1942. It lost its streamlined casing in 1947 and was withdrawn prematurely from service in October 1963 during British Railways' swivel-eyed crusade for 'modernization', whatever the cost. Meanwhile the glamorous crimson lake and gold-striped carriages arrived home in 1946, and could be found mixed randomly with conventional express train stock until 1964.

Speeds of West Coast expresses accelerated very slowly from 1945 to 1955. Between 1957 and 1959, the *Caledonian* express saw 3,000-hp Princess Coronation Pacifics cantering to and from Euston and Glasgow Central under easy steam in 6 hours and 40 minutes, at an average speed of just over 60 mph. Piccadilly and dry martinis became the stuff of passengers' dreams, as they remain today.

Josiah Stamp, by now Lord Stamp, was killed in a German air raid that blew his house in Bromley apart in April 1941. The cityscape the *Coronation Scot* set out from and the landscape it paced through have changed considerably since 1937. Lord Stamp's plan to replace Euston station was brought to an end by the advent of the Second World War, by which time the LMS chairman had agreed to keep the Euston Arch by moving it closer to the Euston Road. To no avail. Euston station and its Arch were demolished in 1961–2. A delegation to 10 Downing Street led by J. M. 'Grim' Richards, editor of the *Architectural Review*, failed to win over the prime minister, the arch-modernizer Harold Macmillan. 'He sat without moving,' recalled Richards, 'with his eyes apparently closed. He asked no questions; in fact he said nothing except that he would consider the matter.' A statement was later issued to the effect that the government had decided not to intervene.

A lacklustre air terminal-style building, designed by a team led by William Headley (architect for the London Midland Region of British Railways) and R. L. Moorcroft, opened in 1968, and the trains at Euston were now hidden from view down long ramps leading to glum concrete platforms. There has since been talk of replacing the Sixties station, as a programme to bring a new generation of fast trains designed to shave a few minutes off journey times from Birmingham and Manchester to London at ineffable cost barges its doltish way through unspoilt English countryside. A plan to re-erect the Arch – led by the Euston Arch Trust – might succeed, although a reproduction Neo-Greek monument there would be a proverbial fig leaf, quite unable to hide the pumped-up panoply behind it.

Beyond Euston, an effluence of crude and cynical new housing has been dumped in fields alongside miles of railway line. Smokestack factories have gone, yet their demise is no compensation for the visual denigration of Shap Fell, where crude electric catenary for electric trains and the accompanying brute savagery of the M6 motorway have done their worst to eviscerate this otherwise lyrical landscape. The sight and sound of a Stanier Pacific climbing Shap Fell or Beattock, through wild countryside all but innocent of cars, lorries and coaches, must have been rather like a Turner landscape coming to thunderous life: the elemental power of steam meeting that of nature.

One Princess Coronation – 6229 *Duchess of Hamilton* – has been re-streamlined and placed on display at the National Railway Museum. There are those of us who still hope she will be put back into steam at the head of a new set of streamlined coaches, but the past is indeed a different country – and, try as we might, it would be impossible to recreate this journey on board the *Coronation Scot* in the lead-up to the Second World War. If I had the choice of riding the West Coast Main Line at speed by any steam other than the *Coronation Scot*, which I have dreamed of since I was four or five years old, it would have been aboard the special train run one day in 1953 taking 180 VIPs from Euston and Glasgow – including military top brass and Duncan Sandys, Minister of Supply – on a visit to a new Rolls-Royce aero-engine factory at East Kilbride. The party went down overnight on a 14-car sleeper with 46241 *City of Edinburgh*, one of *Queen Mary*'s 37 siblings, at the head of the train. The following day, the VIPs had to be back in London in time for dinner. A train of seven coaches was marshalled, and with Camden shed's George Pile at the regulator and 'Nellie' Wallace on the shovel, the special's running time to Euston was 4 hours and 10 minutes – an average of 72 mph. As locomotive inspector W. G. Fryer later recalled:

> At Bay Horse we were on the limit and going well. Nellie gave me the thumbs-up sign. George held his pipe in his left hand still unlit. So far he had not been able to spare the concentration to light up. I looked over the side to see the connecting and side rods; at speed they were just a blur. In the moonlight I could just see the mileposts. With my stopwatch I made it 8 sec for the ¼ mile [112½ mph]… The locomotive was running like a sewing machine, the click of the rail joints barely audible; the steam from

the exhaust clung to the boiler and drifted over the tender. It was as if some gigantic hare was running with its ears laid back.

SIX

Dundee to King's Cross via Edinburgh: *Coronation*

6th July 1938

I t would be wrong to say our timber-lined shooting brake comes down from the Cairngorms this morning like a mountain goat. The Rolls-Royce Phantom II is far too big a car for the comparison to stand, but she does descend the hills with a purring assurance. And just as well. Unseasonably, it snowed heavily yesterday, and the going is slippery in sleet. My driver, a former sergeant major in the Royal Scots Fusiliers, hums 'Highland Laddie' as an aid to concentration as much as a salute to the white-hemmed tartan landscape.

With little leeway, we canter into Dundee. I can see my Edinburgh train threading towards the station, a long string of varnished-teak coaches behind an imposing streamlined eight-coupled apple-green express passenger engine. Numbered 2006. 'That's *Wolf of Badenoch*,' says my driver. I run after her, a porter shutting the door behind me as the train departs.

I look for a seat as we cross the Tay Bridge, before *Wolf of Badenoch* accelerates rapidly towards Kirkcaldy. This train, from Aberdeen, connects with the 4.30 p.m. from Edinburgh

133

to King's Cross. The run from Dundee to Waverley is a little less than 60 miles. The timetable allows 85 minutes. This might seem overly generous, especially with a powerful Gresley P2 2-8-2 at the head of the train, its American chime whistle resounding across the sleet-whipped firth. This, though, is a saw-tooth line, all demanding gradients and speed-denying twists and turns. I wipe the condensation from the window of my first-class compartment to glimpse *Wolf of Badenoch* swinging into bends – so many green wheels blurring – and pounding south, pluming dense white clouds of steam over the heavy train.

But for the middle-age couple snoozing contentedly in a bracken of dense tweeds, and despite the unseasonal weather, I would happily open the ventilator above my compartment window to better hear the chattering three-cylinder beat of the P2. These locomotives – their highly efficient flow of superheated steam much influenced by the work of M. André Chapelon of the PO (that's the Compagnie du chemin de fer de Paris à Orléans) – have revolutionized services on the Aberdeen route. I hope to see many more of them at work in coming years.

From Kirkcaldy we meet the Firth of Forth, and at this time of day and year we should enjoy glorious views across the water to Edinburgh itself. Today, though – as wintry a July day as anyone can remember – it's hard to make out the masts and funnels of ships, let alone the increasingly heavily defended garrison islands of Inchcolm and Inchkeith. And yet the scenery along the line, or what I can see of it, is so very compelling that my case remains closed and the pile of newspaper cuttings – prepared for me while I was escaping the world for a week in the Highlands – stays unread.

Turning tightly, we climb towards North Queensferry and the Forth Bridge, our speed no more than 20 mph. A hollow rumble of axles and wheels announces the world's greatest bridge. Opened nearly half a century ago, the Forth Bridge is world-famous – and justly so. Its orange-painted girders and imposing cantilevers flick hypnotically across the window. Curving slowly through South Queensferry station, we accelerate through the new Edinburgh suburbs and so into Waverley, hidden under its expansive glass roof in a ravine between the Georgian New Town and medieval Auld Reekie.

Here, the two-tone blue *Coronation*, the 4.30 p.m. to King's Cross, is waiting for us, unmistakable and impatient for London. A vision of the future of sorts, the train is streamlined from the nose of its locomotive to the beavertail of its observation car, its paintwork as lustrous as that of a bespoke Rolls-Royce. Passengers can lounge in plush armchairs in the futuristic observation car, cocktails to hand, watching the tracks of the LNER main line speeding into the distance as trains thunder past in the opposite direction.

Not having had lunch, and with some wintry summer hours and miles behind me, I'm very much looking forward to my trip on the streamliner. Even then, I feel I must walk to the head of the train, where a crowd of passengers, railway enthusiasts and LNER staff alike are gathered to admire our A4 Pacific 2510 *Quicksilver*. Garbed in a coat of garter blue – she was silver and grey until May – with red wheels and burnished steel rims, and name and numbers picked out in stainless-steel Gill

Sans, *Quicksilver*, built at Doncaster works three years ago, is a superb-looking machine, purposeful and clearly shaped for speed.

I do know just how fast these locomotives are. On the press run of the LNER's first streamliner, the *Silver Jubilee*, in September '35, A4 2509 *Silver Link*, with driver A. Taylor and fireman J. Luty on the footplate, ran the 76 miles from King's Cross to Peterborough in 55 minutes, with a mean speed over 25 miles of 107½ mph, an average speed over 43 miles of 100 mph, and a top speed (reached twice, at Arlesey and then at Sandy) of 112½ mph. The locomotive could have run even faster than this, but because the new coaches – although quite safe – bucked and swayed rather wildly on some of the curves, Mr Gresley, the locomotive's designer, made his way through *Silver Link*'s corridor tender to instruct driver Taylor to 'ease his arm' on the regulator, as there were 'some elderly gentlemen on board'.

The *Silver Jubilee* went into regular service between London and Newcastle-upon-Tyne, covering the 268 miles in four hours. The average speed of 67 mph deserves to be higher, but between Darlington and Newcastle the LNER main line runs over collieries with the ever-present threat of subsidence. These last 36 miles occupy 40 minutes and, as the speed of the A4s is recorded, drivers must pay strict regard to the leisurely timing over this section.

Hugely popular, reliable, and profitable, too, the *Silver Jubilee* was followed last year by the longer and heavier *Coronation* racing between London and Edinburgh – 393 miles in 6 hours; 80 minutes faster than the *Flying Scotsman*. The average speed is 65½ mph, with the really fast running made between York and London – where, although the line limit is normally 90 mph, speeds of 100 mph have become commonplace. Colour-light signalling has replaced mechanical semaphores over long stretches of the East Coast Main Line, while canted curves – where one rail is higher than the other – allow trains to run smoothly through them at greater speeds than they did just three years ago.

Walking back along the nine-car train, I admire its sheer sleekness, noting the rubber sheets – in the same lustrous garter and Wedgwood blues – smoothly concealing gaps between coaches. Observation car aside, the train is formed of two pairs of articulated four-car sets. Sharing bogies, the purpose-designed coaches are lighter than they would otherwise have been.

Inside, my two-tone grey-green, Rexine-walled first-class carriage is rather like some Art Deco cocktail bar. Pairs of jazzy fawn moquette armchairs face one another in alcoves across tables. The chairs swivel to 45 degrees, so passengers can stretch their legs out without interfering with their neighbours'. There are plump moquette footrests, while the carpet is deep plush, the architraves and other fixtures and fittings are aluminium, and the coach is air-conditioned. There is no dining car, as meals are served at every seat, in first and third. This is a much more modern train than the LMS's *Coronation Scot*, and yet – although comfortable and well thought out – I find the decor a little, dare I say it, garish.

I order a Scotch from an attendant and, as the whistle blows, the A4's cylinder cocks roar. At 4.30 p.m., the *Coronation* begins to move. I open my case and start sifting through the cuttings that, hopefully, will bring me up to speed with the last week's news. Up to speed? I feel both thrilled and a little foolish as we accelerate smoothly – Edinburgh Castle on our left-hand side where I'm seated, and Princes Street with its deluxe shops to the right – to discover that, on Sunday, the brand-new A4 Pacific 4468 *Mallard* broke the world speed record for a steam railway locomotive. She thundered down Stoke Bank towards Peterborough at a maximum of 126 mph. True, that last 1 mph was gained over just 185 feet, yet *Mallard* had reeled off five consecutive miles at over 120 mph, her 6-foot, 8-inch driving wheels rotating more than eight times every second at that great speed. I change my order to Champagne.

Sitting opposite me is a French lawyer, although he says he is also a journalist, on his way back to London from a state occasion at Holyrood Palace. Tomorrow he is attending a reception at the German embassy, where Herr von Ribbentrop, the Third Reich's foreign minister, held court until earlier this year.

My French companion sees me reading cuttings on *Mallard*'s exploits and says, 'But have you seen that last Sunday, the French Grand Prix was won by von Brauchitsch? Caracciola was second, Lang in third place! All driving Silver Arrows.' He enthuses so much over the indomitable prowess of the Mercedes-Benz team, citing the manager Herr Alfred Neubauer and Herr Rudolf Uhlenhaut, designer of the triumphant supercharged three-litre V12 W154s, that I offer him my hearty congratulations and ask the attendant to pour him a glass of Bolly.

By Dunbar, as the train closes in on the North Sea, I have learned over Champagne that in January a streamlined 725-bhp

Mercedes-Benz V12 driven by Herr Rudolf Caracciola on the Reichsautobahn A5 between Frankfurt and Darmstadt set a world speed record on public roads. How fast? Over the flying mile, 268.7 mph. 'And we can expect much greater things.' Mercedes-Benz is apparently working on a new streamlined car with an aero engine designed to reach 750 km/h (470 mph). 'Much faster than your new Spitfire.'

'Makes old *Mallard* seem a bit of a slow coach,' I say, excusing myself to walk down to the observation car, where I am lucky to find an empty armchair among the sixteen here – on payment of a shilling for an hour – to watch the rails rush by as we streak alongside the sea in strong winds and squalling rain. We canter into England over Robert Stephenson's Royal Border Bridge at Berwick-on-Tweed, the town looking as handsome as ever. I wait for Holy Island to heave into view. And, as it does, sunlight gilds the swell of the sea. Guillemots bustle over Lindisfarne Castle.

I order dinner and return to my seat, where Monsieur 'Le Boche' is deep in a bowl of mock turtle soup. He has chosen a '29 Margaux and has filled my glass. I note the flat-handled cutlery – designed, the steward tells me, to keep railway rattles to an absolute minimum. M. Le Boche says he has been in conversation recently not just in Scotland with the Duke of Buccleuch, but also with the US ambassador, Mr Kennedy, in London, and they both say that Germany is doing extremely well and that one mustn't pay too much attention to those in England who criticize Herr Hitler. As for the Jews, the American ambassador says they have brought it on themselves. I can't help thinking that M. Le Boche looks rather like Peter

Lorre, the Hungarian-born star of Hitchcock's *The Man Who Knew Too Much.*

Over cantaloupe melon and grilled salmon with piquant sauce, served soon after our departure from Newcastle and the dramatic exit across the Tyne, and lamb cutlets chased by strawberries and cream, I encourage my companion to ask me why I'm racing to London. Tomorrow, I tell him, I am invited to the opening of the 20th Century German Art exhibition organized by Mr Herbert Reid at the New Burlington Galleries. It was going to be called 'Banned German Art', but the Foreign Office thought differently.

'*C'est juste, n'est-ce pas*? I was at the *Entartete Kunst* exhibition, the "Degenerate Art Show", in Munich last year,' says my companion. 'Adolf Ziegler, president of the Reich Chamber of Visual Arts himself was kind enough to send me a personal invitation.'

Of the 270 works to be shown in London, I say, knowing that he has got the wrong end of the stick, there are those by Kandinsky, Otto Dix, George Grosz, Käthe Kollwitz and Emil Nolde. Many are by German Jews exiled in Britain. Proceeds from the show will be paid to distressed artists from Nazi Germany.

He looks a little pale as I watch Durham Cathedral and its attendant castle pass by. 'And Paul Robeson will be singing at the opening.'

'Robeson, the communist Negro?' Now M. Le Boche is quite put out.

Better known to the public at large as the handsome American bass-baritone star from *Show Boat*, the Drury Lane musical – and the film, too – and as Othello to Peggy Ashcroft's Desdemona, Mr Robeson has recently been to the Soviet Union, courtesy of the film-maker Sergei Eisenstein. Mr Eisenstein, I enjoy informing my companion as we gallop south through Yorkshire, is apparently completing his long-awaited film *Alexander Nevksy*, or the story of how the German knights under the command of Prince-Bishop Hermann of Dorpat were defeated by the Russian prince at the Battle on the Ice in 1242.

Who knows if Eisenstein's film will be released in Britain? What the public is really looking forward to, though, is next month's premiere of *The Adventures of Robin Hood*, with Errol Flynn in the lead role and Olivia de Havilland as Maid Marian. The film has been made in Technicolor. Perhaps I should tell my companion that Mr Logie Baird, the Church of Scotland minister's son from Helensburgh, gave a demonstration of colour television earlier this year at the Dominion Theatre on Tottenham Court Road. Beat that, Goebbels!

Believing he may have been seated with an ardent communist, especially when I ask if he has read Edgar Mowrer's Penguin Special *Germany Puts the Clock Back* – I have a copy of the sixpenny paperback in my case – my companion excuses himself. He will, he says, smoke a cigar in the observation car. I wonder, do communists ride the *Coronation*? Spies, perhaps, and the wealthier of Stalin's 'willing fools'.

Lenin, the late Soviet dictator, ordered a number of Rolls-Royces from the Crewe factory. Communists like to travel in aristocratic style. They would never settle for a *kulak*-class Humber or Rover – these are cars for the despised bourgeoisie. I haven't been to the Soviet Union, although my railway-industry informants tell me that the *Red Arrow* express from Moscow to Leningrad is quite luxurious in the 'soft-class' compartments reserved for senior politicians and Communist party apparatchiks. I did see a rather impressive streamlined Soviet Railways class IS (or Iosif Stalin) 2-8-4 on show in Paris last year, at the *Exposition Internationale des Arts et Techniques dans la Vie Moderne*, and there is news of a streamlined 4-6-4 that may well have run some time this year at 112½ mph – but, as we have come to expect, the comrades like to keep things top secret. There is also, in my clippings, further news of Stalin's Great Purge.

We come to our second stop, under the curving glass roof of York station, a masterpiece of railway design by the North Eastern Railway architects Thomas Prosser and William Peachey that opened a little over 60 years ago. Here, waiting passengers, platform staff and boys taking down numbers in notebooks wave as if we were an ocean liner coming in to berth. Freed of my Frenchman, I take stock of my other travelling companions. A senior businessman puffing at a corona is dictating to a fashionably coiffed secretary. There are many business travellers on board. The speed of the streamliner has encouraged them to swap letters for face-to-face meetings in Edinburgh, Newcastle, York and London. A well-dressed mother is reading Daphne du Maurier's *Jamaica Inn*. Across the table, her daughter – a glass of pale green cordial in hand – is deep in the bright pages of *The Schoolgirl*, following the adventures of Bessie Bunter and her friends at Cliff House.

Thirty miles south, we pass Doncaster in the high seventies, *Quicksilver* chiming loud and long. This is where she was born in '35. The famous railway works puts on an impressive show of LNER locomotives – new, middle-aged and old – from fleet Pacifics to hard-pounding goods engines. South of 'Donnie', we flit away from the realm of heavy industry through a landscape of rolling farmland: shorn lambs here, haymaking there, heavy horses, traction engines, the latest tractors, and, if only we could hear them, the joyous solos of skylarks hovering ecstatically over high summer fields. From Scotland to England we have streaked from a realm of sleet and snow to a land of sun and rain.

Nearing Grantham, its approach signalled by the skyrocketing spire of St Wulfram's, I slip my Venner split-second stopwatch surreptitiously from a waistcoat pocket. Like many passengers, I have to admit to being excited by the idea of the run down Stoke Bank to Peterborough, and the Swiss stopwatch will allow me to see just how fast *Quicksilver* runs this evening. This is the stretch of track *Mallard* flew down at German-beating speed on Sunday. Even the senior businessman takes time from dictation and the signing of documents and letters, as *Quicksilver* exits Stoke Tunnel and bolts down towards the low-lying Lincolnshire villages of Little Bytham and Essendine. Faster than fairies, faster than witches, we crest 106 mph, the countryside on either side a blur of rain-flecked, summer-sunset greens, browns and greys.

In her stride, some four and a half hours from Edinburgh, *Quicksilver* would undoubtedly pace on at a very high speed for many miles yet. But we have to slow to 20 mph through Peterborough before drifting past brickworks and picking up speed over the Cambridgeshire fens. Almost dark now, we are up to 100 mph again somewhere close to Hitchin, then after the climb to Stevenage – the small town on the A1 where the mighty 110 mph Vincent Rapide motorcycle is made – and up to Potters Bar, we drop down to London.

My Frenchman comes back to his seat. To show him there are no hard feelings between us – although, of course, there are – I order him a bottle of Löwenbräu, a lager beer from Munich more than twice the price of a Guinness or a Bass. He is clearly delighted. But just before we re-join our stilted conversation of a hundred miles or more back, an LNER locomotive inspector I have met several times asks if I'd like to visit the footplate. The answer is a foregone conclusion. This indeed is a privilege.

At the corridor gangway at the end of the first coach, the inspector hands me a boiler suit that I pull over my own. He opens a steel door, says, 'Mind your head, you'll have to bend,' and disappears into a low and narrow metal passage no more than 5 feet high and 18 inches wide. This is *Quicksilver*'s 5,000-gallon, eight-wheel tender. Although noisy, it rides like a coach.

A second door opens onto the operatic drama of the A4's footplate, all black-on-white dials, pipework, levers, a fierce orange-white blaze from the firebox, a low hiss from the safety valves, the smell of coal dust and hot oil; driver Ellis and his fireman, our crew since York, leaning out from leather-trimmed bucket seats on both sides of the swaying cab, hunting for signals. Our speed is 90 mph. But now, the hard work is done. The fireman has stowed his shovel, swept and hosed the coal dust from the footplate floor. There is sufficient steam pressure to see us to the buffer stops at King's Cross.

The suburbs encroaching on either side are a panorama of electric lights. Headlamps shine from cars and buses on wet roads below, and from the fast-flicking windows of suburban trains passed at speed. *Quicksilver* flashes past them all, her purring three-cylinder beat mesmerizing. A clock tower points to 10.20, so it's time to thank the crew and the inspector, take off the boiler suit and return to my seat, shortly before – brakes applied firmly and smoothly – we plunge into the smoky recesses of Copenhagen and Gasworks tunnels and draw into King's Cross, a stable of lithe Gresley Pacifics and stalwart Ivatt Atlantics and their varnished-teak trains. We are on time, as expected of the *Coronation* as a matter of course.

We leave the train in a loose-knit file of hats and coats and porters, all on our way home or to hotels. My French diplomat walks alongside me. 'My friend, some of your fellow Englishmen take pride in the new Germany. And some of them like speed, too. Look out for news later this month of the German Grand Prix. Your fellow countryman, Richard Seaman, will be driving for Mercedes-Benz.'

Good luck to him, I say, offering a parting '*Vive la France!*' at the platform end, even though I can't help thinking that if my saturnine French companion ever burst into song it would be with 'Horst-Wessel-Lied' rather than 'La Marseillaise'. Europe can certainly seem an odd place these days, with old loyalties divided, but then, looking back at *Quicksilver* and the beautiful streamlined train that has sped me through volatile July weather in imperturbable style – despite the slightly questionable decor of my first-class carriage – Britain does hold the world speed record for steam traction. And, although Germany offers some fine trains, none can match the sheer élan and silver service of the *Coronation*. I walk out of the stock-brick terminus to find a taxi. It's stopped raining.

*

The *Coronation* made its last run from Edinburgh Waverley to London King's Cross on 31st August 1939. Its sibling streamliners, the *Silver Jubilee* and the *West Riding Limited* (King's Cross to Leeds) were withdrawn, too. There was a fourth LNER streamliner – the *East Anglian*, running from London Liverpool Street to Norwich Thorpe with a call at Ipswich. In this case, appearances were deceptive, and the main-line locomotives – although resembling Gresley A4s, and complete with those distinctive chime whistles – were in fact fashionably dressed and smaller Gresley B17 4-6-0s. Intense traffic on the East Anglian Main Line between Colchester and London meant that the *East Anglian* was not really very fast, but it looked the part and, collectively, the streamliners were a superb public relations coup for the LNER, a railway that in its 25-year life was rarely less than hard-pressed financially.

Speed returned slowly to the East Coast Main Line after the Second World War. From the mid-1950s, the much-loved A4s, now with their driving wheels exposed, were running at up to and over 100 mph again. In 1956, the A4s were the locomotives chosen to work the new *Talisman* express, with up and down trains leaving Edinburgh Waverley and King's Cross at 4.30 p.m. as the *Coronation* had – and covering the distance between the two cities in 6 hours and 40 minutes, with a stop at Newcastle. The seven-coach *Talisman* might not have been as fast as the pre-war streamliner, yet, delightfully, it included a pair of articulated first-class coaches – now painted the British Railways maroon – from the *Coronation*. These survived in service until the early 1960s. On its first run up to London, the net time of the *Talisman*, with 60018 *Sparrow Hawk*, was 236 minutes against a schedule of 265 minutes – or one minute faster than the *Coronation*.

The *Coronation*'s two observation cars were rebuilt in the late 1950s. One – 1719 – was often attached to trains on the Scottish Region line from Inverness to the Kyle of Lochalsh, and can be seen at the preserved Great Central Railway. Its twin, 1729, has been restored to its original condition by Nemesis Rail of Burton-on-Trent.

From 1954, the A4s performed splendidly on the summer-only *Elizabethan*, an 11-coach train running non-stop in both directions between London and Edinburgh in six and a half hours, an average speed of a shade over a mile a minute. A 20-minute documentary, *Elizabethan Express* (1954), directed by Tony Thompson and produced by Edgar Anstey for British Transport Films, includes stirring footage of 60017 *Silver Fox* at speed, and captures life on board a train that – while not as glamorous as the *Coronation* – was certainly special at a time when ration books had just been withdrawn after nearly a decade of post-war austerity.

In May 1959, Bill Hoole, a legend among East Coast engine drivers, attempted to break *Mallard*'s record at the regulator of A4 60007 *Sir Nigel Gresley*, racing down Stoke Bank with a Stephenson Locomotive Society enthusiasts' special at 112 mph – an official post-war record for British steam – before being instructed to slow down. Some while earlier, Hoole may have reached 117 mph with *Sir Nigel Gresley*.

When replaced by the well-regarded 100 mph Deltic diesels on the East Coast Main Line in the early 1960s, several A4s were transferred to Glasgow (St Rollox depot) and Aberdeen (Ferryhill), where they cut the schedule of trains between the two Scottish cities via Dundee to three hours flat. Though restricted to the Scottish Region's maximum speed of 75 mph, the A4s showed their pace uphill as well as down, and were much missed when they went in September 1966. Ever since, the service between Glasgow and Aberdeen has been lacklustre. Although a little faster, contemporary diesel trains are glum, cramped, ungenerous things that are lacking the griddle car which served hot food on the A4-hauled trains that made the Scottish landscape as romantic as it can still be. Six A4s have been preserved, two running on main-line specials today. *Mallard*'s speed record has yet to be broken.

Richard Seaman, a wealthy young man from Chichester who was educated at Rugby School and Trinity College, Cambridge, won the German Grand Prix on 24th July 1938. Leading the Belgium Grand Prix in the rain in June 1939, ten weeks before Hitler invaded Poland, he crashed his Mercedes-Benz into a tree and died. He was 26 years old. He is buried in Putney.

My French companion is based on Fernand de Brinon, a French lawyer and journalist who befriended the French-speaking Joachim von Ribbentrop. He was a keen advocate of Nazi Germany and a leading light of the Groupe Collaboration that, after the German invasion of France, sought a union of European states following a Nazi victory in the Second World War. Tried by a French court of justice for war crimes, he was executed by firing squad in March 1947.

The journey along the East Coast Main Line from Edinburgh to Newcastle, some unforgivable new housing aside, remains a marvel – even if today's express trains share little of the glamour of the LNER streamliners. Meanwhile, the P2 Steam Locomotive Company – based at the A1 Steam Locomotive Trust's Darlington works – is building a new P2 2-8-2. Named *Prince of Wales* – the flesh-and-blood Prince Charles is a keen steam enthusiast – this powerful, and improved, locomotive is scheduled to steam in 2021, a partner to the Peppercorn A1 class 60163

Tornado, engineered by the same team, that since 2008 has been busy at work on Britain's main lines at speeds of up to 100 mph.

Poster by Norman Wilkinson for the London Midland and Scottish Railway celebrating its fast, new North Channel steam turbine ferry service established by *Princess Margaret* (1931) and *Princess Maud* (1934).

TRAVEL TO IRELAND BY
THE SHORT SEA ROUTE

STRANRAER-LARNE

MAGNIFICENT NEW TURBINE STEAMERS
'PRINCESS MAUD' AND 'PRINCESS MARGARET'

GREATLY ACCELERATED SERVICES

PARTICULARS OF TRAIN AND STEAMER TIMES FROM
ANY L M S STATION

Burtonport station, Donegal, June 1937. The 8.30 a.m. Londonderry train is ready to depart. Locomotive, No. 12, is one of two impressive 4-8-0 tender locomotives built for this quixotic narrow-gauge railway.

June 1935. A London Transport Brill branch train waits for connecting Metropolitan Line services at Quainton Road, Buckinghamshire. Its locomotive dates from 1866, its single carriage, although re-bodied, from 1863.

Between 1932 and 1937, the 770-foot silver German airship *Graf Zeppelin*, seen here over Guanabara Bay, flew a regular transatlantic summer service carrying twenty select passengers to Rio de Janeiro.

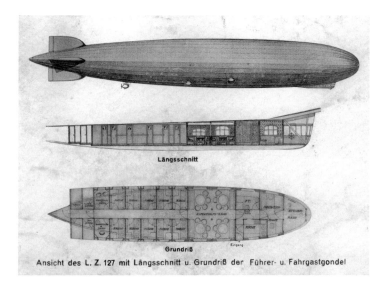

Längsschnitt

Grundriß

Ansicht des L. Z. 127 mit Längsschnitt u. Grundriß der Führer- u. Fahrgastgondel

Drawings of the *Graf Zeppelin* reveal how small the gondola – with its 'flight deck', kitchen, dining room and cabins – was compared to the sheer scale of the aircraft.

Wine and card play on board *Graf Zeppelin* interrupted for views of the South American coast. The climate is tropical, yet shirts and ties are the order of the day.

Flanked by tugboats and the Manhattan skyline, SS *Normandie*, as long as the Art Deco Chrysler Building was high, and very fast for an Atlantic liner, negotiates New York Harbor.

Normandie's ambitious interiors – the first-class dining room was longer than the Hall of Mirrors at Versailles – sported fine contemporary French décor, including softly lit Lalique glass columns.

Seen from the footplate of 6220 *Coronation*, the northbound and southbound *Coronation Scot*, bound for Glasgow and London in May 1938, cross paths at the southern end of Preston station.

Club car designed for an improved *Coronation Scot* service scuppered by the Second World War. In 1939, the new train was displayed at Euston station before touring the United States.

The sleek two-tone blue *Coronation* express, with A4 Pacific 4490 *Empire of India* in charge, glides south from Edinburgh Waverley in the summer of 1938 on its six-hour run to King's Cross.

Coronation dinner menu, July 1938. Meals were served at passengers' seats rather than in a dining car. The accompanying wine list offered a choice of eighteen wines and five champagnes.

Model *Coronation* passenger seated in a swivelling armchair, complete with ottoman, on board a two-tone green first-class saloon. The Art Deco steam streamliner aimed to outdo contemporary British Pullmans.

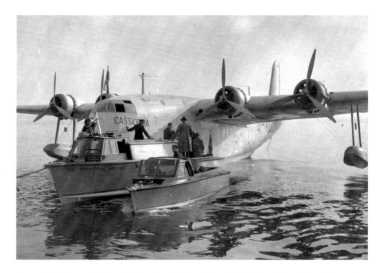

Imperial Airway's Short Empire Flying Boat *Cassiopeia* at Southampton Docks, January 1937. Passengers and post bound as far as Singapore, and perhaps on to Australia by Qantas, board from tenders.

Drinks and cards, this time in the leather-lined smoking cabin of a Short Empire Flying Boat. Fresh flowers replaced at ports of call, menus pinned on the wall, enveloping armchairs.

The sublime 1938 Henry Dreyfuss-designed *20th Century Limited* gallops into the sunset on its way from New York to Chicago, its locomotive a powerful New York Central Class J-3a Hudson.

Lounge and observation car of the 1938 *20th Century Limited*. Behind the banquette seat and curved Manhattan skyline wall are seats facing views of fast disappearing tracks, trains and landscapes.

SEVEN

Southampton to Singapore: Imperial Airways

12th–18th July 1939

A hush-hush afternoon meeting at Whitehall Court with members of the Air League holds a real surprise. I am introduced to the Marshal of the Royal Air Force, Hugh 'Boom' Trenchard. Although Lord Trenchard, a never-less-than-controversial figure, has long retired from the RAF and from his recent role as commissioner of the Metropolitan Police, he remains a formidable presence in the world of military aviation. From as early as '32 he has been pressing successive governments over the defence of Singapore. 'When you get out there,' he booms, as we stare out from high Victorian windows over the Victoria Embankment to the wharves and workshops on the south side of the Thames, 'you're pretty damn sure to be drenched by a complete shower. And I'm not talking about the weather.'

The official view is different from that of 'Boom'. The ambitious new military port and dockyard are, I learn, all but ready for action – 16 years down the line, and at a cost of no less than £60 million. The government's line is that should the

Japs ever be so foolhardy as to nip this way, they'll be met by the full force of the Royal Navy and some big new shore guns that, together, will blast them from here to kingdom come. Others think differently, which is why my bags have been sent on to Waterloo this afternoon and I have a ticket in my pocket for Singapore.

I leave Whitehall Court at five-thirty and stroll along the narrow walkway across Hungerford Bridge. Performing their sulphurous ministry inches from me are Southern Railway suburban trains flashing electric fire, pugnacious ex-South Eastern and Chatham 4-4-0s, and a powerful three-cylinder Schools class 4-4-0 at the head of a Hastings express. There are plans to move Charing Cross station east along the Strand and to build a replacement double-deck railway and road bridge, yet despite Mr Chamberlain's continued assurances to the contrary, war is looming and projects like this are already on the back burner.

Stepping up through its stirring war memorial arch – a reminder of the last show – between Portland stone goddesses representing war and peace, presided over by Britannia bearing the torch of liberty, I join the commuter throng of Waterloo. This is London's busiest station and it has an air of real excitement about it. The coaches of my train, the 7.30 p.m. to Southampton, have yet to arrive, so I weave my way along the concourse, pick up newspapers and journals at W. H. Smith and catch the latest newsreels at the News Theatre opposite Platform 1. Germany's Hermann Paul Müller has won the French Grand Prix at the wheel of a 200-mph D-Type Auto Union; Pan American Airways has launched the first flights by aircraft across the Atlantic

– New York to Southampton, Boeing 314 flying boat; and the Japs have invaded Mongolia.

I'm all for Mickey Mouse, yet I leave the theatre before the cartoon. My train is in. I spot a pair of umber and cream Pullman cars attached, along with a luggage van to the rear of the Southampton boat train. Wooden boards above the Pullman windows read 'Empire Service Imperial Airways'. My flight to Singapore starts here. My bags are stowed, so I walk briskly along the parade of smart malachite-green coaches to find our locomotive, 862 *Lord Collingwood*, one of the four-cylinder Lord Nelson class 4-6-0s designed under the direction of Richard Maunsell, former chief mechanical engineer of the Southern Railway.

I'm pleased to see Lord Collingwood's name. As Nelson's second-in-command at Trafalgar, he sped *Royal Sovereign* to first engage the French. And successfully so. But the story I like most about the decisive and very decent Collingwood is how, when at home in Morpeth, he would walk his dog Bounce (who also served at Trafalgar) over the hills, planting acorns as they went so that these might grow into the mighty oaks the admiral saw as necessary for the future defence of his beloved country – and of liberty, too, of course. Our warships are made of steel today, yet Collingwood's oaks, fully mature now, are still there at Morpeth to remind us of his fighting spirit.

Lord Collingwood, the locomotive, is in fine fighting mood. Her driver tells me that Mr Bulleid, the Southern's new CME – Gresley's former second-in-command at the LNER – has fitted the Nelsons with Lemaître multiple jet exhausts, and that the new French devices have improved the performance of these once sluggish, if powerful, engines to no end. But it's 7.20 p.m., so I walk back the length of the train to be shown my armchair seat in the last carriage.

I hang up my hat. It's been a warm day and I'm tempted to remove my jacket and loosen my tie. Of course, I don't. In a few days, though, all going well, I'll be in Singapore and looking forward to sinking a Singapore Sling or two at Raffles. I settle for a whisky and soda as whistles resound under Waterloo's expansive ridge-and-furrow roof and *Lord Collingwood* pulls us out from the station, the engine's unusually fast exhaust beat suggesting we're accelerating with something of the alacrity of Müller's Auto Union. Well, not quite.

Rumbling through Clapham Junction, I settle down to read my brief for Singapore. What are the air defences? What are the Japanese up to? What needs to be done? A tap on my shoulder prompts me to turn my papers face down on the table. I look up and, as if on cue, it's Bob, a New York journalist with the Associated Press. I met Bob in town for drinks at Brooks's a couple of years back. The last I'd heard of him, he was on assignment in Chunking – the provisional capital of Generalissimo Chiang Kai-shek, the Chinese leader – reporting on the situation with Japan. Bob has been back in New York for a few weeks, and now, following hot on the Jap invasion of Mongolia, he's heading China-wards.

'Of course, you'll hate me,' he says, taking the empty seat opposite mine and ordering more whiskies. We whistle through Surbiton at over sixty.

'Now, why should I do that?'

'Flew over the pond, Pan Am, the new Boeing.' Bob is flying to Hong Kong via Singapore and then across the Chinese border, and continuing overland to re-join his colleagues in Chunking.

I decide not to talk military aircraft so early in the trip, and ask Bob about the transatlantic Boeing. We eat mixed grills between Woking and Eastleigh. The ventilator is open. Cantering down towards Southampton, soot particles spray like ground pepper across our plates. The train brakes to crawl through the town to Terminus station, a firm favourite. Fronted by a handsome white stucco design of 1839 by Sir William Tite – architect of the Royal Exchange and, from 1855, a Liberal MP – the station offers direct access to the imposing French Renaissance–style South Western Hotel.

Inside its gilded lobby, Bob says, 'Like an ocean liner.'

'It really is. See the stair? That was the model for the central stair of the *Titanic*.'

'You don't say!'

'I do. And what ghosts, Bob, will be here in the hotel with us tonight. Thomas Andrews of Harland and Wolff, who designed the *Titanic*, and Joseph Ismay, chairman of the White Star Line, both spent their last night on land here.' Both went down with the ill-fated liner.

'We'll drink a toast to them,' says Bob.

After a quick scrub and a weight check for tomorrow's flight, we meet in the bar. Here are quite a few of the faces we saw on board the train from Waterloo. Most will be sailing tomorrow morning. Just a very few will be flying. I bring up the subject of the Japanese air force. Bob is quick to follow my cue. 'It's not the air force you need to watch, it's the Imperial Navy. I don't have any particularly useful details, but from what I can gather Mitsubishi has been working on a new carrier-based fighter that's meant to be the real McCoy. And – listen to this – you guys have played a part in its design.'

'Pull the other one,' I say as our brandies arrive.

'Before the Japs invaded Manchuria, I was posted in Tokyo. I had wanted to do an interview with Admiral Togo' – the 'Nelson of the East' who took out the Russian fleet at Tsushima in 1905 – 'you know he was at King George V's coronation? Togo was an ardent Anglophile. Fatally ill by the time I tried to get in touch. But, in the process, I did get to meet an ex-British air force officer who'd been close to Togo and the Imperial Navy.'

'Who the heck was that?'

'Lord Sempill, Order of the Rising Sun.'

'William Forbes-Sempill...'

'The very same. Sempill was and perhaps still is close to the Imperial Navy. Led the mission to Japan in '21, taking Gloster something-or-the-other...'

'Sparrowhawks.'

'Thanks – Sparrowhawks, out east. When I met him, Sempill was a technical and commercial consultant to – guess who? – Mitsubishi.' We down our brandies and order the other halves. 'Meanwhile, he'd kept channels of communication open between Gloster and the Jap military. Hinted that they'd recently had sight of blueprints of an experimental Gloster monoplane fighter. These were handed on to Mitsubishi. Does this make any sense or is the brandy doing the talking?'

'Come on, time for a bit of shut-eye,' I say. 'We take off at first light tomorrow.'

A typed Imperial Airways memo informs us reveille will be at 0415 hours. Light breakfast in our rooms, 0430. Bus leaves for the port, 0500. Take-off, 0530 hours. I find it hard to sleep. The experimental Gloster fighter Bob mentioned must be the F.5/34, designed by Folland and Preston to meet the same specification as Camm's Hawker Hurricane and Mitchell's Supermarine Spitfire. I saw the F.5 being put through its paces last March. Test pilots liked it. A little underpowered, perhaps, with the Bristol Mercury IX, but it certainly had the makings of a fighter well suited to Far Eastern ops. As for Sempill, I'll ask about him when I'm back from Singapore.

I must have dozed off eventually, because I'm woken with a morning tea tray. Up, splash, shave, dress, and downstairs to meet the bus that gargles out into sunrise Southampton. There are nine of us aboard. Over the whine of gears, we nod to one another and exchange quiet good mornings. So, down to the docks, where liners are being loaded in a realm of cranes, derricks, smoking funnels, and small tank engines puffing up and down beside freighters towering above them; of raucous, wheeling gulls, sonorous hooters, bustling tugs, pilot boats and tenders.

Ushered onto the pontoon at Berth 108, we meet G-ADUX *Cassiopeia*. The porpoise-like Short S.23 C class Empire flying boat might not be big by the latest American standards, but she is certainly an impressive machine: a high-winged, four-engine double-decker, her silver-aluminium alloy fuselage rippling with reflections of the morning sun cast across the water.

We step from the floating deck into our 'boat. It smells of cold metal and cool leather, with just the hint of petrol. The steward settles us in our seats, the nine of us in three cabins. Upstairs, the first officer and flight clerk are busy with last-minute preparations as Captain 'Jackie' Harrington offers us a brief welcome. He's back upstairs as we fasten our seat belts. The 920-hp Bristol Pegasus XC air-cooled radials fire up one after the other, spitting fire, port and starboard. Away from our berth, we make two circles in the water as the engines warm, before turning into the wind and, with a glorious spray of Solent tide over the windows, *Cassiopeia* rushes through the tidal water like some outsize speedboat. I feel her lift, yet the captain holds our 18-ton machine low before she has gathered sufficient momentum. Up we go, engines blaring, flap motors whining, turning south-west over Calshot. Turning again over the Needles, I have a cinematic view of the Isle of Wight, which is etched around with the snow-white wakes of a shoal of ships.

We climb slowly towards Cherbourg in the early-morning chill. The steward does the rounds, offering tea, coffee, Oxo, Bovril, blankets, cigarettes and foot muffs. Ahead of me, I can see Bob tipping the contents of a hip flask into his coffee. Getting up from my generous and comfortable reclining armchair, I go for a stroll, stepping down from the aft cabin into the lofty promenade deck, where I stand for a moment to stare out across the Channel, then continue on through the cosy midship cabin and into a passageway – the kitchen to starboard;

gents' and ladies' lavatories on the port side – leading to the forward smoking cabin and its convivial interior.

The colour scheme throughout our flying boat is a soothing palette of grey and pale green, with walls and ceilings lined in Connolly hide. Bottle-green leather below dado level. Aluminium-alloy fittings. Carpets, mottled black and green. The decor is the work of Brian O'Rorke, a Kiwi architect and engineer who was, I believe, responsible for the elegant, free-flowing interiors of the Orient Line's RMS *Orion*, launched in '34. The *Architectural Review* described her as a 'landmark in the evolution of the modern liner'. She sails between Southampton and Sydney, so we might even pass her on the way to Singapore.

Although this is my first trip aboard a flying boat, I was down at the Short Brothers Seaplane Works at Rochester last year to see C class machines under construction. Arthur Gouge heads the design team. Son of a Methodist minister and from Northfleet, he left school at 13 to train as a carpenter in the building trade. Night school led to a bachelor's degree in maths and engineering, and a job in the carpentry workshop at Shorts during the war. He was chief designer by '26, doubling up as general manager in '32. There's a career that took off.

Gouge also designed the Sunderland, the big military flying boat – there are 40 in service, I think, with lots more to come – and the Stirling four-engine bomber. It made its maiden flight in May, but it's in competition with Supermarine's four-engine Type 317. This promises to be a lot faster than the Stirling. We'll see.

We pass over the 250-foot-high, early-nineteenth-century lighthouse on Pointe de Barfleur. Last year at Rochester, Gouge showed me the drawing office at Shorts. Seventy draughtsmen at work – including, he couldn't help telling me, 'young Conrad over there'. One of Joseph Conrad's sons. I've read Conrad's *Heart of Darkness* several times. Can't help feeling we're heading that way today. After what the Japs did at Nanking, what else should one think?

The steward interrupts my thoughts. 'Captain asks if you'd like to see the "office", sir.'

I most certainly would. I climb a ladder to the spacious cabin up top. At his busy desk, the flight clerk is rattling away on a Baby Empire typewriter. Compartments crammed with mail separate him from the equally busy radio operator. Captain Harrington leans back from his seat to extend a hand. The first officer nods and flies the ship.

'Good to have you aboard. What do you make of her?'

'She's quite something, I have to say.'

Cassiopeia certainly is. The flight deck – 'cockpit' is too confining a word – is an airy, generously glazed space. We chat about the route to Marseilles. South to La Rochelle. South-east from there, to Blaye, Villefranche-de-Rouergue and Millau. Over the Rhône delta, landing on the lake at Marignane – for Marseilles – where we'll refuel before our next stop, Rome. We talk about the weather, too, of course. Calm today, all the way. The first officer engages the automatic pilot.

'We probably won't need to put down for fuel before Marseilles today,' says Captain Harrington. 'We've a run of 641 nautical miles and fuel for 760, cruising at 143 knots.'

'What's she like to fly?'

'Piece of cake, for the most part. Some limitations, though. We won't fly above 10,000 feet unless we have to. Unfair on passengers. Cold. Lack of oxygen. And taxiing can be a bit taxing! Fast currents – that sort of thing.

'Last June, Captain Gurney made a forced landing with *Ceres* on Lake Dingari on the way from Karachi to Gwalior. Got stuck in mud. Night on board, five-course dinner. And crocodiles, dozens of them by all accounts, rubbing their backs against the aircraft. They were looking for a rather different dinner. *Ceres* was towed out in the end, but it took some days and the crew were supplied with food and water dropped by parachute from passing 'boats. All good fun.'

Captain Harrington has been at the controls of flying boats since '32, and intensely so since '34 when the Empire Air Mail Scheme was opened up to no end and the C class flying boats were commissioned to cope with rising demand. Mail takes precedence over passengers, and Captain Harrington tells me that there is talk of turning the smoking cabin into a secondary mailroom and moving the flight clerk's office downstairs to the midship cabin. If so, passenger accommodation will be very limited.

Who are the nine of us approaching Marignane this morning? The flight clerk gives me the lowdown. Aside from Bob and myself, there's Mrs Sidders and her 14-year-old daughter, Alice, flying to Calcutta to meet Brigadier Sidders who has been posted to Kohima. The Siamese gentleman is the racing driver Prince Bira, en route to Bangkok. Two high-ranking civil servants flying to Singapore, and Mr Furlow, an Australian in the tinned-meat business, and his pretty wife, Joyce, who are flying through to Sydney.

'Mr Furlow told me a funny story last night,' says Captain Harrington, 'when I popped in to the hotel to check everyone had arrived. He was at Gallipoli. An Anzac soldier threw a tin of bully beef into the Turkish trenches. It came flying back with a note scribbled in English: "Cigarettes, yes. Bully beef, no". Since the armistice, Furlow's made a fortune flogging the stuff to us. Don't worry, it's not on the menu.'

I go back to the aft cabin and strap in as *Cassiopeia* makes a graceful landing. Up in front, the first officer is busy in the mooring compartment. Opening the forward hatch, he ties *Cassiopeia* to a buoy. A launch pulls alongside and we step down into it for a quick spin to the docks to stretch our legs and have a smoke, while a Shell tender burbles out to meet our aircraft. Bob races Alice Sidders up and down the landing stage. I chat to Prince Bira, Mr and Mrs Furlow, and Mrs Sidders. The high-ranking civil servants have remained on board.

Back on our 'boat, the steward announces a 12 o'clock lunch. Once we're up and in level flight, heading due east towards Saint-Raphaël, the steward serves drinks followed by white linen–covered trays and lunch. I choose roast guinea fowl and salad, followed by a sherry trifle and Gruyère toast. The wine list is extensive. The steward explains that hampers are brought on board at most stops, so there's always a supply of fresh food, drinks and water. Hot food and drinks come in vacuum-sealed containers and flasks.

We pass over the northern tip of Corsica and, tables and trays swept away, sweep low between the islands of Pianosa and

Monte Cristo. Crossing the Italian coast, we drop down to Lake Bracciano where we splash into the water a little before two o'clock. A member of the British embassy staff at Rome joins our small company, taking a seat in the promenade deck. Hugh, in pale green tweeds, has been given a three-year posting to Singapore. He's glad to get away from Rome and the braggadocio of the Fascists, but I wonder what he'll make of Singapore.

'The Japs will have taken over Malaya and even Australia by the time you're next packing your bags,' says Bob, two Airways Specials, half a bottle of claret and a brandy down.

'What rot!' laughs whey-faced Hugh.

We climb hard away from Rome towards the Apennines. The steward offers boiled sweets as well as Italian newspapers. Stories in *Il Messaggero* are surely censored. They seem slightly vague anyway as we reach 10,000 feet, a fact we know from a typed memo sent from the flight deck shortly before take-off. It's cold at this height, but we're quickly over the spine of Italy and dropping towards the Adriatic coast over Campobosso and Foggia to Brindisi, where the port is chock-a-block with Italian warships. Our British Civil Air Ensign is flown defiantly as we taxi in and out of harbour. Up again, tea is served. We fly at 2,500 feet towards Albania, skirt Corfu and the Greek coast, hasten with Homeric gods along the Gulf of Corinth, and put down with Athens in view on Phaleron Bay. It's 7 p.m.

A tender and a small bus take us to the lavish embrace of the Hotel Grande Bretagne on Constitution Square. The view from my window is of the Parthenon. I rather wish I could end my trip here and now. But I wash and go up to the rooftop restaurant for dinner. Only the high-ranking civil servants are absent.

I suggest a walk around the Acropolis. Only Alice and her mother, Mrs Sidders, seem keen. A taxi whisks us to the foot of the Acropolis and we walk for an hour up and among these splendid ruins. Odd to think this was all pretty much intact until the Venetians lobbed mortar shells at the Parthenon at the time of an assault on Ottoman Athens in 1687. Mind you, the Turks had turned the Greek temple into an ammunition store.

We walk back to the hotel. It's midnight and we need to be in the lobby at 5 a.m. for our six o'clock flight. But I sit for a further hour in the bar. The hotel, I know, was formerly a particularly grand Neo-Classical mansion, built in 1842 for a Greek tycoon by the Danish-born architect Theophil Hansen. Hansen also designed the Musikverein in Vienna. I have happy memories of the New Year's Concert of '33, held in its pitch-perfect Golden Hall. The conductor was no less than Johann Strauss III, nephew of Johann Strauss II of 'The Blue Danube' fame. Carefree days.

I sleep soundly with the windows wide open and the Parthenon to greet me when I rise. Another fine day spells a non-stop leg to Alexandria. I was planning to read Raymond Chandler's *The Big Sleep* but I fall asleep in my armchair, awoken now and then by the occasional rise and fall of the flying boat as we ride the air waves. The steward serves me a quick coffee before we nose down to Alexandria's Eastern Harbour and its parade of Royal Navy warships.

Refuelled, we fly east along the Mediterranean coast. After a dry martini, lunch today starts with a fresh grapefruit followed by lamb cutlets and a fruit salad with cream. I eat with Prince Bira and we talk great races and great cars. He remains a fan of the English Racing Automobile's terrier-like cars. He set up his own team with his brother, Prince Chula, who bought him an ERA R2B as a 21st birthday present. 'It's called *Romulus*,' says Bira. 'We got 166 bhp from the supercharged 1.5-litre six. But we weren't able to compete with Dick Seaman's straight-eight Delage.'

We think we should drink a toast to Dick Seaman, a contemporary we've both known. I find it a little hard, though, to raise my glass with true enthusiasm. Spoilt rotten – his mother bought him a country house for his 20th birthday – Dick was an utterly brilliant driver. He died last month, frightfully burnt, after crashing his W154 Merc while leading the Belgian Grand Prix. By his own deathbed admission he'd been going far too fast. Signed up with Mercedes-Benz from the '37 season, he was the only British driver to sport a swastika on the tail of his car. Won last year's German Grand Prix and gave the Hitler salute on the podium. Seemed odd. Somehow tasteless. Dick's funeral was held in town at the end of last month. Herr Hitler sent an enormous wreath.

We cross the coast of Palestine south of Haifa, and splash down into Lake Tiberias just before 3 p.m. 'This where JC walked on the water?' says Bob.

'Fed the five thousand, calmed the storm and chose his disciples, too.'

'Actually,' says Bob, 'I find it pretty awe-inspiring. Go for a walk in Tiberias?'

When Jesus practised his ministry here, the lake, also known as the Sea of Galilee, was surrounded by a ribbon of villages. It may have been better off than it is now. I wish we had time to see Capernaum. I have to remind myself that I'm on a work trip and in a hurry to get to Singapore. This is the quickest way, yet there are diversions, it seems, all along the way. Even so, we manage a swim in the biblical lake before take-off.

Heading due east from Tiberias, we climb steeply. 'Sandstorm, sir,' says the steward. 'Still, better than a thunderstorm. They can reach up to 35,000 feet and are no fun at all.'

Turbulence rocks *Cassiopeia* this way, that way and every other conceivable way over the Syrian desert. The cabins are quiet. The Bristol engines drone on. We come down three hours later on Lake Habbaniyah, the storm unabated. *Cassiopeia* bucks and sways. It's a hard job to moor her. Alice says it's been the most terrific fun and she rather wishes we could do it all over again. Quite the girl.

It's absolutely baking here: 110 degrees Fahrenheit. It's a relief when the storm fades and we rush down the lake and climb into clear, if hot and turbulent, skies. We follow the Euphrates south-east through ancient Mesopotamia, spotting the ancient Ziggurat of Ur on our way, and so on, down to Basra on the Persian Gulf. Our hotel for the night is the Iraqi State Railways guesthouse at the land and sea airport, on the west bank of the Shatt el Arab. I play cards with Hugh and Alice, a terrific game Alice calls 'Cheat'.

'Learned it from the nuns at school. It gets better, Sister Josephine says, the more you drink.'

'Does it?'

After Alice has gone up, I play 'Cheat' with Bob, Bira, Hugh and Mr and Mrs Furlow. Two packs of cards. Perhaps a little too much J&B. We must be unwinding from the storm.

*

Saturday morning, 0530 hours, and we're up over the Persian Gulf flying low, with plenty of bumps to please Alice. We refuel at Bahrain and then make the short hop, 90 minutes or so, to Dabai – or Dubai – a former fishing village famed for its daring pearl divers. Captain Harrington, who is dressed now, as are the rest of the crew, in tropical gear – short sleeves, khaki and shorts, rather than Navy-style uniforms – says that it's rather exciting, first time around, if you have to spend the night here. The hotel is the Sharjah Fort, surrounded by barbed wire. 'Godforsaken place, Dabai,' he says, 'but don't let the locals hear you say it! We've a long leg from here to Karachi, but the weather's good and I don't think we'll need to put down for fuel.'

We don't. Bob regales me with stories from China as we drink cold white wine and tuck into a lunch of roast chicken and mint sauce, served with a beetroot and apple salad with cream cheese and crackers to follow. At the captain's suggestion, we step up to the promenade deck to stare, astonished, at the bizarrely sculpted peaks of the Makran Coastal Range, as we skirt the Gulf of Oman and cross the Indian border. We land in Korangi Creek at the RAF flying boat base and are driven from shore to Karachi's Carlton Hotel, a pleasant enough hole serving an excellent curry, and with arcades sheltering rooms from a ruinously fierce sun. When I try to fall asleep under the mosquito net, my drifting mind confuses the whirr of the ceiling fan with that of the *Cassiopeia*'s spinning airscrews.

We cross India west to east on Sunday, flying as low as 300 feet. We have marvellous views of villages, forests, temples and rivers. In one river, women in bright saris washing swathes of coloured fabrics look up and wave as we drone over. Our first refuelling stop, 437 miles from Karachi, is the lake at Raj Samand. Flanked by white marble pavilions, and its water level controlled by a white marble dam, the lake was built by Maharana Raj Singh in the late seventeenth century. We fly low again on the short leg across Rajasthan to Gwalior. If we climb higher, *Cassiopeia* will be met by powerful headwinds that could lower our cruising speed by up to 40 knots.

Turning over the Aravali Hills, we land on Lake Man Sagar on the fringe of Jaipur. What a sight awaits us. We moor against a backdrop of the fairy-tale Water Palace, or Jal Mahal – built in the 1790s, I've been told, by a local maharajah, Jai Singh II, for duck-hunting parties. The lake is adorned with birds.

Captain Harrington says what we can see of the palace is just the top floor. There are four more underwater. 'Why did they build it like that?' asks Alice. 'Can we have a picnic there?'

'It's a folly,' says Captain Harrington. 'I do agree it'd be fun, if we had the time, to see if we could organize lunch on the roof garden. But we'll be off as soon as we've refuelled.'

We're taken by boat to the shore, where Imperial Airways has built a small office with staff accommodation. We are offered refreshments. I wonder what it would be like to be posted here for a spell?

'Are there tigers nearby?' asks Alice, hungry for lunch and devouring a cheese and chutney sandwich. The answer is yes. This is tiger and temple territory.

Airborne again, we eat lunch flying at little more than 500

feet over lush riverine landscapes. It's just well we keep low, as the monsoon lets rip shortly before we come to land at Allahabad on the confluence of the Ganges and Jumna. An electric storm engulfs the aircraft. Hail from improbably tall clouds beats an urgent tattoo on the airframe. The current we land in is fierce and fast. It takes some play with the engines to bring us to our mooring.

A lull in the storm sees us back in the hot air on the final 437-mile stretch to Calcutta. The steward brings drinks; our tables are refreshed with vases of flowers from the market in Allahabad that were brought to the 'boat by boys in punts. I'm excited to see Calcutta heave into view. My father was brought up here, and I came this way in '33, after Oxford. But we have to steer around the bases of towering, anvil-headed cumulonimbus clouds before setting down on the Hooghly close to the Howrah Bridge. Lightning zigzags down through a saturated sky. It's intensely humid. Hugh will do well in Singapore, his first posting to the Far East. His tweeds are unruffled.

'Call me effete if you like,' he says to the casually dressed Furlows, 'but I'm quite impervious to heat.'

More than 6,250 miles from Southampton, I feel on home turf. Boats take us to the east bank of the Hooghly. A bus is waiting at the quay, but I hire a pair of rickshaws for Bob, Hugh, me, Alice and Mrs Sidders. We idle along to Old Court House Street, narrowly avoiding a tram as we pull in at the entrance to the Great Eastern Hotel. While our bags are unloaded, I look up and down the street, terminated at one end by St Andrew's Church – a St Martin-in-the-Fields lookalike – and at the other by the Ochertlony Monument, a classical column much the same height as Nelson's in Trafalgar Square, I'd have thought, although all the more exotic with its Syrian detailing and Ottoman dome. If it were possible to swap climates, central London might be mistaken for downtown Calcutta, and vice versa. The journey to here from Southampton, I can't help thinking, has been made in a very English bubble.

Just as we're about to go in, a black Humber pulls up and out steps a gentleman who can only be Brigadier Sidders. The family is reunited. We shake hands. Brigadier Sidders has rooms at the nearby United Service Club, so father, mother and daughter are soon in the Humber. 'We'll write to you from Kohima,' says Alice, and off they go in a cloud of dust – and via a rather exclusive club – to one of the remotest corners of the empire.

Bob's in the bar, beers lined up in frosted glasses. 'Can't get these in England. Long way to fly for a cold beer. Cheers!' The beer is certainly refreshing. 'I've been reading Kipling's *The City of Dreadful Night*,' he says. 'Came across this sentence about the Great Eastern: "A man could walk in at one end, buy a complete outfit, a wedding present, or seeds for his garden, have an excellent meal, a *burra* peg and if the barmaid was agreeable, walk out at the other end, engaged to be married."'

I've seen this quote repeated quite twenty times, but as I don't want to spoil my travelling companion's fun, I raise my glass. 'To Mr Rudyard Kipling, India's finest correspondent.'

Over dinner, I talk to Captain Harrington about the Short Sunderland. This, I'm sure, is a machine we could do with in Singapore. 'The RAF flew one to Singapore last year,' he says. 'It's got a tremendous range. Airborne for up to fourteen hours, and can be armed to the teeth. But I don't think Singapore is in the running for Sunderlands. At least, not so far as I've heard.'

Captain Harrington thinks the Sunderland would make a great mail plane, too. The C class machines, as he reminds me, were ordered after Shorts won a competition for the design of a flying boat that would guarantee the delivery of Royal Mail overseas at a speed liners couldn't possibly match. It is first and foremost a mail plane. Now imagine the Sunderland fetching and carrying even more mail than *Cassiopeia* and her siblings. 'We'll have to see how events pan out over the next few months. The C class has a ten-year life. After that, perhaps we'll have much bigger flying boats than the C class and Sunderland put together.'

It's windy on Monday morning as our reduced company joins the 'boat. The high-ranking civil servants make a last-minute entrance in the company of a new passenger, a military man who I take to be equally high-ranking. They take the three seats of the midship cabin and are in earnest discussion even before *Cassiopeia* races down the Hooghly and, climbing, turns towards the Ganges Delta and the Bay of Bengal. We steer around thunderclouds. I try to read past page one of James Joyce's *Finnegans Wake*, but put it back in my bag and opt for Joyce Cary's *Mister Johnson* instead.

With coffee, cigarettes, conversation and a few chapters of Cary's spirited novel – and a guarded silence as I walk through the midship cabin with Prince Bira and Bob on my way to the smoking cabin – the Burmese coast south of Cox's Bazar is under our wings. We put down at Akyab.

The rest of the morning takes us over dense rainforests and snaking river valleys to Rangoon, a city announced some miles off by the spine-tingling sight of the gold-leafed Shwedagon pagoda. As if weaving a magic spell, we circle three times around this picture-book *stupa* before landing on the river some miles north of the city.

Rangoon is a beautiful garden city. If only we had the time to go into town. I have to remind myself again that this is not a sightseeing trip. In any case, some post for me has arrived from Singapore. This, and writing letters to London, keeps me busy before we're back on board. We're up again shortly after midday. Lunch is a consommé princess followed by cold chicken and salad. We fly over the Gulf of Martaban, cross the Thai border and follow the Menam river down to Bangkok. A rather vicious wind scythes across the river and, deftly, *Cassiopeia* sideslips into land.

Passengers and crew, we are ferried to the Oriental Hotel. Prince Bira is hastened away in a dove-grey 3½-litre Bentley. Bob and I collect mail and papers from the concierge. We'll meet in the bar and digest these over cocktails. One 'top secret' letter – which, by the looks of it, has probably been steamed open – might as well have a Black Dragon symbol stamped on it. Members of this ultra-nationalist Japanese organization are secreted across East Asia.

The note lists RAF aircraft in Singapore. This comprises two squadrons of Vickers Vildebeest torpedo bombers. There are no fighters to protect them. I order a second dry martini.

'Bob, will you let me know if you can find out anything more about that new Jap navy fighter?'

'Sure thing. You'll talk to Sempill?'

'Not me, but someone should.'

'What you want in Singapore,' says Bob, 'is a dozen squadrons of Spitfires. Now, that might keep you safe.'

'I'll wire the Air Ministry and tell them to forward them, chop chop.'

Singapore, however, is as likely to get Spitfires as Lord Halifax, the foreign secretary, is to stand up to Herr Hitler. We go in to dinner.

In the morning, Mr and Mrs Furlow snooze in the promenade cabin. Again, the secret threesome occupies the midship. I sit upstairs with the captain and first officer as *Cassiopeia* thrums due south over the Bay of Siam, with the long, thin Malay Peninsula to our starboard side, on the long leg to Penang. Climbing high to avoid low turbulence, I borrow the first officer's Zeiss Deltar binoculars and, for several mesmerizing minutes, look right across to the Andaman and Nicobar Islands. While we think we are so clever – with our cameras, wirelesses and flying machines – there are Palaeolithic tribes in this archipelago that stretches across the Bay of Bengal and the Andaman Sea who have yet to see an Indian, let alone a pale face. What might they make of *Cassiopeia* should we fly over them?

We set down to refuel at Glugor Marine Aerodrome on the shores of Penang Island, before taking lunch on the three-hour flight to Singapore. A clearly marked channel on the straits indicates our landing spot. I thank the crew, who will return to Southampton from here on an incoming flight from Sydney, and say goodbye to Bob, who is in good time to make the Imperial Airways connection to Hong Kong, a two-day adventure on board a ten-seat, four-engine de Havilland DH.86A Express, a biplane infamous for its wayward handling. Before Bob's launch burbles away, I make him a present of Evelyn Waugh's *Scoop*, a savagely funny satire on the world of foreign correspondents published last year.

A second launch is for the secret three, who finally introduce themselves and ask me to join them aboard. Their mission, it turns out, is a version of my own. They had not been sure until this morning about just what I should be told concerning Singapore and its defences. We will, they say, meet this evening for dinner to discuss the matter. It will not take too long, says the gentleman I take to be a senior general, rather ominously. Half an hour later, I'm settled in the Long Bar at Raffles, Singapore Sling in hand. I drink a silent toast to *Cassiopeia*. The flight from Southampton has been an utter delight. Has this all been rather too much like a paid holiday? Perhaps, yet my work out East is about to begin, and after all – I think as I order a second cocktail – tomorrow is another day.

*

G-ADUX *Cassiopeia* first flew in service in February 1937. On 29th December 1941, the aircraft crashed on take-off from Sabang, Indonesia, after striking debris. She had been carrying a cargo of ammunition bound for Singapore. Four passengers drowned. Of the 42 C class flying boats built, fifteen crashed, three were lost to fire, three were destroyed at their moorings, two were shot down by Japanese fighters and one was lost without trace. Having spent half their brief lives at war, the survivors were out of service by the end of 1947 and were broken up either immediately or soon afterwards. The era of the flying boat was largely over. No C class was preserved.

Imperial Airways was incorporated into the new British Overseas Airways Corporation (BOAC) in April 1940. Captain 'Jackie' Harrington became BOAC's deputy director (operations) and Grand Master of the Guild of Air Pilots and Navigators. London's Science Museum turned down the airline's offer of G-AFKZ *Cathay*. Aquila Airways operated Short Sunderlands and Short Solents from Southampton to Madeira and the Canary Islands from 1948 until 30th September 1958, when its last flight to Madeira marked the end of British commercial flying boat services. The world's last scheduled flying boat service was Ansett's 2½-hour flight from Sydney Rose Bay to Lord Howe Island. The 42-seat Short Sandringham *Beachcomber* flew this route until 1974.

Imperial Airways' Southampton to Sydney service had been disrupted by Italy's entry into the Second World War on 10th June 1940. It was no longer possible to follow the Mediterranean. Singapore fell to the Japanese in a shockingly short time, on 15th February 1942. In August 1940, the aerial defence of Singapore had amounted to 84 first-line aircraft. Joint Far East commands said they needed 336. However brave the pilots of the RAF and the Royal Australian and Royal New Zealand air forces, a few outmoded Brewster Buffalo and dogged Hawker Hurricane fighters were no match for, among other Japanese fighters, the superb Mitsubishi Zero. When 51 Hurricanes arrived at the last moment, 17 were destroyed in their first week with 13 under repair. Arguments still rage over whether or not Jiro Horikoshi's supremely nimble fighter was based in any way on drawings of the Gloster F.5/34. Lord Sempill continued to pass secrets to the Japanese during the Second World War, but was never prosecuted.

Since 1939, countries overflown and visited by *Cassiopeia* on this journey have changed names as new states have emerged. Siam is Thailand, Burma is Myanmar, and Bangladesh – formerly East Pakistan and East Bengal before that – was recognized as an independent country in 1971. Since 1947, Karachi has been a part of Pakistan. In 1948, Lake Tiberias moved to the new state of Israel.

Of the hotels en route, Raffles has been much renovated; while in Bangkok, although a wing of the old hotel survives, the Oriental is very different from how it was in 1939. It was used as a Japanese officers' club during the Second World War. Calcutta's Great Eastern is largely unrecognizable today, and property developers in the city now known officially as Kolkata continue to win permission to replace handsome historic buildings responsive to the local climate with air-conditioned global-style horrors. The original Carlton Hotel in Karachi has long been demolished. The Iraqi State Railways guesthouse served as a headquarters for British troops in the 2003 Bush/Blair invasion of a country that is currently unsafe to visit. The Hotel Grande Bretagne overlooking the tourist-encrusted Parthenon remains impressive, if perhaps a little too shiny today. In 1940–41, it housed the Greek General Headquarters. Then the Germans took over, followed by the British military in late 1944. The South Western Hotel in Southampton has been redeveloped as flats.

Southampton serves cruise liners today. Airliners and airbuses land on wheels at Heathrow, Gatwick and elsewhere. Seven months before the C class Empire flying boats took to the air, the Douglas DC-3 made its aerial debut. The precursor of pretty much every airliner and airbus since, the DC-3 spelled the end of flying boats even as they climbed to their zenith. Today, all traces of the Short Brothers' Seaplane Works at Rochester appear to have vanished.

EIGHT

New York to Chicago:
20th Century Limited

3rd–4th April 1940

A green and cream Checker cab drops me off at Grand Central on 42nd Street. It's been quite a day, what with the long Pan Am flight from Southampton to the brand new Marine Air Terminal at LaGuardia, two intense meetings straight after that in Manhattan concerning potential Anglo-American cooperation in military aircraft procurement, then a quick wash and off to catch the overnight train to Chicago.

Grand Central is as busy, as exciting and as grand as ever, inundated with a rush-hour surge of hats, coats, newspapers, bags, bright lipstick and cigarettes, to homeward-bound tracks for Long Island and Westchester County. There is no station like this in London. It's not just the sheer scale and busyness of the Beaux Arts building, but its opulence that impresses. I look up to the 125-foot vault of the main concourse – adorned with the constellations – and, slightly enviously, downstairs to the Oyster Bar, with its promise of a very dry martini and trademark caviar sandwich. This ocean liner of a station dates from before the First War, when it was rebuilt to outdo rival Penn Station between Seventh and Eighth avenues, a railway-era evocation of the Baths of Caracalla with hurried commuters standing in for leisurely bathers.

We – Britain, I mean – have been at war with Germany for the past seven months. Grand Central, Penn and Manhattan seem more than an ocean away. People at home are talking of a 'Phoney War', as not much seems to be happening that directly affects us, aside from ration books. Meat was added to the list last month. Perhaps caviar will be next. Göring's Luftwaffe, however, has had a crack at the fleet at Scapa Flow, while a month ago a Heinkel bombed the *Domola* cargo liner ferrying Indian seaman repatriated from Germany to England via Antwerp. Of the 108 killed, 81 were Indian. The seas are becoming unsafe. I feel lucky to have crossed the Atlantic in the comfort of *Atlantic Clipper*, one of the giant new Boeing flying boats.

Looking for my platform, I bump into a journalist friend from CBS who says, 'I won't keep you if you're boarding the *20th Century*, but here's a funny story...'

Editors in the CBS newsroom were sent into a spin two days ago, apparently, when the BBC broadcast a speech by Herr Hitler. When the German protectorate embraces the United States, the Führer said, the Statue of Liberty will be removed and the White House will be renamed the Brown House in honour of Hitler's 'Brownshirts'.

'What they didn't know,' says my friend, laughing before his punchline, 'is that it was April Fool's Day! Luckily I was out on assignment, so I don't have to wear a red face. Turns out it was some Limey comedian impersonating Adolf. Does Martin Miller ring a bell?'

Martin Miller. Yes he does. I've seen the Czech-Austrian émigré impersonating Hitler at his Lantern cabaret theatre on Westbourne Terrace. Miller is a Jewish refugee. Got out of Vienna a year ago. He's very funny. Vienna's loss is London's gain.

My train, the *20th Century Limited*, is announced. Track 34. And, already, the platform gates are flanked by a phalanx of press photographers armed with battery of Speed Graphics. The New York Central Railroad's premiere train is patronized by moguls and stars. Whoever famous is boarding the train this evening is invisible in the staccato light of popping flashguns. A redcap takes my suitcase; a conductor checks my ticket. Platforms at Grand Central are underground and, after the architectural theatre of the concourse, almost surprisingly grim. There is, though, no functional need here for the cathedral-like train sheds of other great railway stations, as steam locomotives are banned from Manhattan. In January 1902, fifteen commuters died when a New York Central express from White Plains rammed into the back of a New York, New Haven and Hartford commuter train stopped in Park Avenue Tunnel. Lingering smoke obscured the NYC driver's view of several successive signals. It was the city's worst railway accident. From the outset, the new Grand Central was designed for electric trains.

And yet my catacomb-like platform is made glamorous by its procession of well-dressed passengers, by the red carpet we parade along – emblazoned with the legend '20th Century Limited' in unswervingly modern lettering – and by alluring lighting glowing from the windows of the sleekest of trains. The carriage at the platform end is an observation car. The New York Central has no doubt that this two-tone grey and blue and aluminium-striped Pullman is the world's finest train. All of a piece, it looks like the future and is one up, says the NYC, on the *Broadway Limited*, the rival Pennsylvania Railroad's luxury overnight express styled by Raymond Loewy, which has the more demanding of the two routes to Chicago, over and around hills rather than skirting lakes and rivers along what adverts call the 'Water Level Route'.

When he has placed my case in my 'roomette' aboard *City of Detroit* – each of the cars is named – I tip my redcap, step back onto the platform and walk past two more sleepers, a lounge car and a travelling post office to look at our locomotive. She is not one of the photogenic New York Central J-3a Hudsons engineered by Paul Kiefer and styled by Henry Dreyfuss that feature on posters for 'The World's Greatest Train'. Instead we have the boxy and slightly ungainly 277, a 3,040-hp, 75-mph T-3a electric loco built by Alco-General Electric in 1926. Picking up power from a third rail, like a Southern train from Victoria or Waterloo, she will tow the 13-car *20th Century Limited* through the low-roofed Park Avenue Tunnel and on across the Harlem River to Harmon, on the east bank of the Hudson, where we'll meet our eye-catching streamlined steam loco.

Walking slowly back beside this svelte train, as long perhaps as the Empire State Building is tall, the conductor's call 'All aboard!' echoes along the platform. It's one minute to five. I step aboard *Century Inn*, where my American colleague is waiting for me to join him for a cocktail. For all the charms of our British streamliners, this train is clearly in a different league. The club lounge is reached through a low-lit semi-circular vestibule, its walls inset with illuminated flush-faced glass cases displaying models of two famous American railroad locomotives. On my left is NYC 4-4-0 999, designed by William Buchanan and built in 1893 to run the *Empire State Express* to and from New York and Chicago at 100 mph. This was the year of the Chicago World's Fair, and the NYC wanted to show visitors to the show that its trains were faster than those of its rival, the Pennsylvania. On 10th May 1893, 999 was reported as having reached 112½ mph between Batavia and Buffalo. In popular imagination the legend has stuck, even though Mr J. P. Pearson, an experienced train-timer, was on board. He noted a maximum of 81 mph. 999 is at work still on light duties, but she was rebuilt some while ago with 5-foot, 10-inch driving wheels in place of the high stepping 7-foot, 2-inch drivers she sported in the Nineties, so she is unlikely now to reach 80 let alone that fabled 112½.

In the right-hand case is the DeWitt 0-4-0 locomotive of 1831, and the train she ran in 1831 from Albany to Schenectady – 16 miles in 38 minutes – along the Mohawk and Hudson, a railroad absorbed by the NYC in 1853. She was designed by John B. Jervis and built, I believe, by David Matthew at the West Point Foundry. Scrapped less than two years later, for the '93 Chicago exhibition the NYC built a replica of engine and train that is owned by Henry Ford today.

'Looked like you were lost in a dream for a moment.' I was, but I tell William that it's been a long day. William, who is very much on Britain's side – not a sentiment shared by many of his colleagues in Washington – says I need a drink and steers me through a maze of seats to the corner of a leather banquette. He orders a Manhattan, and an Old Fashioned for me, while I take in the ambience of this ultra-modern carriage, its rust- and grey-coloured furniture, cork-lined walls, Venetian blinds, copper trim and, most strikingly, its sculpted ceiling and concealed cinematic lighting. Windows are double-glazed, the train air-conditioned and its ride as smooth as a skate on ice, the clickety-clack of rail joints a soft distant drumbeat somewhere underfloor.

'Hey, you're in for a surprise,' says William as our drinks are placed on coasters on a circular glass table. 'Well, two surprises in fact. Number one, London wants you to go on to Minneapolis from Chicago to stand in for the fella who was meant to be discussing transatlantic grain supplies. And, number two, we're going to have dinner with Paul Kiefer and Henry Dreyfuss. I told them about your interest in railroads. We'll join them in the dining car at Albany. Now, tell me the latest on Churchill. Do you think he'll be prime minister any time soon?'

As we talk, my colleague is happy to answer incidental questions about our route. We cross the Harlem River and curve north-west to meet the east bank of the Hudson. The NYC's main line is mostly four-track – meaning we are unlikely to be held up by freight trains – all the way to Chicago, 960 miles, a distance we'll cover in 16 hours at an average speed of a mile a minute.

To the west, we look out over the green stretch of the Palisades as the Hudson widens and freighters make their way downstream to Manhattan. We pass Sleepy Hollow to the east, although it's too early in the day to glimpse a headless coachman, and roll right through the grounds of Sing Sing, the penitentiary dating from the 1820s, 30 miles north of Grand Central. William is telling me a funny story of how earlier this year he promised his girlfriend, a postgraduate in American literature at the University of Chicago, they'd see *The Grapes of Wrath*, John Ford's interpretation of the Steinbeck novel, at a movie theatre while in New York, but he had chosen *Pinocchio*, the new Disney feature instead. 'I can't lie about it. If I did, my nose would give me away!' The train brakes smoothly across a bridge over a bay and makes its first stop, at Harmon, 33 miles in 46 minutes.

We get out to see 277 uncouple and thrum into a siding. And then watch the most impressive locomotive I have seen to date – 5451, a superbly streamlined 4,700-hp J-3a Hudson – backing quietly towards the *20th Century Limited*. The 12-wheeled tender has been styled and painted to blend seamlessly with the look and form of the train, its store of coal hidden from passengers' eyes. The grey locomotive herself is a work of art. Unlike some recent streamlined locos, her many wheels are all on show. But what wheels! The 79-inch drivers are painted aluminium Scullin discs, ultra-modern. William says they light up at night.

Ahead of the driving wheels are vast cylinders with polished aluminium faces. The loco's headlamp extends from a bullet nose intersected by an arc or comb of aluminium that, side on, has the look – as William says – of a Trojan helmet. There is no visible chimney or dome, let alone safety valves, sanding boxes and whistle. These are all concealed in a casing – ventilated at the front – stretching from nose to cab. 5451 is evidently a perfect marriage of function and style, a machine that serves as a gift to the NYC's advertising department and yet one that is easily serviced by crew and depot staff. We wave to the engineer and walk back along the entire length of the train. William wants me to visit *Manhattan Island*, the observation car.

On board, we pass the 'de luxe suite' which, says William – who has ridden the *20th Century Limited* as much as anyone over the past year – features a drawing room, bedroom, bathroom (as in the English use of the word) and even a wireless, although none of this is visible as the blinds are down. We pass through into the busy lounge, with its blue leather sofas set amidst gunmetal columns, grey leather walls, concealed lighting, gently swirling cigarette smoke, Venetian blinds and piped Glenn Miller Orchestra. A curved floor-to-ceiling screen at the far end of the lounge features a photograph of the Manhattan skyline and what I take to be a clock but proves to be a speedometer. It registers 20 mph as the train eases over points and crossings out from Harmon.

Behind the screen, we are invited to sit on a curved grey sofa at the very end of the car held for us by two obliging NYC managers. Before the setting sun gets too low and bright, we watch the track disappearing in a serpentine unravelling of steel as the train swings around fast bends, through tunnels, and across bays over bridges shadowing the Hudson River. Now we're moving, probably at the line limit, 85 mph, a speed we'll maintain, I'm told, wherever possible all the way to Chicago. Track pans, or what we call water troughs, are sited every 40 miles along the line to assuage our locomotive's thirst on the hoof. There is nothing to hinder our smooth and rapid progress.

The scenery is mesmerizing, the places we swing past memorable. Bear Mountain. West Point. 'The Springwood estate is just over there,' says William, pointing inland to sun-drenched hills. 'FDR's family home. The president was born there. Spends a lot of time up here still.' A steward asks if he can adjust the Venetian blinds. As he does, we cross the Hudson and slow for Albany, coming to a stop shortly before 7.30 p.m. in the handsome Beaux Arts–style Union Station.

We make our way to the dining car. Americans tend to dine early, so it's second sitting as we enter a further domain of discreet modern styling. Mirrors between windows punctuate grey leather walls. The rust leather of dining chairs offsets grey leather banquettes. The carpet is rust-coloured, too. Some diners sit facing into the car; others in groups of four around tables. I can't help noticing Paulette Goddard, who I recognize from *The Cat and the Canary*, the comedy horror film she starred in last year with Bob Hope. At the end of the car we join Mr Dreyfuss and Mr Kiefer around a table laid with exquisite modern plates, glasses, cutlery and napkins. The ashtrays, matchboxes and even the wrapping around sugar cubes have been designed to be in keeping with the seamless style of the train. There are fresh cut flowers in modern vases and displays of dry flowers in curved glass cases in the bulkhead.

The two serious men in well-cut suits – Mr Dreyfuss in his mid-thirties in tweed with a colourful tie, and Mr Kiefer in his early fifties in sober charcoal wool – are gallant hosts. It's agreed we should order food before conversation. The fixed price for dinner, I note, is $1.75 – unless anyone is prepared to splash out on the 'Lobster Newburg, 20th Century', which is an extra 50 cents. As meat is rationed at home, I choose roast prime ribs of beef au jus, with new Brussels sprouts polonaise and Lyonnaise potatoes, as well as a fresh shrimp cocktail Lorenzo to start, a selection of Roquefort, Camembert and Liederkranz cheeses to follow and 'Imported Claret' to wash down this feast.

We drink toasts to Great Britain, the United States and the *20th Century Limited* as the train eases through Schenectady – where 5451 was built, less than two years ago – and accelerates alongside the Mohawk River. I tell Mr Dreyfuss that I very much like the design of the train and wonder what style best describes it. 'I don't think of it as a particular style,' he says. 'In a word, I describe my work as "cleanlining".' He shows me photographs of his recent designs: the Hoover Model 150 vacuum cleaner, Westclox Big Ben alarm clock, Bell 302 telephone and the John Deere Model A tractor. I understand his point and choice of word. There is nothing essentially Art Deco nor even Bauhaus about his designs. How can one describe them?

Mr Dreyfuss tucks the photographs back into a folder as our starters are served. 'I wrote this down for our New York studio,' he says, reading from his pocket diary. 'We bear in mind that the object we are working on is going to be ridden in, sat upon, looked at, talked into, activated, operated, or in some other way used by people... When the point of contact between the product and the people becomes a point of friction, then the industrial designer has failed. On the other hand, if people are made safer, more comfortable, more eager to purchase, more efficient – or just plain happier – by contact with the product, then the designer has succeeded.'

I ask if our train really needs to be streamlined. It looks good and Mr Dreyfuss's styling is impeccable, but if our maximum speed is 85 mph, does streamlining matter?

Mr Kiefer laughs. 'Does it have to be? Not for engineering reasons, no, but railroads have been facing increasing competition from automobiles and airlines. Streamlined trains are glamorous, and streamlining has given the steam locomotive a fresh lease of life. The streamlining that really matters is inside the locomotive, getting steam to flow as efficiently as possible.

'What really got the railroads keen on streamlining was the *Flying Hamburger*. Over here, the Chicago, Burlington and Quincy responded with the *Pioneer Zephyr*, a stainless-steel three-car diesel that made its trial run in May '34, Denver to Chicago, 1,015 miles in 13 hours, an average of 77½ mph. That's going some.

'That led on to the *Twin Zephyrs* between Chicago and the Twin Cities, and a race to streamline express trains both steam and diesel. But a J-3a Hudson like ours today doesn't need to be streamlined to maintain our schedule. Of course, it looks good. On test we've had a J-3a running at a steady 100 mph on level track with a 700-ton train. With a booster engine in the rear truck it accelerates well from stops, too.'

It's dark now as the *20th Century Limited* gallops on towards our next stop, Syracuse, where we're due just after 10. Mr Dreyfuss tells me about an exciting new work by Charles Sheeler, the 'Precisionist' painter and photographer. 'It's called *Rolling Power*, an oil painting that shows the drivers, side rods, pistons, cranks and levers of a J-3a in photographic detail.

It's one of six paintings on the theme of power that *Fortune* magazine is publishing this year.'

The Dreyfuss-styled locomotives really are works of art. I ask Mr Kiefer about future NYC steam locomotives. Is the diesel train on the way? Not yet, he tells me, or at least not on the NYC. He believes the railroad will go on to develop more powerful and more efficient steam locos into the foreseeable future. Meanwhile, the J-3a Hudson is a perfect ambassador for steam.

Our train, however, changes its locomotives and crews twice along the long road to Chicago, so 5451 will have been replaced by the time tables are cleared and the dining car is transformed into the 'Club Century', a late-night joint with soft red lighting, drinks, food on demand and swing music.

Mr Kiefer and Mr Dreyfuss need to meet with other people. William decides to stay up late. Paulette Goddard and Rosalind Russell – one of her co-stars in last year's hit *The Women*, directed by George Cukor – have just arrived with an entourage. I am truly beat, though, and while I'd much enjoy a sprinkling of Hollywood stardust over cocktails, I call it a day and head to my sleeping car.

My compact and immaculate cabin offers privacy, a fully made fold-down bed, a fold-down washbasin, discreet lighting, and a curtain to draw across the door to the corridor, so that it feels like a snug hotel bedroom. In Britain we are used to sleeping in cabins on night trains, yet on this side of the Pond, the idea is new. In fact, the *20th Century Limited* sells itself on the fact that it's the first 'all room' sleeper on US railroads. For most overnight travellers, an American sleeping berth means a bed strung up in an open saloon, hidden from fellow passengers behind curtains.

My plan to read briefing documents before Chicago meetings dissolves into dreams. Somewhere in those dreams I hear the chime whistle of a speeding Hudson, the muted thrum of fast-receding rails, the distorted clang of the engine's bell. When we stop in the early morning somewhere outside Cleveland, I raise the window blind to look out over a yard where mighty steam locomotives, including our own, are being serviced.

I am up for breakfast, taken in the dining car, where I join a slightly bleary-eyed William for juice, coffee, ham and eggs over copies of the *New York Herald Tribune*. 'What time did you go to bed?' I ask him.

'Four, I think.'

Shortly before we pull into Englewood, a suburb on the south side of Chicago, at 7.45 a.m., William wakes up to the world. There is something he has to show me. He leads me to the observation car, quiet at this hour.

The Pennsylvania's *Broadway Limited* has pulled in next to us. And we leave for Chicago together. For the next 10 minutes, the two trains race one another, our locomotives flat out, before we fork away on our different tracks to Chicago Union and Chicago LaSalle Street stations. For a glorious couple of minutes, we draw alongside the *Broadway Limited*'s locomotive. She's one of the railroad's 425 K4 Pacifics, engines it has used to power most of its expresses since 1914. The Brunswick green engine is a muscular, functional machine with little of the svelte grace of our polished grey J-3a, and yet how these punchy engines can run. She begins to overhaul us just before turning away along the Pennsy's line into the Windy City. This is an exciting end to our 16-hour trip.

We pull into LaSalle Street in Chicago's financial district on time at 8 a.m., the station's skeletal platforms – it lost its glass roof some years ago – overlooked by the Chicago Board of Trade Building, a 600-foot Art Deco skyscraper designed by Holabird & Root. I decline a carnation buttonhole and, with a 'thank you' to the crew of 5453, I walk into the cavernous lobbies of the Beaux Arts station and out with William into a street clamorous with honking cabs and the rattle and squeal of 'L' trains – 'elevated', that is – cutting across the hemmed-in facade of the station. The refined hush and aesthetic of the *20th Century Limited* is trounced by the morning rush-hour din of downtown Chicago.

*

The era of the streamlined steam-hauled *20th Century Limited* was short-lived. The demands of heavy wartime traffic saw L-4 class 4-8-2 Mohawks in charge of the train from 1943, and by March 1945 pairs of new General Motors EMD E7 2,000-hp diesel-electrics. The J-3a Hudsons lost their streamlined casing in 1946–7, and the last was taken out of service in April 1956. Although none was preserved, the Hudson Steam Locomotive Revival Project is planning to build a fully operable replica. The 1938 cars were sold on to a number of railroads, including the Canadian National and Ferrocarriles Nacionales de México, and some were still at work as late as 1968.

Paul Kiefer retired in 1953. His last steam design was the herculean 6,500-hp Niagara class 4-8-4, which substituted on occasion for the diesels from 1945. But the 4-8-4s, despite their prowess and easy progress with the 15½-hour schedule from 1947, led short lives. A single Niagara would run all the way from Harmon to Chicago, turn around and run the distance back again. Equipped in 1948 with a new set of Dreyfuss-designed cars, the overnight express lost out, year by year, to airlines and automobiles lumbering at speed along the new Interstate Highway System. In the 1950s and '60s it was only on days of deep snow, when planes were cancelled and driving conditions hazardous, that the *20th Century Limited* was ever truly busy again. It last ran on the squally night of 2nd–3rd December 1967.

Today, through trains between New York and Chicago are few and far between. Amtrak's *Lake Shore Limited* sleeper leaves the Stygian depths of the grim 1960s Penn Station at 3.40 p.m., arriving at Union Station, Chicago, at 9.50 a.m., more than three hours slower than eighty years ago and with none of Henry Dreyfuss's impeccable style. Dreyfuss was one of the twentieth century's great industrial designers. In 1972, he committed suicide in a pact with his terminally ill wife, Doris Marks Dreyfuss.

Renovated in recent years, Grand Central remains a deeply impressive building and a place to meet, eat and catch trains. Chicago's LaSalle Street station was demolished in 1981. It was replaced by an undistinguished commuter-line station and a new building for the Chicago Stock Exchange. In terms of design, style and service, no train has yet bettered the *20th Century Limited* as it was in 1940.

NINE

Chicago to Minneapolis:
Afternoon Hiawatha

10th April 1940

Swift of foot was Hiawatha;
He could shoot an arrow from him,
And run forward with such fleetness,
That the arrow fell behind him!

S natches of Longfellow's *The Song of Hiawatha* flit through my mind while I walk to Chicago Union station after a morning spent in productive meetings with American colleagues keen to support the British war effort. News of Winston Churchill's appointment as chairman of the Chamberlain government's Military Coordinating Committee has been well received by the small – though key – pro-British lobby in Washington.

Tomorrow I have meetings in Minneapolis concerning grain and other food supplies to Britain. This is not my normal beat; I'm covering for colleagues. But I'm happy to go.

The quickest way to Minneapolis is by train. There are three rival routes between Chicago and the Twin Cities – that is,

Minneapolis and St Paul, the pair divided, more or less I think, by the Mississippi. A 'gentleman's agreement' between the three railroads concerned means that, since 1935, each of their fastest trains takes an equal six and a half hours for the 400 miles from Chicago. But what different trains they are. The Chicago and North Western's *400* is, I'm told, a comfortable old-school train pulled by E-2a Pacifics – modified but dating from 1923 – that, although innocent of streamlining, have been timed at speeds of up to 108 mph. The Chicago, Burlington and Quincy's *Twin Cities Zephyr*, a streamlined stainless-steel diesel with a power car at each end, has recorded 112½ mph.

The train I'll take today, the *Afternoon Hiawatha*, is the most exciting of the three. Streamlined and steam-powered, because of the nature of its route, the number of stops it makes, the slow entries and exits from towns en route, and numerous speed restrictions, it must gallop for many miles at 100 mph and more if it is to run on time. Its locomotives, the F7 4-6-4s, new in '38, are said to have been timed at 120 and even 125 mph in regular service. No other steam locomotives run this fast, day in day out, with such heavy loads and over such long distances.

The prospect of this fast steam running is exciting. Union Station is something of a thrill, too. The size, I'm told, of nine and a half city-blocks, with tracks terminating here from both north and south, it looms on the west side of the Chicago River just outside the Loop, a concatenation of giant Corinthian columns, Indiana limestone and marble. The complex includes the Chicago Daily News Building and the city's gigantic Main Post Office – two Art Deco designs of recent years. A grandiloquent marble staircase leads up to the station's Great Hall. A vast Beaux Arts cavern, its 110-foot-high vault is lit from one end to another by an enormous skylight. Primed on the architecture, I look up to find Henry Hering's allegorical sculptures of *Day* carrying a rooster and *Night* holding an owl, the two of them symbolizing the station's around-the-clock activity.

Since its rebuilding after the Great Fire of 1871, Chicago has invested on a Roman scale in impressive and innovative architecture. Union Station was designed, before the First War, by Daniel Burnham, a larger-than-life character famous for his aphorism 'Make no little plans; they have no magic to stir men's blood'. Chicago architects Graham, Anderson, Probst & White completed this stirring station in 1925 after Burnham's death, and at immense cost.

This is a quiet time of day, relatively speaking, for Union Station, so I stroll in appropriately relaxed fashion to find my train, the 1 p.m. *Afternoon Hiawatha*. It is hard to miss. The tail of the nine-coach, orange, red and silver-grey express is a dramatic observation car styled as if for Flash Gordon rather than Midwestern businessmen. Beyond handsome saloon cars styled to suggest speed, a dining car, and a car with porthole windows is our hugely impressive streamlined F7 Hudson 100. Locomotive and tender appear to flow seamlessly into the cars. Like the *20th Century Limited*, my *Hiawatha* is all of a piece.

William, my American colleague, catches up with me on the platform. 'Didn't think you could get rid of me in Chicago, did you?' he jokes. 'I've been pressed into service to give you every assistance in Minneapolis.'

We step aboard, finding comfortable swivel armchairs upholstered in a subdued Art Deco pattern of rose and green velour. The walls of the car are lined in American walnut and bleached maple. Gunmetal fixtures and fittings. Subtle, indirect lighting.

While not as sophisticated stylistically as the *20th Century Limited*, this will be a delightful place to spend the next few hours. Once we've placed our bags and overcoats on the overhead rack, William escorts me to the 'Tip Top Tap' bar. It's in the car with the porthole windows. Our martinis are poured as the Hudson gives a blast on her chime whistle and draws our high-speed train from the platform, leaving a trail of white steam in the cold afternoon air.

The Hudson accelerates rapidly as we scythe a colourful path through Chicago's northern suburbs, stretching along the west banks of Lake Chicago. 'Our first stop's Milwaukee,' says William. 'Eighty-five miles, scheduled for seventy-five minutes. We could do it in an hour flat apparently, but we mustn't get ahead of the North Western or the Quincy. By the way, the F7 isn't a Hudson. I'm reliably informed that Charles Bilty, the Milwaukee's chief mechanical engineer, calls his 4-6-4s "Baltics", as you do in Europe. I guess he thinks of Hudsons as NYC engines and he's doing something different.'

'How do you know this?' I ask William, impressed by his knowledge of Milwaukee Road terminology.

'I met Otto Kuhler, a very persuasive fellow – gift of the gab – for a possible federal government advertising commission. He's an adman and industrial artist. German-American. Styled this and the earlier *Hiawathas*. As far as I could make out, there's not much he doesn't know about the Milwaukee. Oh, and I got you this, a brochure on the *Hiawatha* courtesy of Frederic Tellander.

Works for the Milwaukee's ad agency, Roche, Williams and Cunningham. Came up with the word "Speedliners" for the *Hiawathas*, designed the posters, and assisted Mr Kuhler with the colours of the locomotives.'

Crossing the Illinois–Wisconsin state border at Wadsworth, we're up to 100 mph and more. Sturtevant flashes by at closer to 110 mph. 'Racine's just a few miles to the east, by the lakeshore,' says William, considering a second martini. 'Now you really need to go there sometime. Frank Lloyd Wright has built this humdinger of a new headquarters for Johnson Wax. Saw it last year shortly after it opened. The office is a big open-plan design with these lily-pad columns – that's what Mr Wright calls them – holding up the roof. Like something out of *Astounding Science Fiction*. Would make a swell train depot!'

I make a mental note to visit when the war's over, whenever that will be. I pump William for a little more Milwaukee gen. 'So Kuhler came to the States from Germany in '23, set up a design studio in Manhattan, caught the eye of the American Locomotive Company at Schenectady and got into railroad styling. Apparently, our loco will have a plate somewhere on her side saying "Speedlined by Kuhler". Now that's what I call on the beam.'

'On the beam?'

'I mean cool,' says William. 'Kuhler certainly got the attention of the Milwaukee folk. The principal characters there in terms of the look of the trains are Bilty and Karl Nystrom, a Swedish-American in charge of car design. They worked together on the '35 *Hiawatha*, which was six or seven cars with a Bilty A class Atlantic in charge. The A class is still about, but not on the *Hiawathas*. They got these longer streamlined trains in '38. The Atlantics were as fast as the new Baltics, but not powerful enough to cope with growing demand. The train's been on a roll, which is why there are two trains in each direction today. I think I'm beginning to run out of facts. Drying up. I need that second drink.'

We slow for Milwaukee, an industrial town on Lake Michigan at the confluence of the Menomonee, Kinnickinnic and Milwaukee rivers. Bell ringing, 100 guides our train through unfenced streets and into the station, with its curious 1880s Gothic Queen Anne–style buildings by E. Townsend Mix. Crowned with a 140-foot-high clock tower, it overlooks the business district. We eat a soup and sandwich lunch in the bar car as we thunder out of town, the landscape giving way to prairies, the train dashing in the high 90s past a blur of telegraph poles, and chiming over gateless crossings and bridges over rivers. Columbus, our next stop, is a small town served by a small station with a rather grandiose pediment over its platform building.

The landscape is wholly rural now, our pace rapid. William returns to his seat for forty winks. I head on down to the observation car and, slipping out my chronograph, time the train over the 28.2 miles to Portage, a small railway town on the Wisconsin River. We cover the distance start-to-stop in 22 minutes and 29 seconds, an average of 75¼ mph. It really is impressive just how quickly 100 accelerates up to speed, and how smoothly the cars ride on their coil springs.

We reel off the 78.3 miles from Portage to Sparta, where we arrive early, at an average of just over 82 mph, running for mile after mile at between 100 and 105 mph. We charge through sparsely populated country – the Wild West to me – to scenic La Crosse, all tree-covered mountains and limestone bluffs. Here we meet the Mississippi with its double *S*s and double *P*, its steamboats and Huckleberry Finn, although we are so much further north than I expected the Mississippi to be. We accelerate again at a phenomenal rate to Winona, all lumber and milling, and on to Red Wing, our last stop before St Paul. We arrive there at 7.30 p.m. and then make slow and stately progress over the last 11 miles to Minneapolis.

William is awake and, as we twist towards Minneapolis, where I spot the Foshay Tower, a 447-foot Indiana limestone–clad Art Deco office tower modelled on the Washington Monument, he tells me how the city and the region we've been 'speedlining' through are as German as they are American. Immigration from Germany to Wisconsin and Minnesota was an intense affair from the late nineteenth century. 'I might be wrong,' says William, 'but this might go some way to explaining why the Silver Shirts have done so well here.'

'Silver Shirts?'

'A Nazi-style organization founded by William Dudley Pelley in '33. White supremacists. Anti-Semitic. Being watched closely.'

100 brings the *Afternoon Hiawatha* to a stand at Minneapolis's Milwaukee Road Depot dead on time at 8 p.m. The station is small, although its architecture – with a clock tower modelled on the Giralda, the twelfth-century bell tower of Seville Cathedral – seems curiously out of place in this city of flour mills, breweries, German Americans and cold Aprils. It feels a very long way indeed from Grand Central. And yet what a ride, by a steam express that seems charged with electricity.

William and I measure ourselves against 100's 7-foot driving wheels. I find it fascinating to know that, alone, the tender of this eye-catching locomotive carrying 22 tons of coal and 20,000 gallons of water weighs more than a complete LMS Princess Coronation class Pacific. Could one of our British streamlined Pacifics keep pace with Charles Bilty's Baltics? I don't think so. I find myself muttering, *'With his moccasins enchanted . . . At each stride a mile he measured.'*

'What's that?' asks William.

'*Hiawatha*, of course,' I answer as we button up our overcoats, don our hats and walk from the station into the bitter spring chill.

*

The racing days of the steam-powered *Hiawathas* were short-lived – diesel-electrics took over in 1951 – yet what days they had been. With as many as 16 cars in tow in wartime, the fleet and powerful F7 Hudsons could run ahead of time on the train's tight schedules. During 1943, an F7 with just such a train, weighing 780 tons, ran the 85.6 miles from Milwaukee to Chicago in 63 minutes, with 60 consecutive miles reeled off in 37 minutes at an average of 100.7 mph. On a day-to-day basis, the Milwaukee's F7s were the world's fastest steam locomotives. But, as American train timing was rarely as rigorous a discipline as it has been in Great Britain, we are unlikely to know if one of these glorious machines beat *Mallard*'s 1938 record. We do know they ran for miles on end at between 100 and 120 mph, so perhaps one of the six F7s, none preserved, may have done so.

Post-war Interstate Highways and the allure of car ownership, plus the debut of inter-city airliners, spelled the demise of long-distance high-speed trains in the United States. The *Afternoon Hiawatha* was withdrawn in 1970; the morning train the following year. The journey over the Milwaukee Road can still be made from Chicago to St Paul – Minneapolis station closed in 1971 and is now a hotel complex and event space – and on to the Pacific Coast by Amtrak's *Empire Builder*, a sleeping-car train that cannot be classed as an express. The Chicago to St Paul section of the ride occupies 7 hours and 48 minutes, a lot slower than the 1940 timetable. In design terms, the *Empire Builder* is not a patch on the *Hiawatha* as it was in steam days, yet it does offer an alternative way of crossing the continent, with bedrooms and all-American meals along the way. Its top speed is 79 mph.

Much of the landscape along the Milwaukee Road route remains defiantly rural. As for Minneapolis, wholesale and unforgivable destruction of the city's historic Gateway District in the 1950s and '60s makes it look as if the Luftwaffe managed to fly this far after the USA declared war on Germany in December 1941. St Paul survived the rapacity of this neophiliac era relatively unscathed.

Chicago Union Station remains impressive, although it hosts few long-distance express trains today. Founded in 1991, the Friends of the 261 operate a 1944 Milwaukee Road 4-8-4 together with a fleet of 1948 *Hiawatha* cars. Excursions with this powerful locomotive have kept alive something of the spirit of the Milwaukee Road in its prime.

TEN

Bristol to Paris: Bristol 405

3rd–5th October 1955

Wrapped in my overcoat, I'm eating breakfast alone on the terrace of the Avon Gorge Hotel, with its irresistible view of Brunel's suspension bridge, when a telegram arrives. *FERRY NEW BRISTOL FILTON HÔTEL LE BRISTOL FOR 6TH OCT? REWARD. TOM +*

Tom is an old friend on secondment to Paris, who knows I've been in meetings with the Bristol Aeroplane Company at Filton, twenty minutes from the hotel by taxi, and plan to be in Paris within the next few days to visit Dassault Aviation at Saint-Cloud. I'm looking forward very much to meeting M. Dassault himself. Refusing to collaborate with the Vichy regime, he landed up in Buchenwald in '44. He was not expected to live, yet made a more or less full recovery after liberation. Born a Jew and originally named Bloch, M. Dassault's new surname was adopted from his elder brother's Resistance *nom de guerre* 'Chardasso', a play on *char d'assault* or 'tank'. Although anything less tank-like than Dassault's dart-like Mach 1.6 prototype Mystère-Delta jet fighter is hard to imagine.

My plan was not to fly to France but to take the *Bristolian* to Paddington and the *Golden Arrow* from Victoria. But Tom's telegram promises a new adventure. As Bristol's car division is next door to the aircraft factory at Filton Aerodrome, I finish breakfast and ask reception to call a cab. Half an hour later, and over a cup of tea, I'm in conversation with Mr Dennis Sevier, head of engineering at Bristol Cars, and Mr Dudley Hobbs, the company's chief designer and stylist. An aerodynamicist by training, Mr Hobbs spent several years developing wings for Bristol Aircraft before joining the car division here, in what used to be the Filton laundry.

Tom's new car, a four-door Bristol 405, is ready for immediate collection. I telegram Tom to say I'll be at the Hôtel Le Bristol in Paris for dinner on Thursday. Mr Hobbs says they can ring Silver City Airways and make a booking for a flight tomorrow from Lydd to Le Touquet. If I leave today, I could be in Paris in time for dinner, but as I don't have to be there till Thursday, I could stop overnight in Kent or the Pas-de-Calais. The latter sounds the better option. I know the Hôtel Windsor at Le Touquet, and a small restaurant nearby serving the kind of delicious meal all but impossible to get in England beyond Soho, Mayfair and the grander London hotels.

My meeting at the aircraft factory is at 11 a.m., so, very kindly, Mr Hobbs takes me on a brief tour of the factory before introducing me to Tom's distinctive gunmetal 405. The model was first shown at the Earls Court Motor Show last October. Its wind tunnel–shaped body begins with an aero engine–like air intake and ends with a rounded and well-glazed rump, adorned with a pair of residual fins. It's an attractive yet slightly curious design, with its front doors notably smaller than the rear doors, but evidently all well screwed together – as you'd expect from a car designed and built by aero engineers.

'The spec's a little special,' says Mr Hobbs. 'It's fitted with a tuned version of our triple-carb two-litre six, giving 125 brake horsepower – or twenty horsepower more than standard. We've also fitted it with front disc brakes that'll be standard from next year. We've run it in, but remember to let the oil warm up for the first twenty miles or so. Nothing above two thousand rpm. But that's sixty-five miles an hour, so you won't be held back. She's on Michelin SDS radials, so handles nicely. We'll have her tanked up with Esso Extra. You won't need to refuel until well after Le Touquet. It's a little over two hundred miles to Lydd. Not sure how you're planning to go, but you could cut down to Stonehenge, then through the South Downs, to Goodwood and along the south coast.'

I haven't made a plan, but this sounds ideal. We look at the car a little more closely. The front wings conceal lockers that on the one side house a spare wheel and jack and, on the other, the battery, wiper motor, twin brake servos and fuse box. Under the long bonnet, the engine is set well back to ensure the car is nicely balanced. The boot is lined and fitted with bespoke leather luggage. The cabin smells deliciously of Connolly hide, while the choice of light blue leather offsets the gunmetal paintwork to a T.

There are Dunlopillo-filled bucket seats in the front, and a two-spoke Bluemel steering wheel with finger grips and an aircraft-like binnacle of seven white-on-black dials in front of the driver. These include a 140-mph speedometer with trip and total mileage recorder; a 7,000-rpm rev counter incorporating a small clock; a trio of oil temperature, oil pressure and fuel gauges; and an ammeter. On the top of the walnut dashboard is a Bakelite switch for the self-cancelling indicators; while below the dash are the heater controls and switches and buttons for the two-speed self-cancelling windscreen wipers, windscreen washer, self-cancelling overdrive, mixture control, ignition advance and retard, hand throttle, headlamps, fog lamps and the Lucas spot lamp centred in the air intake.

There's a pedal beside the clutch for one-shot chassis lubrication, and a floor button for the dimmer switch. There's also an HMV radio, with speakers in the headlining and rear parcel shelf. This really is a well-equipped car – and rightly so, given the price. I think Tom has paid close to £3,500 for the Bristol, a lot more than a new Aston-Martin DB2/4. For this money, he could have bought a pair of truly fast XK140 Jaguars. But then, how many of today's cars are built by former aircraft engineers and mechanics? And who else makes a grand touring four-door four-seat saloon?

As to how fast Bristol cars are, Mr Hobbs tells me that five years ago Bristol's sole dealer, Mr Crook, drove a new 401 from his home in Caterham via Silver City Airways and on to the Montlhéry Autodrome south of Paris, where he clocked 104.7 miles in a solid hour around the track before returning to Surrey within 12 hours of leaving home. Until his retirement from the track and a spell in hospital earlier this year after a collision with Stirling Moss at Goodwood, Tony Crook had won 370 events since 1946 – among them hill climbs, sprints and circuit races. He'd also raced in two Formula 2 Grand Prix.

Aerodynamics aside, Bristols are fast cars because their engines are among the very best. Mr Sevier, who has joined us again, explains that these are modified versions of the two-litre engines that powered the highly successful BMW 328 from 1936. That car, designed and engineered by BMW's Fritz Fiedler, was sold in England before the war as a Frazer Nash BMW. With the right to manufacture the free-revving six-cylinder engine after the war, Frazer Nash enticed Dr Fiedler to its factory in Isleworth. This led to Fiedler working from Isleworth on Bristol's first car, the 400. The chassis of this excellent machine was essentially that of the BMW 326, its body that of the 327 and its engine that of the 328. The 400 was, I suppose, the 100-mph fast-touring saloon that BMW might well have built if only the Führer had refrained from invading Poland. Dr Fiedler has since returned to Munich, where he is BMW's chief engineer. With his immense experience, who knows what excellent cars he might produce in coming years?

As I leave, Mr Sevier hands me a May copy of *The Autocar* featuring a road test, he says, of the 405. I'll read this when I get back to the hotel this evening. Returning to the airfield, I watch one of BOAC's double-deck Boeing Stratocruisers coming in to land. These big American airliners are serviced here, alongside BOAC's Lockheed Constellations. Inside the hangars, Bristol is busy building its new transatlantic Britannia turboprops. While I'm here to discuss a future Bristol supersonic airliner, this revolutionary machine won't fly for some years yet. I do worry that Boeing is busy at work on a swept-wing long-distance jet airliner, developed from the exciting Dash 80 prototype that made its maiden flight last year, and this may well corner the subsonic transatlantic market for the next decade or so. In August, the Boeing made what the Americans would call a 'special guest appearance' at the Seattle Seafair, where, I'm told, it performed two barrel-rolls over Lake Washington. That was impressive. When it appears, the Boeing's 'jetliner' is likely to be a very competitive aircraft. I don't know anyone who is taking bets against it being otherwise. Bristol, for all its wartime success with Blenheims, Beauforts and Beaufighters, will need to make a quantum leap into the future. We'll see.

As I leave Filton for Clifton, a pair of Vampire jets of the Royal Auxiliary Air Force's 501 (County of Gloucester) Squadron comes in to land. One of the squadron's pilots is Flight Lieutenant 'Hoppy' Hodgkinson, who, like the celebrated Douglas Bader, flies with tin legs, and has done so since his Tiger Moth was in collision with another trainer aircraft in 1939. 'Hoppy' tells me he is tempted to shoot down the Avon Gorge and fly under Brunel's bridge. Now, that would be fun.

Tuesday morning sees me back at Filton. Bag in the boot, I fire up the Bristol and off we go, nursing the car down towards Batheaston through thundery rain on the southern hem of the Cotswolds, before opening her up as far as the wet road allows and making good use of the 'rifle-bolt action' gearbox and the engine's willingness to rev. All-round visibility is excellent – not for nothing has the car been dubbed the 'Flying Greenhouse' – while the view straight ahead between the curves of the pronounced wings is compelling whatever the scenery.

On to Box, en route to Melksham and Stonehenge, along gloriously rural roads splashed with sunlight. We make spirited progress, overtaking the occasional tractor, farm lorry and slower car. I enjoyed reading *The Autocar* road test in bed last night. 'One starts to throw this car into corners after a very few miles of motoring. The high geared steering responds to a single quick turn of the two spoke wheel, and the 405 goes round, as uncompromisingly upright as a Calvinist pastor...' Exactly so. It brakes well, too.

On my way along lanes proffering sweeping views of rolling farmland through the interstices of trees still very much in leaf, I stop at Box station to watch a Castle class 4-6-0 pounding up the 1-in-100 grade towards the grand classical entrance of Brunel's tunnel – the best part of two miles long – on her fleeting way from Bristol to Paddington with an express train of glistening chocolate and cream coaches. The Great Western was nationalized seven years ago, yet it's hard to notice any particular change.

The stop at Box gives me a chance to open the rear quarter-lights slightly, so that, with the front quarter-lights already ajar, I can enjoy a subtle flow of air through the car and, as a bonus, hear the exhaust. Pulling away in second – first is unsynchronized and best left for hill starts – and changing up quickly, the sound of engine and exhaust morphs from a chattering ruffle to a growl, before smoothing out into a deep, honeyed purr. On all-but-empty Wiltshire roads, I have the Bristol up to 80 mph in overdrive and find myself humming 'The Dam Busters March'. That tune, by Eric Coates – from the film starring Michael Redgrave and Richard Todd, which I saw in town a few months ago – is annoying only in that it's hard to switch off from if I'm at the wheel of a car racing towards a narrow horizon or, of course, flying low over water. Luckily no one can hear me.

The countryside, sunlit between squally rain, seems especially beautiful. Unmitigated England. Driving alone along blissfully quiet roads, there is time to think. Not so if I had chosen to take the obvious A-roads east from Bristol; increasingly, these lead through towns clogged with smoky nose-to-tail traffic, marred as each year passes by dismal new development as if the English have abandoned the art and science of elegant architecture, crafted building and intelligent planning. These old roads may seem slow, yet they are free of traffic – although with the number of cars rising quickly now that the economy seems to be on its feet after the long years of austerity, rationing, slow trains and low-octane fuel, who knows what things will be like in 1975, let alone 2000.

The June issue of the *Architectural Review*, labelled 'Outrage', was an excoriating vision of the 'subtopian' England that is taking shape, according to the young writer Ian Nairn, anywhere in front of our eyes from Southampton to Carlisle. He drove between these two towns in a Morris Minor, noting the careless destruction of landscapes – urban and rural – that we say we love yet are in danger of smothering with dismal new development. Nairn, I discovered from flying colleagues, is a former RAF pilot who must have watched the English landscape changing from the cockpit of his Gloster Meteor before he turned to architectural journalism. His father was a draughtsman on the R101 at the Royal Airship Works under Lieutenant Colonel Richmond. I swerve to avoid a Morris 8 pulling out blindly from a farm cottage in in Shrewton. Richmond was killed along with pretty much everyone on board when, on its first overseas flight 25 years ago, R101 crashed into a field to the southwest of Beauvais. That was the end of the British airship industry.

Motoring across lonely Salisbury Plain on the undulating road above Stonehenge, I join the A-road for a sprint down to Micheldever, where I turn off for Alresford. I like this Hampshire market town, and it's a good place to stop for a late-morning char and wad. The town's wealth of graceful Georgian architecture is a delight, almost as if some enlightened eighteenth-century landowner had created Alresford from scratch. Far from it. In fact, it was three devastating fires between 1690 and 1736 that prompted rebuilding in an era where no one seemed able to design a bad building.

It's all so peaceful today, yet in the build-up to D-Day, Alresford was awash with GIs practising with tanks and landing craft shipped here by the Southern Railway's Mid-Hants line. The Hampshire landscape is bucolic onwards to Steep, the village where Edward Thomas, the First War poet, once lived, although most of us remember him for 'Adlestrop', a moving poem invoking the ancient spirit of the English countryside and inspired by his Great Western express train halting 'unwontedly' at the Cotswold station.

Down past Petersfield, I speed through the sheep-studded South Downs to Goodwood, where it would be fun to give the Bristol a blast round the famous racing circuit opened by the Duke of Richmond in '48. Before becoming the duke, when he was still known as Freddie Settrington, he ditched Christ Church just before finals for Cricklewood, where he was apprenticed to Bentley Motors. In '31 he ran his own MG Midget racing team, then served with the air force during the war when RAF Westhampnett operated from the Goodwood estate.

Driving an Aston-Martin DB3S, Peter 'Skid' Walker and Dennis Poore won this year's Goodwood Nine Hours trophy. Walker, of course, won the Le Mans 24-hour race four years ago with a C-Type Jag. This year's Le Mans was marred by the terrible accident when Pierre Levegh hit and flew over the back of an Austin-Healey that had been forced to swerve in front of him. Levegh was killed when his lightweight Mercedes-Benz 300 SLR disintegrated and burst into flames. Pieces of the car including the engine shot into the crowd, killing 83 people and injuring many more.

With this rather morbid thought in mind, I press on, picking up the A27, cantering along the hem of the South Downs and overtaking some rather smart cars among the Fords, Morrises, a Jowett Javelin and a three-wheeled Bond Minicar, all pottering along in the centre of the carriageway. I stop to visit the church of St Mary the Blessed Virgin, Sompting, sadly cut off from the village it serves today by the A27. I know this church from books I had at school on the history of English architecture, but have never been to see it. Its fame is twofold: first for its Saxon tower crested with a 'Rhenish helm', the architectural equivalent of a twelfth-century knight's helmet and unique in these islands; and, second, for its chapel built by the Knights Templar.

Onwards past Shoreham Airport, with its charming Art Deco terminal designed by the Brighton architect Stavers Tiltman. This was a particularly civilized base for Spitfire, Hurricane and other squadrons in the war. I'm tempted to stop for more tea in Rye, but push on to meet the Channel at

Camber Sands. Quiet on an October weekday, this five-mile stretch of sand and shingle is very popular indeed throughout the summer. When I last came here, before the war, a 3-foot narrow-gauge tramway ran from here to Rye. A tiny petrol locomotive, more like a lawnmower than anything normally found on rails, drew a single wooden four-wheeler carriage. But the tramway's shed housed two Caledonian-blue 2-4-0 tank locomotives, built by W. G. Bagnall, Stafford, for the line in the mid-1890s. This somewhat Heath Robinson tramway closed in September '39. It was used, though, for Operation Pluto, the 'Pipe-Line Under The Ocean' project, an ingenious scheme devised by Arthur Hartley, chief engineer with the Anglo-Iranian Oil Company, to supply petrol to Allied forces in France during and after D-Day.

Shortly before 5.30 p.m. I roll into Lydd's Ferryfield Airport, set in splendid isolation on Romney Marsh. A marshal guides me into a parking space, says good evening and takes the car keys. He points me to the terminal entrance, although I stop to watch a silver, white and blue Bristol Freighter take off thunderously, with puffs of smoke from its twin Bristol Hercules radials, turning slowly towards France as it climbs.

The smart modern terminal, with its picture windows overlooking the runways and restaurant, is quiet this evening. But when I check in and ask how busy it gets, the steward laughs. 'We've had our busiest summer yet this year, sir. One day in July we made a record 222 flights, making us busier than Gatwick.'

'That many? How many crews do you have?'

'Quite a few, although not quite so many as you might think. They make six return flights a day.' Which is going some. I think of all the procedures involved each time an aircraft takes off, and all for a 20-minute flight.

The idea of an air ferry to France has certainly proved popular. Flights are frequent, safe, reliable and fairly cheap. Silver City Airways was founded in '46 by Air Commodore 'Taffy' Powell, formerly of RAF Ferry (later Transport) Command. The Duke of Edinburgh opened the new terminal last summer. I sit and catch up on some briefing documents in the terminal's bright waiting area. The seats are of a lightweight design, in keeping with the spirit of flight. The windows are open to let in the Channel breeze. A boy stands outside behind a fence overlooking the runway, noting down the reporting numbers of the flock of Silver City Bristols.

I watch as Tom's 405 is driven into the wide-open steel jaws of Bristol Superfreighter G-AMWB *City of Salisbury*, followed by a left-hand-drive pearl-grey Mark VII Jag with Swiss plates and a brightly polished black Lanchester Fourteen Roadrider, one of the cars built in the late '30s. When the Lanchester has climbed the ramp, we are invited to walk to the aircraft. What bulbous machines these Superfreighters are. Twenty-ton mechanical pelicans designed especially for Silver City. Ours, built the year before last, is leased from the Bristol Aeroplane Company.

Inside the small matter-of-fact cabin at the rear of the fuselage, we join a quartet of foot passengers and a solitary cyclist whose Claud Butler is stowed with the cars. As soon as we're settled, the 14-cylinder Hercules engines whirr, rattle and roar into life. The crew is at work above the aircraft's nose. I note that the props are in line with the pilots' ears. The cockpit must be noisy.

Very quickly, we're airborne, the Superfreighter climbing to 1,000 feet, her cruising height for this brief flight. Through the big and all-but-square windows, I can see the track of the Romney, Hythe and Dymchurch miniature railway, a barrage of bungalows along the coast road, the lighthouse at Dungeness, trails of steam from freighters, tankers and ferries, and the choppy waters of the Channel.

With no need to lower the wheels, as the Bristol's undercarriage is fixed, we land at 'Paris-on-Sea', as Le Touquet is known. Engines off. Doors open. Ramp attached. And out come the cars. A quick passport check. At 7.30 p.m., I park the Bristol in front of the Hôtel Windsor on rue Saint-Georges, where there's a warm welcome, a glass of wine, a calm old room and a bath. I eat a quiet beefsteak dinner in the small restaurant close by that I've known for some years, before putting my feet up to read. It's pelting down. A walk along the prom in the October dark doesn't appeal.

After a *café crème*, I nose the Bristol out onto the D940 and motor south through the low-lying landscape to Abbeville, cruising at 100 mph along stretches where I can see far ahead. The morning is dry. With the 125-bhp engine, the 405's top speed is around 115 mph. The car rides confidently at the ton, although wind whistles around the A-pillars, quarter-lights and door handles. Threading through Abbeville and crossing the Somme, I sustain a brisk pace all the way to Beauvais, overtaking lorries and Simcas, Renaults and tractors, Citroën vans, bicycles, horses and carts, coaches, and a big American car I can't recognize at speed. While you see few of these in England except on roads close to US air bases, they are surprisingly popular in post-war France – as are Westerns, comic books and American pulp fiction.

Beauvais, two hours on from Le Touquet, comes as a shock. As much as eighty per cent of the city centre, I've read, was blown to pieces by the Luftwaffe during the Battle of France. It certainly looks that way. There are few surviving buildings – the cathedral aside – from much before then. I pass the mid-eighteenth-century town hall and the gatehouse of the sixteenth-century bishop's palace, and drive along a street where half-timbered medieval houses seem out of place among new buildings under construction at every turn and junction. It's time to stop and walk this battered city.

Last night, I marked a page about Beauvais in the book I was reading – *The Wounded Don't Cry* by Quentin Reynolds, a correspondent for *Collier's*, the popular American weekly that Martha Gellhorn, Ernest Hemingway and Winston Churchill wrote for in the 1930s. I've enjoyed its long-running series on space travel written by, among others, Dr Werner von Braun, the former Nazi rocket scientist whose wartime mission was to destroy our cities with his V2 'revenge weapons'. It does seem likely that a man will walk on the moon within the next 50 years.

Published in '41, Reynolds's book is a sequence of memorable impressions of the falls of France and England at the time of the Battle of Britain. I sit on the steps of the cathedral's south transept and read:

> At first it is hard to watch men die, but after a while you get quite accustomed to it. Actually they make it easier for you

because they die very quietly. The wounded don't cry. In a way it is hard to watch a city die. Beauvais was a middle-aged city still in the prime of life and it died very gallantly but not at all quietly.

Between 5th and 8th June 1940, the Luftwaffe flew wave after wave of bombers over Beauvais with the broadcast aim of destroying it completely – even the cathedral. Hitler was not a fan of Gothic design, although he was impressed with Strasbourg Cathedral for some reason. Planned to turn it into a national monument after the war. Beauvais was evacuated on 6th June as all hell let loose from the bomb bays of Heinkels and Dorniers.

Curiously, it has been hubris rather than high explosives that has done the most damage over the centuries to the truly extraordinary Cathedral of St Peter. Stepping inside this thrilling casket of light, it is easy enough, I think, to understand why the cathedral was never completed – in addition to the sheer cost of the thing and, of course, the Black Death that raged through Europe in the fourteenth century. It was, quite simply, too ambitious a building project for its own good. All that was built was the choir, part of which imploded in 1284, twelve years after its dedication, and the transepts. There is no nave. There was a central tower, and at 502 feet it was the tallest building in the world – but for just four years. Completed in 1569, it collapsed in 1573. But, the choir! Its vault is 157½ feet above the stone floor.

To support itself, the choir is surrounded on the outside by flying buttresses. I have an Eric Gill engraving depicting a monoplane circling around these very buttresses. The association with aircraft makes a kind of sense, as the medieval architects and masons were experimenting here not just with stonework per se, but with the effects of wind on their improbably tall cathedral. They used iron in the structure, while for a number of centuries the flying buttresses were connected to one another and to the walls of the choir by iron rods. I imagine the entire structure is moving slightly and needs to be held in subtle check. If only those medieval masons had been able to test the design of this daring structure in a wind tunnel.

Over a late-morning coffee and croissant, I sit outside a café to stare at this dumbfounding fragment of a cathedral. Back behind the wheel of the Bristol, I thrum down to Paris, entering the city by Saint-Denis and Clichy. Its population has grown rapidly since liberation, and it certainly shows. Streets are chock-a-block with people and traffic. I follow the open-platformed green and cream Renault TN buses and the latest Somua OP5s with folding doors, and weave slowly across thronged junctions, hugely enjoying the sight of French automobiles – a truly Gallic show of Citroën Traction Avants and 'tin snail' 2CVs, rear-engine Renault 4s, Simca Arondes that look like American cars shrunk in the wash, and the Citroën U55 Cityrama tourist coaches that appear to have been let loose from the sets of the Flash Gordon films.

Here's the rue du Faubourg Saint-Honoré. Getting out, I hand the keys of the Bristol to a doorman of the Hôtel Le Bristol. At the reception desk I ask for Tom, who, I learn, is in the bar.

'Now, about that reward,' I say to him.

While ordering champagne, Tom slips a small envelope from

a jacket pocket. Inside is a ticket for tomorrow's opening of the Salon de Paris. 'You just have to see what Citroën has on its stand.'

'Exciting?'

'Let's put it this way: if the Bristol comes from aviation, the new Citroën is from – what's the *mot juste*... Aerospace! I know you'll want to see it.'

We've both met and spoken to Citroën's chief engineer André Lefèbvre, who started out with Gabriel Voisin, the French aviation pioneer and maker of those glorious pre-war Avions Voisin cars loved by pilots, engineers, racing drivers, the most fashionable socialites and the architect Le Corbusier, who had his pre-war white Parisian villas photographed with his Voisin C7.

What chumps we are, though, with our chatter of cars and planes and trains. It's time to eat. Tom insists on Bofinger, so we walk to Champs-Élysées–Clemenceau and, stepping down into that familiar and faintly repugnant underground world smelling equally of cigarette smoke, urine and disinfectant, we board a Line 1 train to Bastille.

With its growling traction motors, slatted wooden seats and huddle of passengers in damp overcoats, the experience of riding this 1930s Sprague-Thomson Metro train is very unlike that of travelling by Bristol 405, yet what character it has. The metal clasps that send doors flying open at stations. The first-class cars with leather seats, although we brave third. Notices saying '*Prière de céder la place aux mutilés de guerre*', a request for passengers to give up their seats to wounded veterans.

At Bofinger we drink toasts to 'Bristol'. To the city, to Bristol Cars, to Bristol aircraft and to Frederick Hervey, 4th Earl of Bristol and Bishop of Derry, whose insistence on travelling in comfort and style in the eighteenth century prompted the building of luxurious hotels named Bristol. I'm very much looking forward to see if the French can do one better than we *rosbifs* tomorrow, though. Can Citroën possibly upstage Bristol? Perhaps I can drive one of the new Lefèbvre cars back to England and subject it to a Maigret-like investigation.

*

The Citroën DS was revealed in all its chic aerodynamic glory at the Paris Motor Show on 6th October 1955. Citroën took 12,000 orders for the *Déesse* (meaning 'goddess') on the first day of the exhibition. The futuristic car, with its self-levelling hydro-pneumatic suspension, steering and transmission, was like no other. It rode like a magic carpet. Made in Paris – and Slough, a rather glum Berkshire town on the Great Western Railway line from Bristol to London – the DS was manufactured for a period of over 20 years, by which time nearly 1.5 million had been sold. For Roland Barthes, the structuralist philosopher who compared the design and structure of modern cars to those of Gothic cathedrals, the DS was nevertheless a prostituted idea, a creation of the media designed to promote the petite bourgeoisie. *Bien sur.*

First-class Metro cars vanished in 1991. Bofinger survives, although often full of tourists in search of an Instagram 'experience'. Eye-wateringly expensive, Hôtel Le Bristol is more bling than Bristol fashion today. The condition of Beauvais cathedral remains a concern. The Hôtel Windsor, Le Touquet, fell into a slow decline and is now closed.

The GPO ended its telegram service in 1977. A total of 265 Bristol

405 four-door saloons were built, many of which have survived. Bristol Cars went into administration in 2011. Bristol Superfreighters went on to serve British United Air Ferries on the Lydd–Le Touquet route after Silver City Airways ceased trading in 1963. G-AMWB *City of Salisbury* was withdrawn in March 1968 and broken up the following month. Put out of business by the lack of a suitable replacement aircraft type and by the success of new Ro-Ro (Roll-on, Roll-off) cross-Channel car ferries, the last air ferry from Lydd to le Touquet flew in 1970. LyddAir operates a scheduled service in nine-seat Piper PA-31s between the two destinations.

Since 1994, many motorists have opted for the 35-minute crossing by Eurotunnel Le Shuttle trains between Folkestone and Calais. Travelling at 300 km/h (186 mph), anguilline Eurostar trains have made air travel between London and Paris largely redundant. The journey from St Pancras to Gare du Nord takes two and a half hours. A road journey from Bristol to Paris today could be driven, the Channel crossing aside, all but exclusively on motorways and *autoroutes*. Both were still in their infancy in 1955.

ELEVEN

Liverpool Street to Hammersmith: Route 11

19th April 1958

My boat train, the *Hook Continental* from Harwich Parkeston Quay, arrives two minutes early at Liverpool Street. It's Saturday morning and so, although the train is heavy – 520 tons, says the guard – our locomotive, the handsome British Railways two-cylinder Britannia Pacific 70035 *Rudyard Kipling*, has enjoyed an unchecked run into the London terminus.

I'm back to London from Bonn via the Hook of Holland, our ferry SS *Arnhem* chock-full with some 600 overnight passengers. We stream down Platform 9 – a motley crew of English, Dutch, Scottish, German, Irish, Danish, Welsh and Swedish nationals, among others – under the station's glorious though soot-fretted Gothic roof. Liverpool Street is as impressive, if confusing, as ever, its layout devised as if by a half-cut spaghetti chef. It seems somehow appropriate that it was built on the site of old Bethlehem Hospital. At busy times, it can certainly feel like Bedlam.

I skip up to the footbridge for breakfast in the café, an Edwardian gem in Neo-Jacobean style. Its menu consists of eggs, tea and toast, and it offers views of arriving and departing trains through its oriel windows. If I hadn't a late-morning meeting in Hammersmith, I'd be more than half tempted to take a train straight back up to Colchester behind another Britannia, and ride gently from there across rural Suffolk, far from the madding crowd, in a veteran varnished-teak coach, all horsehair-stuffed cushions, leather-strap window releases and sun-bleached portraits of half-forgotten East Anglian resorts between faded mirrors and below string luggage racks. I can just imagine the train swaying gently behind a former Great Eastern Railway E4 2-4-0 built in the 1890s and still – in the Jet Age and three years after the publication of British Railway's exhaustive modernization plan – going gently about its work.

My reverie is broken by an unfamiliar two-tone air horn and the alien appearance of a brand-new English Electric 2000-hp diesel-electric leading an express from Norwich towards the buffers. 'It's one of the new diesels,' says a man at a table next to mine, as he looks up from the *Daily Herald*. 'They started running just yesterday. The steamers will be gone soon enough.' He says this as if he's pleased and about to doff his cap. I settle the bill and leave.

Outside the architectural ambition of 1870s Liverpool Street, with its steam-age quatrefoil plate tracery and elaborate facades – the work of the Scottish engineer Edward Wilson, with an 1890s extension by John Wilson and his architect assistant William Neville Ashbee – I watch passengers climbing up and down the arcaded 1860s Lombardic Gothic stair of neighbouring Broad Street station, a hunched and characterful building by William Baker, chief engineer of the London and

North Western Railway. I'm not in a great hurry, so I join them and even put a penny in the venerable glass case in the station's raised concourse, to watch the wheels of a model North London Railway 4-4-0 tank engine turn round and round. I remember as a child taking a train to Kew Gardens from here, behind one of these pugnacious black locos.

Unhurried this morning and in nostalgic mood, brought on I think by the ominous sight and sound of that bland and blaring green diesel at Liverpool Street, I opt to catch the bus to Hammersmith. The number 11 starts from here and, because this is Saturday, my favourite London Transport RT double-deckers are in charge. I stop to watch them parade in and out of Liverpool Street. In their immaculate scarlet, black, cream and gold uniforms they resemble guardsmen keeping step along the Mall. And how uniform they are. The RT fleet, some 7,000 strong, is the biggest of its kind anywhere in the world.

I remember the first batch put into service just before the war, although nearly all of these singularly handsome buses were built between 1946 and 1954. London Transport's aim was to establish a fleet of standardized double-deckers. It certainly succeeded. Today, you are hard-pressed to see anything other than an RT on central, suburban and even country routes. What I like very much is the fact that, although mass-produced, the engineering, design and Rolls-Royce build quality of these 7½-ton buses is second to none. And, even better, they are part of a fully integrated design programme incorporating not just the world's finest double-deck buses, but also Underground trains, station architecture, signage, uniforms and so on, down to the very last detail. This wholly convincing corporate identity has become synonymous with London itself. And I think that whatever grumbles commuters might have day-to-day about trying to find a seat or a non-smoking car on the Tube, Londoners are rather proud of their public transport system.

We owe this highly considered and very effective network to the noble efforts of the London Passenger Transport Board, a public corporation – rather like the BBC – created in 1933. Its first vice-chairman and chief executive officer was Mr Frank Pick, a brilliant if slightly awkward man with a mission not simply – as if this were simple – to create a fully integrated and peerless city transport network, but also to shape it in a way that would civilize life in new ways for everyone from City bankers to Fulham milkmen, smart lunching ladies in Knightsbridge to chars on their knees in Stepney and Bow.

'Underneath all the commercial activities of the Board,' said Mr Pick in one of his annual reviews of the work of the LPTB, 'underneath all its engineering and operation, there is the revelation and realization of something which is in the nature of a work of art... it is, in fact, a conception of a metropolis as a centre of life, of civilization, more intense, more eager, more vitalizing than has ever so far been obtained.' In an appreciation of Mr Pick in a 1942 issue of the *Architectural Review*, following his sudden and early death, the architectural historian Dr Nikolaus Pevsner described the former LPTB chief executive as 'the greatest patron of the arts whom this century has so far produced in England, and indeed the ideal patron of our age'.

From lettering, posters and station buildings, to the design of trains and buses, and encompassing platform clocks and litter bins, seat fabrics, wall tiles, the lighting of escalators, waiting-room benches, bus stops, cap badges, staff canteens and locker rooms, everything had to be a part of a creative, legible, immediately recognizable and joyous whole. Mr Pick may have been a puritan in many ways, and yet he had an exuberant streak revealed in his catholic choice of co-conspirators: artists, designers and craftsmen.

The lettering Mr Pick commissioned from the calligrapher Edward Johnston in 1913 has revolutionized typography worldwide. Charles Holden's Underground stations are indeed as true and pure as a Bach fugue, just as he intended these architectural sonnets to be. The posters commissioned by Mr Pick have long been a public art gallery, introducing millions of people to talents – some traditional, some humorous and others truly avant-garde. Even Sir Kenneth Clark, the energetic former director of the National Gallery, who worked for Mr Pick at the Ministry of Information in the early stages of the war, has been hard-pressed to bring art to the wider public in such a convincing manner.

Through Christian Barman, former editor of the *Architectural Review* and the LPTB's publicity officer from 1935, I was lucky enough to meet Mr Pick in early '39 at the Reform Club one evening before a talk he was due to give at the Athenaeum. I nearly said we met for a drink, but Mr Pick was teetotal and content with a cup of tea. I followed suit. He was a big man, evidently extremely intelligent, yet oddly shy for such a powerful and effective captain of industry. He looked tired and, in any case, had no small talk. I asked him if, through all his commissions – from Johnston lettering and Holden stations to the new RT bus – he was somehow trying to blur or even abolish the distinction between fine and applied art. He spoke of democratizing art and trying to build a worthwhile culture on contemporary foundations of trade, commerce and manufacture. He very much hoped this was possible, saying that if we couldn't do so then 'civilization would soon be without form'.

I asked him, too, if he believed cities would continue to progress, assuming we'd be able to avoid a calamitous war with Germany. With an Eeyorish look, Mr Pick said that we might be deceiving ourselves. We had raised the scale of cities, imbued them with greater speed of movement and more sensation than ever before, and yet perhaps there was no fundamental change. No wonder – as Mr Barman, a loyal disciple, had earlier admitted as we walked from 55 Broadway, the impressive LPTB headquarters designed by Charles Holden, to Pall Mall – Mr Pick is known as 'Jonah'.

In his 'Auguries of Innocence', William Blake wrote these unforgettable lines:

> To see a World in a Grain of Sand,
> And a Heaven in a Wild Flower,
> Hold Infinity in the palm of your hand
> And Eternity in an hour.

It might seem an unholy exaggeration to link Blake's numinous verse, much admired by Mr Pick, to the lineaments of an RT bus picking up passengers at Liverpool Street station, and yet here, in a 56-seat microcosm, is the world that Frank Pick made.

The actual design of these buses – special and yet for everyone – was by a team at Chiswick Works led by Eric

Poster depicting a *Hiawatha* train 'speedlined' by Otto Kuhler. From the prows of F7 class Baltics to the Flash Gordon-styling of observation cars, the Milwaukee Road's streamliners spelt unmitigated speed.

Sixty-four years young, former London Transport RT3781, back at work on Route 11 for a day in November 2014, thrums along Lower Grosvenor Gardens on its way to Liverpool Street.

Bristol 405, 1955 Paris Motor Show. This lithe 2-litre sports saloon drew on aircraft engineering. The new Citroën DS, in the same exhibition, appeared to have come from outer space.

Jaws wide open, a Silver City Airways Bristol Superfreighter waits for passengers and their cars heading across the Channel to Le Touquet at the new Ferryfield Airport, Lydd, Kent, 1955.

In October 2004, and soon after leaving Nesafit, a 1930's Ferrovie Eritrée Fiat 'Littorina' railcar on its way to Asmara climbs towards the railway's highest point, 7,854-feet above sea level.

A 442 Mallet Class compound 0-4-4-0T, built by Asaldo of Geneva in 1938, at Massawa docks busy at work shunting a freight train bound for Asmara, December 2012.

A Birmingham-bound 85mph Midland Red CM5T express motorway coach at Victoria Coach Station, November 1959. Although fast, these turbocharged coaches were hostage to slow traffic in and out of London.

'Il Settebello', arrived from Rome, under Alberto Fava's iron and glass trainshed at Milan Centrale. In service from 1953 to 1984, the streamlined ETR-300s were Italy's most glamorous express trains.

The Mk2 Jaguar remains one of the most beautiful of all saloon cars. Designed under the direction of Sir William Lyons, these mechanical cats were built from 1959 to 1967. This 3.8 model was mine.

The most potent Mk2 – the 125mph 3.8 – continues to be raced successfully, yet on the road it is a relaxed, immensely stylish and determinedly English club on wheels.

In March 2001, a powerful Chinese QJ class 2-10-2 accelerates the daily passenger train away from Daban on its 600-mile trek from Tongliao (east) to Jitong (west) across Inner Mongolia.

A QJ powers its train up and away from the curved concrete Simingyi viaduct and around the spectacular, demanding and remote Jinpeng Pass between Jinpeng and Reshui in February 2005.

Late November 2016. A Class 37 diesel-electric – 37406 *The Saltaire Society* – growls past Carrour, Britain's highest main line station, with the Fort William section of the *Caledonian Sleeper*.

A rugged Chevrolet Suburban heads off road to keep a family out of danger and away from a US military blockade in the aftermath of the 2003 invasion of Iraq.

Twenty-first-century steam. A Polish State Railways Ol class 2-6-2 of the mid-1950s sprints towards Wolsztyn at the head of a train of double-deck coaches on its way from Poznań.

Pedro the sea dog. With his barrel chest and rolling gait, Pedro was a natural sailor. Born on the Lancashire coast, he died in sight of the Atlantic Ocean.

Ottaway, Pick's technical officer (buses and coaches). They were built in Southall by Associated Equipment Company (AEC) – a manufacturing arm of the old London General Omnibus Company – which was set up in Walthamstow in 1912 to mass-produce Frank Searle's legendary B-type bus. That plucky open-top double-decker – the one that went to war in France and Belgium – was mass-produced to a high standard, too. Of the 3,000 buses at work in London immediately before the First War, 2,500 were B-types. Records show that just 0.02 per cent of the 55½ million route-miles B-types worked in 1913 were lost to mechanical breakdown. The RT is proving to be a more-than-worthy successor.

The RT has replaced trams throughout London. And though it was sad to see the trams finally go in '52, these new buses are impressive and much-liked replacements. Along with its fluent styling, the RT is nicely engineered. The bus boasts powerful and silent air brakes, air-operated pre-selector gearboxes and the latest version of AEC's 9.6-litre six-cylinder diesel engine. It makes a lovely sound. London Transport's demand for the new bus was so high that Leyland was roped in to build some 1,600 labelled RTL, while the 500 RTWs – which also have Leyland chassis – are 8 feet rather than 7 feet, 6 inches wide. These extra few inches, disallowed for many years by the stringencies of the Metropolitan Police, spell wider gangways that make these buses, allocated to route 11 on weekdays, easier to move around inside – especially during rush hours. Their 9.8-litre Leyland engines, though, sound harsher than those of the mellifluous RTs. They also lack the AEC buses' elegant radiator surrounds, with their distinctive triangular London Transport badges.

Time to step up onto the open rear platform and into the bus. Both lower and upper saloons are finished to an exceptionally high standard. Well-padded seats upholstered in striations of red, green and brown moquette, edged in brown leather and bolted firmly to floors and walls. Seatbacks lined with green leathercloth. Brown lower walls, then green up to the midpoint of the window line and a rich buttery cream for the upper walls and ceilings. Tungsten lightbulbs. Bell cord and framed timetables and fare charts downstairs. Ridged timber floors. Windows that wind open with the lightest touch. The overall effect is bright, modern and all of a piece. The design of most new cars seems crude by comparison.

The standard of engineering and manufacturing is, in fact, up there with that of the very best contemporary aircraft. Perhaps unsurprisingly, LPTB led the London Aircraft Production Group during the war, building 720 Handley Page Halifax four-engine bombers between its Chiswick and Aldenham works and the Duple and Park Royal coachworks where my RT was bodied in 1952. The last of the London Transport Halifaxes, PN 640, made her maiden flight from Leavesden Aerodrome near Watford on 16th April 1945, a fortnight before Hitler shot himself. It was named *London Pride*. In fact, while LT engineers have adapted aircraft industry materials and manufacturing techniques for the RT – and much more so for its new Routemaster, currently undergoing trials – Handley Page learned valuable lessons about the interchangeability of parts from Eric Ottaway and his team.

Every four years at most, RTs are driven up to the huge new Aldenham works – it covers an area of not far off 1,000 tennis courts – at Elstree, where they are taken apart and renovated from top to toe. The interchangeability of components means that the bus that went in to Aldenham as RT1000, for example, may well emerge resplendent with the chassis of RT500 and the body of RT2000 and it won't matter one bit. The RT is a kit of parts. What this great undertaking at Aldenham – employing 1,800 skilled labourers – does is to release what are effectively 50 new double-deckers back on the streets of London every week, as a further 50 are taken off the streets for overhaul. In this way, RTs will last for very many years. Not surprisingly, Aldenham is the biggest and most comprehensive endeavour of its kind in the world.

I take a seat at the front of the lower saloon of RT476, looking out over the long tapered bonnet crowned with a black radiator cap. The driver climbs up into the half-cab on my right and reaches up for the starter lever. The AEC engine settles into a slow, gargling tickover. I'm joined by City types working a half-day, along with railway clerks and cleaners. The conductor, perched on the rear platform, has a quick look around and gives two rings of the bell and off we go, accelerating down to the Bank of England. The City is quiet on the weekend, so we make brisk progress past the Mansion House and St Paul's Cathedral, London's tallest building, and down to Ludgate Circus. The bells of St Paul's ring out from the west tower Wren designed with Nicholas Hawksmoor, his supremely talented protégé.

The RT rides serenely, innocent of squeaks, rattles, vibrations or screeching brakes but accompanied by a leitmotif of bells, the names of stops called out by the conductor – a cheerful young Cockney singing Buddy Holly's hit 'Peggy Sue' as he works the decks – and the click, whirr and rasp of his

Gibson ticket machine. 'Any more fares now... Plenty of room on top...' Up top, though, is for smokers. It's mild today. It'd be a shame to sit in a fug of nicotine and cigarette smoke. I'm even half tempted to wind down the front window, but experience holds my arm. Except on the very warmest days, an open front window tends to cause a veritable Cuban Revolution among passengers sitting further back.

Fleet Street, meanwhile, is waking up for work on its Monday editions. I imagine there'll be further comment on the CND and its four-day, 52-mile march a fortnight ago from Trafalgar Square to the Atomic Weapons Research Establishment at Aldermaston. The Campaign for Nuclear Disarmament has certainly caught hold of the popular imagination, and you can see its 'Ban the Bomb' symbol, designed by Gerald Holtom – a graphic designer with the Ministry of Education, I hear – on railway bridges and other prominent public locations.

Along with rock 'n' roll, consumerism and what Herb Caen, the *San Francisco Chronicle* columnist, has dubbed 'Beatnik' culture – something to do with berets, bongos, dark glasses, turtleneck sweaters, moodiness, words like 'cool' and 'Daddy-o', and the music of Charlie Parker and Dizzy Gillespie – the 'bomb' is somehow all the rage. Children's comics and science magazines alike talk of a future of atomic-powered trains, cars, boats and planes. The RAF is conducting atomic tests in western Australia as de Havilland Propellers develops the Blue Streak ballistic missile. 'You wonder where your mouth has gone,' sing schoolchildren, 'when you brush your teeth with atom bomb.'

After two world wars, though, I can't help thinking that what the majority of people want, including the proverbial 'man on the Clapham omnibus', is peace and prosperity. And, as the prime minister, Mr Macmillan, said in a speech at a Tory rally in Bradford last year: 'Most of our people have never had it so good. Go around the country, go to the industrial towns, go to the farms and you will see a state of prosperity such as we have never had in my lifetime, nor indeed in the history of this country.'

There is still evidence of wartime bomb damage, seen through the windows of my RT bus, and many buildings are blackened and scarred, yet the number of colourful new cars on the road – along with bold fashions, more shopping bags than I've seen since the Thirties, and new cafés and restaurants – are some sort of evidence that things are looking up.

Threading through traffic composed of RTs, black cabs including a brand new FX4, motorcycles and sidecars, Commer and Morris vans, Ford Thames Traders, three-wheeler Scammell Scarabs and throngs of small family saloons old and new, we negotiate Trafalgar Square, where Nelson watches over a fleet of circling red buses.

Whitehall is almost eerily quiet on Saturday morning as our RT, commanding the road, thrums past Horse Guards Parade and Downing Street to turn around by the Palace of Westminster, then along past Westminster Abbey and into that stentorian nineteenth-century canyon, Victoria Street. We pick up some rather pukka-looking chaps – guardsmen perhaps – from outside the Army & Navy Stores and drop off a choir of children at Westminster Cathedral.

We fill up at Victoria with passengers hotfooting it from steam and electric Southern Region trains, crawl along Buckingham Palace Road and turn, past busy Victoria coach station, towards

Chelsea. If I were to have recommended a quick tour of central London to fellow passengers on board the *Hook Continental*, route 11 on board an RT would have been on the top of my list. In just 21 minutes, our bus has taken us with an almost insouciant ease from the City to Westminster, showing us some of the unforgettable sites of London along the way. It has shown us, too, how London – and certainly the London defined by the Circle Line – is a curious marriage between order and, if not quite chaos, then a certain slovenliness, from the charmingly artistic or bohemian to the downright cheap and nasty.

There has been much big talk from the war years concerning the re-planning and reconstruction of London, but little seems to have been done, as yet anyway, to alter the pre-war cityscape, although the Conservative administrations of Messrs Churchill, Eden and Macmillan have all spoken of relaxing height restrictions imposed on new buildings in the capital. Who knows what will happen if they let their chums in property development and the local authorities get their way. One day, perhaps, Victoria Street will look like Sixth Avenue.

Frank Pick visited New York in 1919 and again in 1928, and Manhattan's skyscrapers may well have impressed him. I wish I had asked him. For all its elemental qualities, Pick's Underground headquarters by Charles Holden at 55 Broadway has something of the look of an American building. When opened in 1929, it was at 175 feet high London's tallest office building. Holden, of course, went on to design Senate House for London University. This is 210 feet tall. It seems somehow significant that Pick had his office in Senate House during his short spell as director of the Ministry of Information in 1940.

At Sloane Square, where many passengers alight for the shops, I decide to climb upstairs, where I find the sofa-like rear seat vacant. This is the cosiest seat in an RT, and one favoured by sweethearts returning from a night out on the town. The bus is full again as we gargle into King's Road and pass by Peter Jones – the fondly regarded department store that is often mentioned in the same breath as the words 'wedding lists' and 'school uniforms' – and its curvaceous, streamlined pre-war street front.

Chelsea has long been bohemian, perhaps even before Turner, Rossetti, Whistler and Augustus John, and is constantly reinventing itself. I'm sure the Beatniks and members of a skiffle group clambering up to the top deck of my RT will move on from here as the next wave of artists, musicians and fashion designers moves in. We stop for traffic lights by Bazaar, the fashion boutique opened by Mary Quant and her husband Alexander Plunket Greene three years ago. All the vogue, it's a shrine to the young 'Chelsea set' who drink at the Markham Arms and eat at Alexander's in the basement of Bazaar.

And here's the new Granada TV studio shoehorned into the old Chelsea Palace Theatre. I associate this ornate Edwardian pile with childhood and Christmas pantomimes. In recent years, it's staged risqué burlesques; one, I noted in a flyer, was sponsored by Jeyes Fluid, a disinfectant. Granada is one of the independent new television broadcasting companies. I remember, four years ago, Lord Reith, the former director of the BBC, railing against the creation of the Independent Television Authority. 'Somebody introduced Christianity into England,' he thundered in the House of Lords, 'and somebody introduced smallpox, bubonic plague and the Black Death. Somebody is minded now to introduce sponsored broadcasting...' The zealous John Reith was Minister of Information when Frank Pick was the ministry's director. I'm not sure if Mr Pick ever watched television, but I'm pretty sure that, had he been alive in 1954, he would have been one with Lord Reith. I have to admit that I've watched Granada's *Chelsea at Nine* now and then, a show featuring new musical talent from the sublime to, it has to be said, the risible.

We bustle on past the former Bluebird Garage, now an LCC ambulance station, to World's End, where a kink in the road leads us into another world. This is the poorer end of Chelsea and the beginning of Fulham, a working-class district and home to bus drivers and nurses, milkmen and shop assistants, students and school dinner ladies. New passengers include women in turban hats weighed down with shopping and a girl in NHS specs and pigtails reading *Bunty* – her younger brother is sucking aniseed balls. Two men in open-necked shirts talk about football, still smarting from Fulham losing 5–3 to Manchester United in the FA Cup last month. I wouldn't dare to offer my pennyworth on this pressing issue, although it surely would have been a tonic to the Manchester team after the loss of eight of their players at Munich in February. Flying back from Belgrade, their BEA Airspeed Ambassador tried three times to take off in the snow along Munich-Riem's slushy runway. It was third time unlucky. Among the dead were eight journalists, the oldest being 65-year-old Donny Davis of the *Manchester Guardian*. The crew were ex-RAF pilots with distinguished wartime records.

And then someone – between bells, gear changes and the conductor's banter – talks of Laika, the poor little Russian space dog who died on board *Sputnik 2*, the Soviet spacecraft that burned up on re-entry to the earth's atmosphere this week. 'Why can't the communists go up themselves if they're so keen on space rockets?'

I don't interrupt the conversation, and yet it reminds me of priests who told us when we were children that God gave humans the right to use animals as they saw fit. I thought that tommyrot then, while anyone who has been through the war and witnessed what evil and savagery humans are capable of en masse will only too willingly root for Laika. All living creatures are our brothers and sisters.

Turning into Harwood Road, the bus slows and breaks my reverie. A bus ride gives us time to drift and dream as well as to look out of the windows, listen to conversations that are impossible to avoid and, with careful folding, to read the newspaper. But here's Fulham Broadway, all traffic and Saturday shopping.

Along Lillie Road, we pass Bothwell Street, where Geoffrey de Havilland built his first aeroplane in 1909. It crashed on its maiden flight, yet de Havilland went on to design and make three of my favourite aircraft – the Tiger Moth, Mosquito and Hornet – as well as, of course, the Comet jet airliner. which has had more than its fair share of troubles. Fatalities, too. The new Comet 4 is due to fly next week. Fingers and flaps crossed. Before his first aircraft, de Havilland spent two years in the drawing office of Motor Omnibus at Walthamstow, a company that evolved one way or another into AEC. It might seem a curious thought, yet London motorbuses and English aircraft developed together.

We're running two minutes early, so wait dutifully at a bus stop on Fulham Palace Road. The bus stop itself is one of the many thousands erected from 1937, a shapely thing made of polished aggregate with a built-in timetable and a flag bearing a modified London Transport 'bullseye' designed by Hans Schleger – or 'Zero', as this German-born artist chooses to sign his work. For Frank Pick, a bus stop was at one and the same time a working tool and work of art.

We pull away and into Hammersmith, dead on time, where I hop off the open platform in front of London Transport's Riverside garage. I watch and listen to RT476 pulling smoothly away from the kerb on its way to Shepherd's Bush. Riverside garage itself is a fascinating thing, an English Baroque country house dating from around 1710, conjured into a London General bus garage 200 years later. What I'm looking at on Queen Caroline Street is the former east front of Bradmore House, taken down and rebuilt facing west as an entrance to the bus garage that opened on the site of the demolished house in 1913. The London County Council persuaded London General to do this, and I'm pleased it did. There's something rather special, almost fairy tale–like, in seeing London double-deckers ease their way in and out of what appears to be a stately home and as if to the manor born.

Until recently, busmen enjoyed at least one of the aristocratic trappings of Bradmore House. Their recreational billiard room was housed until this year in a handsome panelled drawing room on the *piano nobile*. I imagine liveried footmen serving tea to Ron, Bert and Harry, as these knights of the road potted billiard balls as bright red as their diesel mounts waiting at the ready in the entrance hall below. The two historic first-floor rooms have now been relocated to the Trinity Green Almshouses on Mile End Road, to make up for damage caused during the Blitz.

I stroll down to the Thames to The Dove, the huddled early-eighteenth-century pub close by William Morris's Kelmscott House. This is where local residents Eric Gill and Edward Johnston would meet. Johnston lived on Hammersmith Terrace, a five-minute walk west along the river. This is where he devised his famous and hugely influential block lettering for Frank Pick, starting just before the war that killed his half-brother, Lieutenant Andrew Johnston, a Royal Flying Corps observer. His machine crashed in Belgium.

Not that everyone was pleased with the lettering that adorns the fronts, sides and backs of London Transport's first-rate RT buses. One of his students, Graily Hewitt, wrote to a friend:

> In Johnston I have lost confidence. Despite all he did for us... he has undone too much by forsaking his standard of the Roman alphabet, giving the world, without safeguard or explanation, his block letters which disfigure our modern life. His prestige has obscured their vulgarity and commercialism.

I hope I'm not being too vulgar discussing aircraft, flying characteristics and production when I meet my aviation contacts for pints and pies in The Dove. I could find nothing vulgar in RT476.

*

RT476 was the last of its type in regular service, pulling into Barking garage, east London, at the end of a route 62 run at Saturday lunchtime, 7th April 1979. RTs had served London reliably and well for 40 years. Their successor, the RM (Routemaster), the last bus designed by London Transport and built by AEC, served London for very nearly half a century. Examples of both types are preserved in running order.

On 2nd November 2014, a fleet of RTs, including RTLs and RTWs, operated route 11 for the day in celebration of the 75th anniversary of these much-loved double-deckers. Later buses, bought off the peg from manufacturers, were far less refined than either the RT or RM. Bigger, heavier, noisier, greedier for fuel – a mass of vibrations and cacophonies of squealing brakes and mostly lacking a conductor – they appeared to stick two fingers up to all Frank Pick and London Transport had stood for. For a while, during the height of privatization madness and deregulation fever in the 1990s, these and a number of humiliated RMs appeared in lurid colours – chosen, it seemed, from the designs of packets of Refreshers and Liquorice Allsorts. Any colour, it seemed, was good, as long as it wasn't red. None of the off-the-peg buses have lasted very long, nor caught the imagination of the travelling public. Because they were not LT-style kits of parts, they could not be overhauled on a mass-production basis at Aldenham. As a result, Aldenham works shut up shop in 1987, and with it came the loss of many skilled jobs.

The original Routemasters had taken over route 11 fully from RTs and RTWs in 1966. A 'New Routemaster' – weighing in at a hefty 12½ tons and cursed with an unreliable hybrid diesel-battery powertrain, gratuitous styling, and a hot and claustrophobic upper deck – took to London streets in 2012. It appears to have been built for the amusement of Boris Johnson, second elected Mayor of London. It took over route 11 in September 2013. Production ended in 2017.

The Hammersmith Riverside garage was closed in 1983. Bradmore House was rebuilt as offices and a restaurant. King's Road became increasingly chic, creative and fashionable in the 1960s. Mary Quant set the pace with her miniskirts and by 1967's Summer of Love, the street was lined with a cornucopia of peacock boutiques – Antiquarius, Bazaar, Chelsea Girl, Garbo, Granny Takes a Trip, Hung on You, I Was Lord Kitchener's Thing, Just Looking, Kiki Byrne, Kleptomania, Lord John, Mates, Mr Freedom, Quorum, the Squire Shop, Take 6, Top Gear, Topper – along with groovy hairdressing salons, far-out clubs like dell'Aretusa, and fab restaurants including Alvaro's and Gandalf's Garden Shoppe (where you could meet the 'gentlest people', and join in playing flutes, sitars and ocarinas). When punk ruled the King's Road roost in the mid to late '70s, Boy, Sex and Seditionaries were the shops of the moment, the spikey realms of Vivienne Westwood, Malcolm McLaren and the Sex Pistols. In 1998, Starbucks opened its first London coffee shop at the same address on the King's Road where the Fantasie coffee bar had opened in 1955. By then, King's Road had become just another chain-store high street, as banal as the latest London buses.

London buses all but disappeared from London streets for seven weeks in May and June 1958. The London bus strike led to the withdrawal of routes, the closure of bus garages and a marked rise, that only increased, in the ownership of cars, motorbikes, motor-scooters and mopeds. From then on, London buses failed to turn a profit. Non-standard RTs were sold as surplus to operating requirements. Traffic congestion led to the introduction, on 10th June 1958, of parking meters in Grosvenor Square. They spread across town with the speed of the Great Plague. Single and double yellow lines appeared at around the same time. Despite attempts to increase the speed of traffic in central London, it has got steadily slower over the past 60 years. The 21-minute off-peak timing from Liverpool Street to Victoria in April 1958 has been extended to 40 minutes. This is due partly to congestion and partly because driver-only buses are slower than buses with both driver and conductor.

The summer of 1958 witnessed the Notting Hill race riots, the screening of *Carry on Sergeant* – the first of a long-running gorblimey series – and the release of what is generally regarded as Britain's first home-spawned rock 'n' roll record: 'Move It', by Cliff Richard and the Drifters. The song was by Ian 'Sammy' Samwell, the Drifters' rhythm guitarist, who said he wrote it on a 715 Green Line bus on his way to Richard's house in Cheshunt. The bus was probably a single-deck RF – an excellent design contemporary with the double-deck RT – but it might just have been a Green Line RT, as these were put to work occasionally on route 715 at busy times. Cliff Richard can be seen learning to drive an RT in a Pathé News clip, a skill needed for *Summer Holiday*, a popular film of 1963 in which four Aldenham works mechanics convert an RT into a caravan and drive to Athens singing songs, including the catchy theme tune that got to No. 1 in the charts.

From 1986, newspapers abandoned Fleet Street for computerized and print union–free premises in Wapping, Southwark and, later on, Canary Wharf, although the Dundee-based *Sunday Post* employed two journalists in what *Private Eye* dubbed 'the Street of Shame' as late as 2016. St Paul's is no longer the tallest building in London. Today, it is bullied by a phalanx of skyscrapers – some much better than others in design – sprouting in what appears to be random fashion. The cathedral has been cleaned in recent years. In 1958 it would have been sooty and shadowy, in a chiaroscuro and curiously appealing way.

Broad Street station vanished to make way for the broad-shouldered Broadgate office development – as did the western range of Liverpool Street station, which underwent a major renovation by British Rail's own architects, completed in 1991. The *Hook Continental* was withdrawn in 1987, by which time the number of foot passengers from Harwich to Holland had diminished considerably. SS *Arnhem* last sailed in 1968 and was broken up the following year, her place taken by car ferries.

Unlike Britannia Pacifics, English Electric Type 4 diesel-electrics were not particularly popular on the East Anglian Main Line, and were positively looked down on by East Coast management and crews alike. Their top-link or elite express passenger locomotives in the late 1950s and early '60s were ex-LNER Pacifics, which were faster, more powerful, more reliable and far more glamorous than the matter-of-fact diesels meant to replace them.

Johnston lettering – a modified version called New Johnston, designed by Eiichi Kono of Banks & Miles, appeared in 1979 – is universally admired. Frank Pick is commemorated by a fine work, *Beauty < Immortality*, by the artists Langlands & Bell in the concourse of Charles Holden's Piccadilly Circus station. The memorial was commissioned by the London Transport Museum and installed by Art on the Underground on 7th November 2016, the 75th anniversary of Pick's death. On that day in 1941, a year on from resigning as a matter of principle from LPTB, he had written to his friend B. J. Fletcher, director of the Central School of Arts and Crafts: 'I am become an idle and useless member of society and so unwell… There is no real living only an existing for a time.' Forty years on from the demise of the RT bus, Frank Pick's legacy lives on.

TWELVE

Massawa to Asmara:
Ferrovie Eritrée

12th–13th May 1958

The receptionist at what must have once been a very smart modern Italian hotel says that Mr Small left yesterday or perhaps the day before. She hasn't been on duty for some days because she's been visiting her family in Nefasit – and, anyway, the clerk who was supposed to be on duty has mixed up the dates in the ledger. Mr Small must have left for Asmara, so I'll follow suit and see if I can catch him there.

Mr Charles Small is an American oil man, and I have some correspondence for him that he missed when he called in at Aden to meet colleagues at what we've learned to call BP, formerly the Anglo-Persian Oil Company. I'm not a postman, but when I told colleagues at RAF Khormaksar, over a dinner with officials from BP's refinery, that I planned to spend the leave I was owed exploring Eritrea, Mr Small's name came up. In his spare time he's writing a book on the world's most far-flung and elusive railways. He wondered if there were any takers for a ride up from the Eritrean coast at Massawa to Asmara, the city

Mussolini built on the plateau more than 7,000 feet up and just 70 miles from the Red Sea. If Mr Small wasn't successful in his career, this might have prompted laughter.

One of the veteran transport pilots at Khormaksar had flown single-engine Wellesley bombers over both Massawa and Asmara during the East African Campaign. 'Wouldn't get me back there again,' he said. 'If you think Aden's hot, wait till you get to Massawa. Up in the air you could get away from the heat, but I could see the trains crawling up the mountainsides. They must have been baked alive inside those old things.'

Being in Aden has been all about replacing old things with new. The de Havilland Venoms are to be replaced by a new generation of jet fighters, and tests have been conducted on three new machines: the Hunting-Percival Jet Provost, the Folland Gnat and the Hawker Hunter. The whole set up seems pretty rum. The Provost's a fine machine, although essentially a trainer rather than a fighter, while much as I admire Teddy Petter – who's given us the Lysander, the Canberra and the new Lightning with his protégé Freddie Page – the Gnat is a tiny aircraft that I can't see impressing the squadrons out in Aden who've been responding to this month's state of emergency. The Hunter is superb in every way.

Even then, I'm secretly excited by the idea of riding the length of the former Ferrovie Eritrée, because I gather it's a brilliant piece of civil engineering, boasts some unusual locomotives and travels through a spectacular landscape. And while I'm up on the plateau, I'd like to pay respects to the thousands of mostly Indian and African soldiers who fell in the Battle of Keran in order to put a stop to the Duce's little game in East Africa. I can remember reading a speech he gave in '39 about 'marching to the oceans' in Europe and Africa. I think he did, although he kept on marching in his big shiny boots until he found himself up to his big jutting chin in very deep water indeed.

I was offered a lift up the Red Sea – blissfully free of pirates since 1839, when the East India Company annexed Aden – on board BP's 32,000-ton *British Victory*. One of the first of a new fleet of tankers, she was launched seven years ago at the Vickers-Armstrongs yard in Barrow-on-Furness. I wonder what the weather is like on the north Lancashire coast today? Here in Massawa, the BP captain told me gleefully, it's just over 100 degrees Fahrenheit, and certain to rise.

I ask the hotel receptionist if she knows what time the next train to Asmara is due. She does. It leaves at 2 p.m. The station is over there, three minutes' walk away. She tells me her uncle works on the railway and writes down his name in English in elementary-school copybook Italian handwriting. 'Italiana?'

'Yes and no. My father is from Lecce, my mother from Nefasit. The train stops there on the way to Asmara.'

I have time for lunch – but, says the receptionist, the hotel kitchen is not what it was before 1941, the year the British took over. She directs me to the Restaurante Primavera, overlooking the old port. This is located on the second floor of an old building that has seen better days, but the welcome is effusive. I'm shown a table covered in a threadbare red-and-white cotton check, on the shaded balcony. The maître d' presents the menu in an ancient leather folder.

'American?'

'English.'

'Ah. We had another foreign gentleman here two days ago. An American. I recommended the shrimps, fresh from the sea, with the spaghetti.'

'I'd like the same if you have it, please.'

'Of course. And perhaps a cold Melotti beer from Asmara? Signor Melotti ate here when he came to the port. He chose the shrimps, fresh from the sea, with the spaghetti.'

'Thank you. And the American gentleman? When did he leave?'

'He took the *Littorina* to Asmara on Saturday.'

The shrimps, fresh from the sea, with the spaghetti, are excellent. And after Double Diamond and quite dreadful lager in the mess at Khormaskar, a cold Melotti beer is liquid heaven. At 1.30 p.m., I make my way to the station, where a small crowd has gathered. In my linen suit, I feel a little out of place, yet people here are welcoming. The goats, too.

At five to two, a high-pitched whistle announces the train. Steaming slowly towards us from the docks, it consists of three unglazed passenger coaches, three bogie goods wagons and a fourth, four-wheeled passenger carriage to the rear, led by a locomotive that cannot fail to win a steam man's heart: a battered and black and only slightly grimy 0-4-4-0 Mallet tank engine, big cylinders out front, tall chimney trailing a thin cloud of dirty smoke, a baroqueness of domes along the top of her boiler. She screeches to a stop next to me as if she wanted me to study her polished builder's plate.

This, it informs me, is 440 class No. 031 – built not in Italy but in Asmara, in XVII. What with the heat and the hustle and bustle it will take me more than a few miles to work out what on earth that XVII refers to. If it means 1917, then why not say so? I clamber into the back of the rear carriage. From here, I'll be able to watch the engine taking the curves. Three soldiers in British uniforms and carrying Lee Enfield .303s climb in with me and take up positions, one at the open back, the other two on either side of the wooden carriage. Then 440 031 whistles shrilly and, with steam hissing from her cylinder cocks and a trail of black smoke, she inches us away from the station and around onto the causeway linking Massawa, an island town, to the mainland.

I speak to the soldiers in Italian. Eritreans, they have been a part of the federal Ethiopian army since the British left six years ago. They tell me they're on the lookout for *shifta* – bandits, revolutionaries and other shifty characters – who may try to hold up the train or take potshots at it. But all I can see as we accelerate up to 20 mph or so across a scorched coastal plain is sparse and spikey vegetation; red, grey, brown and black rocks; heat haze and a gauze of soot. I take off my jacket and roll it into my bag. The soldiers accept cigarettes, although each keeps a finger close to the trigger of his rifle as he smokes.

The *lira* drops now that we've settled into a swaying rhythm. Those Roman numerals on the side of our big tank engine are clearly meant to signal an imperial date. Mussolini's new empire was founded – in the Duce's mind at least – in 1922, when he marched on Rome with his fellow Fascists. To avert violence, King Victor Emmanuel III appointed him prime minister. If I'm on the right track, 440 031 must have been built in 1939, the 17th year since the foundation of the second Roman Empire. And then I fall asleep, awaking only when, rumbling through a tunnel, the engine brakes for Damas with a slight jolting of its train. I have no idea if we've made other stops on the way.

Here, the steam hisses. People crowd the narrow platform. Trading takes place with drivers of a camel train. The locomotive takes water. I go up to see her. The driver invites me on to the footplate. He's Italian – in his late fifties, I'd guess. After he's explained the controls – he's keen I should know this is a compound and not any old engine – I ask him about that date.

'Yes, 1939. I helped build her, from spare parts just before Mussolini's invasion. They wanted all the locomotives they could get to bring military supplies up to Asmara.'

Mr Caputo is more than an engine driver; he's a mechanical engineer. He is also the uncle of the receptionist of the CIAAO Hotel at Massawa. He suggests I ride on the locomotive for the next section as the climb away from the coastal plain begins in earnest. My white shirt and linen trousers already peppered with soot, I'm not exactly dressed for the footplate. Mr Caputo calls from the cab. One of the camel drivers approaches and hands him something like a Mexican poncho. 'Give him something for it. Not too much.' I do, and by the camel driver's expression I've overpaid. Now, though, I feel free to ride an engine I've only been able to half imagine. News and specifications of the Ferrovie Eritrée have not been the stock in trade of either *Trains Illustrated* or *The Railway Magazine*.

We steam steadily up into a narrow valley that, after a rocky pinch point, opens into a green plain. At Ghinda, 3,280 feet above sea level – or so Mr Caputo tells me in metres – and the best of four hours from Massawa, the temperature is almost pleasant. The soldiers disembark and make conversation with a replacement party. A sudden honk and a smart 1930s Fiat *Littorina* diesel railcar approaches from the other direction. Once it's stopped, I look inside. What a lovely thing. It would have been very modern indeed when, according to its builder's plate, it first went into service here in 1935. Clearly, nothing was too good for the railways of the second Roman Empire. Unlike my train, it offers first- and second-class seating. There is no third-class seating. It also boasts a bar stocked with Melotti beer and soft drinks. The soldiers settle comfortably in second.

Mr Caputo has already explained that steam trains are third-class only. Where the *Littorina* does the journey up and down from Massawa to Asmara in 3¾ hours, with steam the trip takes a good six hours, although with the transfer of goods in and out of the wagons, the journey can stretch to seven, eight and even ten hours.

Just as I'm about to step off the railcar I notice a Western gentleman busy with a pile of documents. 'Mr Small?'

'Sure.'

As we have a bare four minutes before departure, I say, 'I'll be back in a jiffy,' and sprint across the platform to find my bag. With the bundle of letters for Mr Small retrieved, I place this on the seat next to him.

'Why, thank you. A fellow steam man! Would you write your address?' He hands me a notebook and pen. 'You'll be hearing from me.' My train engine whistles.

I wave to Mr Small, who waves back – surprised, I'm sure, to find a fellow steam enthusiast out and about on the Ferrovie Eritrée, a line that sees very few foreign visitors.

On to Nefasit, and we climb up the sides of a further valley, the train writhing like a snake. The locomotive, despite her lack of trailing wheels, rides surprisingly well, and her Mallet design means she can swing in and out of bends like an articulated lorry. Mr Caputo handles the locomotive with impeccable skill, making subtle adjustments to steam cut off in both high- and low-pressure cylinders to ensure its efficient use. The fireman, despite initial protests, allows me to swing the shovel for a good number of uphill miles. The coal is horrid, dusty stuff imported from the United States. Perhaps I can ask my BP contacts to find a way of converting the Eritrean locos to burn oil instead.

At Nefasit, I step down from the footplate. A member of the station staff takes me to wash my face and hands. It's starting to get dark now which is a little sad, as it's from Nefasit that the line performs its engineering miracle, climbing the side of an improbable escarpment, thundering through innumerable tunnels, calling at a wayside station cut into the rock face and screeching around three spiral loops and over a magnificent 14-arched curved viaduct. More tunnels, more sheer drops follow, before, in the gloaming, we crest the summit – 7,038 feet above sea level – and drift down the last mile or two to Asmara.

It's 9.30 p.m. Passengers and soldiers disperse. I thank the crew. 'Where are you staying?' asks Mr Caputo. I have no idea. 'I'll get one of the staff to walk you to the Swiss Mission. Very clean. Very good people. They will even give you dinner at this hour, don't worry!'

The spick-and-span station is much like a railway building you might expect to find in Alto Adige. The Swiss hostel, set inside a high-walled and whitewashed compound, is a gem.

They have a phone and I ask if I might ring home. After half an hour, a connection is made.

'How's your African train?'

'Romantic.'

'As romantic as the *Coronation Scot*?'

'That would be impossible.'

The line goes dead. It may be down, or possibly cut, says the Swiss nurse who has brought an evening meal of *rösti* and lamb.

'*Shifta*?'

'We never know.'

What I do know when I wake up the next morning and explore the town is that Asmara is a puzzle. A little worn after years of war and neglect, it is thoughtfully planned, thoroughly crafted and beautifully planted with royal palms, eucalyptus, vines, jacaranda and bougainvillea. I drink a proper cappuccino in the Moderna, a 1930s Italian café. The decor and the coffee machine are exactly as they must have been in 1940. Men doffing Borsalinos to passers-by wear elegant if frayed Italian suits. Women walking past could easily feature on next month's cover of *Vogue* should they want to, and if it were remotely possible. Pre-war Fiats and Alfa Romeos burble along impressive avenues, one featuring a striking 1930s Alfa Romeo showroom and garage, although there are no new Alfas for sale in Asmara today.

I can see that the Italians shaped a place and a way of life here, high on the East African plateau, that might well have made their compatriots – especially in the south or Sicily – feel envious. What I still can't see is why the Italians threw all this away. Our allies in the Great War, they sided with Hitler in the Second and were out for the count here in East Africa little more than a year after they declared war on us. What on earth do such people want?

To take it all in and to ensure I enjoy the marvels of the Ferrovie Eritrée in daylight and to the full, and because of the infernal heat lurking below, I plan to be here for the rest of the week. I'll take the *Littorina* back down to Massawa before steaming south to Aden, Hunters and home.

*

Charles R. Small wrote *Far Wheels* while working in Tokyo. Published in 1955, it had long been on my shortlist of 'desert island' books. I found a copy in a Brooklyn bookshop 30 years ago. The canny bookseller persuaded me to part with $45. Ever since, *Far Wheels* has travelled with me to far corners and remote junctions of the world. Small's *Rails to the Rising Sun* (1965) is a recently acquired treasure, showing what Japanese rail travel, by steam, was like before the arrival of the revolutionary Shinkansen bullet trains at the time of the 1964 Tokyo Olympics.

It took the best part of 25 years and 50,000 unskilled and very highly skilled men to construct the Ferrovie Eritrée from Massawa to Asmara. It was an engineering triumph of the highest order, while the quality of the masonry along the line, especially of viaducts in improbably challenging locations, was second to none. The railway was a showcase of newfound Italian imperial ambition, an imperative prompted by the country's unification in 1859, by the 'scramble for Africa' by European nations between 1880 and 1914, and later by Mussolini's vainglorious attempt to create a second Roman Empire. Competition from road traffic and a gradual loss of skills from the mid-1960s hit the railway hard, yet its closure in 1975 was caused by war. Ethiopian troops did their best to destroy it.

Eritrea won its independence in 1993. The following year, as a sign of how the country might follow its own star and live within its own means, the Eritrean government decided to bring the railway back into use. Veteran engineers, fitters and locomotive crews were asked to join the task. When, in 2003, the railway was re-opened all the way from Massawa to Asmara, these men – many now in their eighties – were still very much at work. I went to Eritrea with BBC Radio 4 producer Rebecca Nicholson in 2005 to make a documentary about Asmara. I met and talked to these veterans as they fettled a 440 class and some of the later and bigger 442 0-4-4-0 tank locomotives at Asmara shed. In town, remarkably little had changed since 1958 – or even 1938. The Moderna still served espressos and cappuccinos, its decor unchanged.

Asmara remains not just an architectural gem, but an African town the continent can be proud of. In 2006, however, the railway was closed again to all but charter trains for rare foreign visitors between Asmara and Nefasit. Charter trains made it further east, to Ghinda, on occasion, but in 2016–17 floods and rock falls destroyed parts of the line. In 2019 it seemed pretty dead, although at least one rare excursion for enthusiasts was planned for that year. In Eritrea you never know what might happen next. The political situation remains fragile.

Remarkably, the railway had once gone even further inland from the Red Sea, running all the way to Bishia, 209 miles from Massawa. Mussolini wanted it to cross the Sudanese border and reach Kassala. This would have opened up trade from Sudan to the Red Sea. The Duce's little war with Britain and the United States put an end to his railway-building. Fascist symbols, meanwhile, can still be seen in the aluminium bodywork of the Ferrovie Eritée's *Littorina* railcars. These took their name from Littoria, one of the Fascist new towns built on land reclaimed from marshes, mosquitoes and malaria south of Rome. In 1932, Giovanni Agnelli, chairman of Fiat and an Italian senator, took the Duce to Littoria for the town's inauguration ceremony on board one of his brand-new diesel railcars. A journalist called the train a 'Littorina'.

In Massawa, the Restaurante Primavera has long gone. So has the CIAAO Hotel, which is a shame as, renovated, it would be a special place to stay – although, as in 1958, the port sees very few foreign visitors save for the crews of Red Sea freighters. The only others have been in search of the railway. BP's *British Victory* was withdrawn in 1973 and broken up in 1977. The RAF chose the Hawker Hunter over the Folland Gnat and Hunting Percival Jet Provost. The air base at Khormaksar closed officially in December 1967. Aden returned to the Yemen. Today, pirates infest the Red Sea.

THIRTEEN

Birmingham to London:
Midland Red

2nd November 1959

igbeth coach station, a dark and dingy 1920s bus depot in central Birmingham, is not where I would normally expect to find myself on a Monday afternoon in November. When I have been to this industrious Midlands city, it's been by train. Spoilt for choice today, there are express trains to London in two hours from both Birmingham New Street and Snow Hill stations.

The London Midland trains sprint down to Euston through Coventry, Rugby and Watford, behind three-cylinder Jubilee class 4-6-0s, while mighty ex–Great Western four-cylinder King class 4-6-0s lead the heavier Western Region trains to Paddington. I prefer the latter route through Leamington Spa, Banbury and High Wycombe, more because of the scenery than because of a preference for Kings over Jubilees. Sir William Stanier, who I got to know from his time at Power Jets, played a key role in the design and construction of both locomotive types during his mechanical engineering days at Swindon and Crewe.

Today, I've been invited to take a coach from Birmingham to London. Normally allergic to coach travel, I have to admit to being intrigued by the idea of Midland Red's non-stop service. The very first express coach leaves from here at 2 p.m., just hours after the opening of the eagerly awaited M1, Britain's first trunk motorway. So, there's quite a bit of excitement here among Midland Red staff and the passengers dressed up in their best hats, coats and handbags. This special occasion demands a pair of coaches, and here they are – Birmingham's finest – numbers 4804 and 4809.

I have to admit that these red and black C5MT coaches are exceptionally smart. Long, straight-lined and with characterful lantern-like windscreens, they look the part – crisply modern and, evidently, motorway-fast. One of Midland Red's engineers is on hand to describe the C5MT to me. Developed from the C5 coach first seen on the road last year, the C5MT has been specially prepared for high-speed motorway work. There is no upper speed limit on the M1 for coaches. Designed and built wholly by Midland Red at its Birmingham Central works, the C5MT – 'M' stands for motorway; 'T' for turbocharged – has been tested at MIRA, the Motor Industry Research Association HQ off the A5 near Nuneaton, at speeds of up to 85 mph.

The monocoque coaches are fitted with Midland Red's very own underfloor six-cylinder, eight-litre diesels producing 138 bhp at 1,800 rpm, and five-speed constant-mesh gearboxes with overdrive on top. The gearbox has been developed with David Brown, who also makes the new Aston Martin DB4, a motorway car if there ever was one. The coach – 8 feet wide and just under 30 feet long – boasts disc brakes, rubber suspension, a one-piece fibreglass roof, soundproofing and a lavatory, deemed necessary for a non-stop service. The only old-fashioned components appear to be the wooden boards that are mounted – railway carriage style – above the windows, bearing the legend 'Birmingham-London Motorway Express'.

Midland Red has long been an innovative company. Founded in 1905 as a subsidiary of the tramway giant BET – British Electric Traction Company – it's the biggest bus company outside London. Its proper name is BMMO, standing for the Birmingham and Midland Motor Omnibus Company. It operates over 6,500 route-miles stretching out to Derbyshire, Gloucestershire and the Welsh Borders. It owns a fleet of 1,900 buses and coaches – since 1954, it has built these itself. I am fascinated to learn that Loftus Wyndham Shire, chief engineer from 1912 to 1940 – whose designs include Britain's first under-floor rear-engine coach in 1936 – trained London Transport's Eric Ottaway, principal engineer of the RT double-decker.

Like London Transport, Midland Red has been innovative in terms of poster design, graphics, architecture – except, of course, for Digbeth coach station – materials and even seat fabrics, although I have to say the leopard-print fabric employed in these new motorway coaches is something of an acquired taste. More Diana Dors than Marilyn Monroe or M1, I'd have thought. But, if fake leopard skin is not quite Hollywood, America has been influential in the design of the C5MT. Midland Red's general manager and chief engineer, Donald McIntyre Sinclair, visited Greyhound Lines in 1948 and would have taken a close interest in the Raymond Loewy–designed PD-3751 Silverside coaches. The Yanks are masters of long-distance buses and, like

Midland Red, Greyhound paid proper attention to architecture and design, too.

It's time to board. On we get, 34 passengers in each of the red coaches and the drivers in smart uniforms crowned with white-topped caps. The faux-leopardskin seats are comfortable enough. There is a magazine rack and an ashtray in the seat-backs, and an overhead luggage rack. It's fun to watch the driver at work, changing up and down the gears as we engage with busy traffic fuming towards the dual-carriageway section of the A45. Bypassing Coventry, we join the eight-mile stretch of the new M45, a Birmingham spur off the M1, where we sprint up to 70 mph, passing under the concrete motorway bridges designed by Sir Owen Williams and overtaking lorries, vans, lesser coaches and cars.

On board, there is a genuine moment of excitement as we negotiate the Kilsby intersection and join the much-feted motorway, although I can't help but crane my neck looking for the decorative and very early Victorian ventilation-shaft towers of Robert Stephenson's Kilsby Tunnel, a three-year project that allowed the London and Birmingham Railway to meet both cities with its steam trains. I suppose that the great white stretches of the M1 disappearing ahead of us are the equivalent of Stephenson's heroic engineering achievement of 120 years ago. With its army of latter-day navvies, and some of the latest earth-moving equipment, the motorway has been built at the rate of a mile every eight days and a bridge every three, which is certainly going some.

Mr Marples, the Minister of Transport, opened it this morning. I find he's all too keen on road construction and not nearly interested enough in the future of our hard-pressed railways, even though plans for the 100 mph electrification of the West Coast Main Line, as far as Crewe, Liverpool and Manchester, are moving ahead. Given that the Conservatives won a third general election in a row last month with a 100-seat majority, and most people appear to agree with the prime minister, Mr Macmillan, when he says that we've never had it so good, I imagine Mr Marples will get his way. The government says we'll have a thousand miles of motorways by 1962.

Not that our cars are up to speed. It is fascinating to see how, as we surge up towards 80 mph, they are swept behind in our wake. Most family saloons – including BMC's intriguing new Austin Seven and Morris Mini-Minor – have top speeds of 70–75 mph, and few will cruise much above 55. We spot several breakdowns on the soft edges of the motorway. And some very bad driving, too, with Vanguards and Crestas (among others) wandering from lane to lane along the concrete carriageway as if their drivers were either grossly incompetent or on the bottle. There is no central reservation or crash barrier, so I can readily imagine these wayward motorists crossing one lane too many and finding themselves facing traffic heading in the opposite direction.

All the way to Watford, where the motorway ends, very few cars pass us. A brace of Jaguars. An Austin-Healey. A Bentley. An exotic Alfa Romeo. We've covered 59 miles of motorway in less than 50 minutes. And then reality hits. Along the A41 and the beginnings of London's ever-expanding suburbs, our average speed drops, the next 10 miles hogging 20 minutes. Mill Hill, Hendon, Kilburn – the going gets ever slower. I'm tempted to try to read. I have Wilfred Thesiger's *Arabian Sands* in my bag. A lady in the seat diagonally in front of me is having a go at *Cat Among the Pigeons*, the latest Agatha Christie. Another has started to knit. The magic of the motorway has been dispelled. And yet we are running well ahead of time. The timetable allows us 3 hours and 25 minutes for the 114 miles to Victoria.

Creeping along the Edgware Road, we join the red-bus, black-cab melee at Marble Arch. Here, though, is Buckingham Palace Road. The early 1930s Art Deco hulk of Victoria coach station heaves into view. We turn in and pull up inside the terminus – so much smarter than Digbeth, although it has seen better days. We are 34 minutes ahead of schedule. This, says the BMMO engineer sitting behind me with a clipboard, is 2 hours and 29 minutes faster than the pre-motorway schedule, with its 'comfort stops' along the way.

Even so, it does seem slow compared to rival express trains. No, I don't think I'm coach-travel material, even though this has been a fascinating trip. That long drag from Watford! I've sprinted the 17 miles from Watford Junction to Euston several times in 19 minutes or less on board London Midland semi-fasts with Fowler, Stanier or Fairburn 2-6-4 tank locos in charge, galloping through Harrow at up to 90 mph. For all its advanced engineering, the Midland Red's C5MT will never manage anything like that, especially as car ownership is growing rapidly. Even the M1, so clear on this mild November afternoon, is bound to be very much busier in the future.

*

Such was the initial success of Midland Red's 'Motorway Express' that the C5MTs soon proved to be too small for the role. From February

1965, 44-seat C6MTs took over the M1 service. The C5MTs lost their 'toilets' and turbochargers, and were used on less busy routes until their withdrawal in 1970–71. No examples are preserved in motorway configuration, although two C5s – numbers 4780 and 4819 – are. The former served for some years as a motor caravan, going on summer holidays – like Cliff Richard and chums in their London Transport RT – to the south of France. An express service, the X44 – using C5s and the new M5 motorway – ran, from July 1962, from Birmingham to Worcester in 50 minutes, faster than by train. In 2018, the fastest trains took 45 minutes.

Gradually, Midland Red lost its identity. It built its last bus in 1970, by which time it had been absorbed by the National Bus Company, a nationalized behemoth created by Harold Wilson's Labour governments of 1966–70. Coach services were provided by a subsidiary, National Express, which was deregulated in 1988. During National Express years, long-distance coaches were painted white, a bizarre choice given British weather and the grime generated by motorway traffic. Throughout these demoralizing years, Digbeth coach station remained resolutely grim. It was finally rebuilt between 2007 and 2010.

The look and character of central Birmingham changed considerably with the Bull Ring scheme of the early 1960s. It was as if the city wanted to become an urban motorway with the car as king, queen and all princes. Much of this brutal scheme was demolished in the twenty-first century as a new Bull Ring – or Bull Bling – 'regeneration' replaced it.

The M1 is dauntingly busy today. Coaches are restricted to 70 mph. All new cars are absurdly fast, yet their average speeds are risibly low. HS2 trains of the future promise to rush Brummies to Euston in 49 minutes. Leopard-print seat fabrics have never quite caught on again.

FOURTEEN

Milan to Rome: *Il Settebello*

6th–7th October 1966

A busy working day in Milan ends with a tram ride from the Galleria Vittorio Emanuele to the central railway station. It's rush hour. I might have taken a taxi but I like trams, and this two-tone green Type 1500 dating from 1930 brims with character – the throaty growl of its 113-hp electric motor, the ring of its bell, the flashes of electricity from the tip of the trolley pole, and the conductor's *bravura* performance working a capacity crowd of what must be more than a hundred homebound commuters in stylish hats and coats.

In any case, we rumble ahead of queues of cars past La Scala and Via Manzoni with its chic clothes and shoe shops. Through one of the twin arches of the Porta Nuova, a much-rebuilt part of the city's medieval walls, we are buzzed by a swarm of motor-scooters, three-wheeler vans and beetle-like Fiats negotiating Piazza Cavour as, wheels squealing, we turn onto Via Turati. Through a canyon of grand early-twentieth-century apartments, we enter the processional route to Centrale station.

I get off at the stop in Piazza Duca d'Aosta before the station, so I can take stock of this monumental building from a suitable distance. I've heard it described as 'Fascist', and I suppose it is. The foundation stone, I've been told, was laid by King Victor Emmanuel III in 1906, after the opening of the Simplon Tunnel had increased rail traffic from Paris to Milan to well beyond the original station's capacity. It took another six years before a new design – by the gloriously named Florentine architect Ulisse Stacchini – was chosen, and a world war and a further 19 years before this behemoth was opened, by which time, of course, Mussolini was jutting his massive jaw over marble balconies and the heads of braying crowds the length and breadth, if you can call it that, of Italy. Stacchini is said to have described the style of Milano Centrale as 'Assyrian-Lombard'. It's certainly operatic, and built on a Brobdingnagian scale.

Walking towards Stacchini's tour de force, through a cluster of well-maintained civic gardens, I catch sight of the Pirelli Tower, a sleek, slim, concrete and glass skyscraper designed by Gio Ponti – the former editor of *Domus* – and engineered by Pier Luigi Nervi, whose exquisite reinforced concrete hangars for the Regia Aeronautica built between 1935 and 1942 in Orvieto, Orbetello and Torre del Lago were destroyed by retreating Germans before I had any hope of seeing them. The Pirelli Tower is not a copy of an American skyscraper. It is clearly its own design and is, I have to say, a convincing symbol of Italy's much-vaunted 'economic miracle' of the past decade, nurtured in part by the kind of advanced engineering, design and architecture I've witnessed here in Milan.

But, look, its nearly five-thirty. Scurrying through the *porte cochère* and its rank of tiny green and black Fiat Multipla taxis, I make my way through the station's voluminous entrance hall and up a flight of escalators to reach its equally vast concourse, its vaults higher than any cathedral I know. This station is like a town in itself, but time is ticking away and there is no time to explore – although I'm intrigued by the 'royal waiting room' that, sealed from the public, is said to be decorated in swastikas, a leftover from Hitler's putative trip by train to visit the Duce in Milan. He got as far as Rome and Florence.

My train, which will take me via Florence to Rome this evening, is unmistakable. Part plane, part speedboat, part sports car – at least in terms of the way it looks – this is *Il Settebello*, Italy's most glamorous and prestigious train. Studying their watches, my Italian colleagues Giancarlo and Benedetta look up and chorus the word '*Eccolo!*' I'm ushered onto the platform under the steel and glass vaults of Alberto Fava's awe-inspiring train shed, and up on board the magnolia, green and mist-grey air-conditioned express. A white-jacketed steward shows us to our compartment.

A floor-to-ceiling Plexiglas partition slides open, revealing a strikingly stylish room. It seats ten – six on blue-cloth sofas with white antimacassars at either end, and four in moveable blue armchairs with 'flyaway' winged headrests. The steward stows our bags above the seats, in lockers disguised by modish 1950s black-and-white illustrations of Rome. We greet our impeccably coutured and well-groomed fellow passengers, and as we do, the train slides effortlessly out of the station. The time on the platform clocks is 1745, these digits reminding me that while Italy adopted the 24-hour clock in 1893, we British have been slow to follow suit. The military switched over at the end of the Great War, but it was only last summer – when British

Railways began calling itself British Rail – that train timetables ditched the 12-hour clock.

As Benedetta and Giancarlo look for documents we need to discuss on the way to Rome, I peer through the Venetian blinds of the double-glazed windows. Here are earlier electric trains and locomotives, some blunt to the point of being gaunt in terms of styling, others semi-streamlined and dashing, all in shades of grey, green and that coffee or toffee colour prevalent throughout Italian railways. Here, too, are a few well-polished steam locomotives: a pair of class 740 2-8-0s, and half a dozen or so class 835 0-6-0T shunters. Our line south to Rome was electrified in 1934, so we won't be seeing much steam along the way this evening.

Benedetta suggests we go for a cocktail as our seven-car, first class–only *Il Settebello* ETR 301 accelerates through Milan's southern suburbs. Walking along the corridors, I note that all seating is in club-like rooms. Before the bar, there is a well-stocked news stand. I pick up copies of *Corriere della Sera* and *Il Tempo*. 'Don't tell Giancarlo,' whispers Benedetta, dressed in Valentino, as she slips copies of *Grazia* and *Vogue* into her handbag. 'He can be a little serious. He finds the *Economist* flippant.'

Serious, yes, but sat over whiskies at the bar – with its racy murals depicting glamorous women, its attentive staff and, of course, an espresso machine – Giancarlo, a top-drawer aero engineer, is happy to brief me on *Il Settebello*, especially when I tell him this is the first time I've ridden the train. The *Settebello*, he explains, was always meant to be a showcase of the latest Italian design and engineering. Although it seems younger, it dates from 1953, when two seven-car train sets, including ours, were built by Breda in Milan, followed by a third in 1959. Development work began as early as 1947, when Italy had barely emerged from the embers of war.

From a technical viewpoint, the ETR 300 is a development of the record-breaking pre-war ETR 200 that, updated a few years ago, is very much in evidence on the line to Rome today. The difference, aside from being longer and more powerful – our train boasts 12 bogie-mounted traction motors generating 3,040 hp, giving the 364-ton *Settebello* rapid acceleration and a top speed of 93 mph (and considerably more if the civil engineers of the Ferrovia Statale would only allow it) – is in the *Settebello*'s showcase styling.

'When it first ran, and for quite a few years afterwards,' says Benedetta, joining in Giancarlo's tutorial, 'they held fashion shows on the train. The aisle of the restaurant was a catwalk. It was a way of letting passengers – including influential foreigners – see new Italian design in the flesh... and, as you'll soon find out, the restaurant is a way of celebrating Italian cuisine.'

We're thrumming along the flat plain towards Bologna at over 90, the train riding serenely. The ETR 200 – continues Giancarlo, knowing I'm keen on this kind of gen – was developed in the mid-1930s, the shape of the three-car train determined by wind-tunnel tests conducted at Turin Polytechnic. In July '39, ETR 212 ran from Florence to Milan at an average speed of 103 mph, reaching 126 mph on the way. Fervent Fascist journalists claimed that the Duce himself was at the controls, although the driver was, in fact, Alessandro Cervellati, one of the train's regular crew.

So, if it hadn't been for the war, Italy may well have had the world's fastest passenger train, I suggest. 'If it hadn't been for Fascism,' says Benedetta, an architect and industrial designer. 'The story had a very sad ending. Perhaps you know that the ETR 200 was styled by the architect Giuseppe Pagano? It was more than styling, though, as he was closely involved with the wind-tunnel tests in Turin. Pagano was very talented. He designed the wonderful Aeronautics Show pavilions in Milan's Parco Sempione in 1934. And he was the editor of *Casabella*. But in 1942 he renounced Fascism and was arrested and tortured. He escaped prison but was recaptured and sent to Mauthausen extermination camp near Linz. He died there less than a week before Mussolini was executed.'

This seems so very sad that, before we go in to dinner, we walk to the observation saloon at the front of the train and, standing at the back by the coffee bar, we watch – as if in a trance – the rails speeding heedlessly beneath us. The sun has just begun to set as we make our way to the restaurant car, where lively chatter, the smell of delicious food, the playful decor and an inviting table dispel our sadness.

Hungry after a light working lunch – olives and breadsticks for me – with journalists at Bagutta in Milan, I order prosciutto with a capriccio salad, a small mushroom risotto, and veal in white wine with zucchini. We choose a Sanct Valentin Sauvignon from the Alto Adige, with the promise of a Tignanello with my companions' main courses and the cheese and fruit.

Before we eat, the *Settebello* pulls into Bologna – on time, at 1938 hours – 136 miles at an average speed of a shade under 75 mph. I use the five-minute stop to get off and take a good look at the train, while Giancarlo takes the opportunity to make a quick call to Rome using the *Settebello*'s radio-telephone. There is just time to walk to the front and take in the train's sleek and unusual look. The crew sit in a cockpit mounted above the front coach, set back from the rounded nose of the glazed observation saloon. Passengers are seated ahead of the leading bogie. The windows, which curve around the train's nose, are protected from the glare of the setting sun by the kind of festive green and white blinds you might expect to find in an Italian seaside hotel. Inside and out, this special train is a happy marriage between serious engineering and playful design.

Platform speakers crackle and, following a *Pim! Pom! Pam!* fanfare, announce our departure. I step back on and into the cheerful restaurant. Our meal is served as we set out on the mountainous section to Florence. Despite the snaking climb ahead through the Apennines, we're allowed just 56 minutes for the next 60 miles. I suggest we can discuss professional matters between Florence and Rome. Just now, I'm keen to know who designed our train. The styling and the interiors, Benedetta tells me, are the work of the Milanese architect Giulio Minoletti. The name rings a bell.

'Didn't he work on Filippo Zappata's BZ.308?'

'Exactly,' says Benedetta. 'You might have met him?'

'No, but I discussed the 308 with Signor Zappata some years ago in Milan.'

'It was quite a success, no?' says Giancarlo.

Now it's my time for a little lecture. 'By the standards of 1948, Zappata's four-engine airliner was a pretty decent machine. On trials, it happily flew the Atlantic, and with Minoletti's input it should have been popular with passengers. The engines, by the way, were English – 18-cylinder, 2,500-hp Bristol Centaurus radials, the ones powering Hawker Tempests and Sea Furies. Sadly, Breda was able to build only a prototype, despite orders from Italy, Argentina, Persia and India. The Allied Commission and Marshall Aid programme wanted to clip Italy's wings. The Americans didn't want competition for their post-war transatlantic airliners, and had Breda's aeronautical division in their commercial gunsights.'

'What happened to the prototype?' asks Giancarlo.

'Scrapped in Somalia after a collision with a cement lorry in Mogadishu in '54. She was a transport plane for the Regia Aeronautica at the time.'

'Well, it looks as if Minoletti had some bad luck, too,' says Benedetta. 'You know he also worked on the shape and the interiors of the *Andrea Doria*? I mean, this ship was the pride of Italy, launched just six years after the war.'

'She sank, didn't she?'

'Not exactly. She was on perhaps her hundredth crossing from Genoa to New York when she was rammed accidentally off the coast of Nantucket by the *Stockholm*, a Swedish-American liner. Something like fifty passengers were killed. I mean, this wasn't the *Titanic*, but it was the end of a very beautiful ship.'

Despite some setbacks, we agree that Italian design took off and reached the stratosphere some time between the maiden flight of Breda's 308 in '48 and the capsizing of *Andrea Doria* in '56.

As we tuck in to a meal that would credit any top-flight Italian restaurant, between courses we rattle off some memorable

Italian design favourites that have impressed the world in recent years. There's Dante Giacosa's Fiat Cinquecento, Corradino D'Ascanio's Vespa motor-scooter for Piaggio, Cassina chairs, Gio Ponti's Pavia espresso machine, Solari digit clocks by Gino and Nani Valle, Marcello Nizzoli's Lettera 22 typewriter – I have one – 'And,' says Giancarlo, 'the new Ferrari 275 GTB/4. Don't tell me you know it, because it was shown for the first time in public today at the Paris Motor Show. I had what you call a "sneak preview" yesterday before taking the *Cisalpin* to Milan.'

'What's it like?'

'The *Cisalpin*? A very smart six-car Swiss electric.'

'No, I mean the Ferrari.'

'Beautiful. Styled by Scaglietti and with a new four-cam version of the Colombo V12.'

I wonder if Señor Scaglietti is an architect? So many Italian products, like my Olivetti typewriter, are designed by architects. Angelo Mangiarotti and Bruno Morassutti have even designed a chewing-gum dispenser. I'm about to ask Giancarlo when we plunge into a tunnel.

'I have a little present for you,' says Giancarlo. He hands me a real treasure, an official guidebook to the opening of the electric line from Bologna to Florence, open on a page showing a tunnel entrance framed by a grandiloquent stripped classical facade complete with stone fasces, with their bundled rods and axe-heads. 'This is where we are now, the Apennine base tunnel.'

'How long is it?'

'Eighteen and a half kilometres, so about eleven and a half miles. After the Simplon, it was the longest tunnel in the world when it opened in '34. You'll see that. It took twenty years to build.'

'I remember coming to Rome as a student,' I say, 'on the old line across the mountains. Steam then, of course. I think it took two and a half hours from Bologna to Florence.'

'Exactly,' says Giancarlo. 'The new line was quite an achievement, especially for Mussolini who promised...'

'... to make the trains run on time.'

We laugh and clink glasses. 'But, there was something sad, too, of course,' says Benedetta with a half-smile. 'The engineer Giuseppe Bianchi, who did much of the planning of the electrification, was dismissed when his first locomotives and even the ETR 200 were unable to go as fast as the regime wanted. He was sent off to the Ferrovie Nord Milano. It must have been like an exile for him. In any case, the building of this tunnel caused the death of many workers, and many more were to suffer from silicosis.'

I think of the many Bianchi locomotives still very much at work on this line, down to Naples and Sicily and across the Po Valley from Turin to Venice. I think, too, of a fast run from Bologna to Venice 10 or so years ago, when this train of battleship-grey coaches – built like battleships, too, by the look and feel of them – was headed by one of the class 691 Pacifics, Italy's fastest and most powerful steam locos. These were late-1920s, early-1930s rebuilds of a less effective class dating back to before the First War. The engineer in charge of turning the steam equivalent of a silk purse into a sow's ear was Giuseppe Bianchi. I feel a bit sorry for Bianchi. Where the 691s would run up to 90 mph and more, his 1934 electrics struggled to top 80.

Out of the tunnel and down in the dark to Florence, 196 miles from Milan in 174 minutes. I say this out loud, possibly for my companions' benefit. A man in his forties who's been polishing off a solo meal looks across and says, in a distinct New York accent, 'You know a car can be quite a bit faster than this train.'

'Really? How so?'

'Well, five years ago *Quattroruote* magazine set up a race from Rome to Milan between an Alfa Romeo Giulietta Spider and the *Settebello*. The Alfa beat the train to Milano Centrale station by thirty-eight minutes. What do you think of that?'

'Frankly, not too much,' says Benedetta. 'I mean, who would want to drive all that way so fast? And did the driver of the Alfa Romeo enjoy a meal on the way like us? I mean, I have a Giulietta Spider myself, but there's no comparison travelling long-distance between my car and this beautiful train.'

'I guess you have a point. Anyway, I heard you folks talking about the new Ferrari. Now, I'm a motoring journalist and I wondered what you made of Ford trashing Ferrari at Le Mans this year?'

I have a feeling we might be quoted if we get too deep into conversation and I can see serious-minded Giancarlo bristling. Ford's GT40s crossed the chequered flag at Le Mans in June in a very impressive 1-2-3 photo finish. This must have been a shock for Ferrari, who'd won the 24-hour race six times in a row from 1960. Beaten by not one, but three common Fords. Though the winning cars were designed and built in England – Slough, actually – and had about as much in common with a Ford Fairlane as the *Settebello* has with a class 835 0-6-0T shunter.

But the prestige of Italian engineering is certainly being challenged. Its fast FS electric trains like the *Settebello* must seem positively slow to the Japanese, whose Shinkansen bullet trains began racing between Tokyo and Osaka at 130 mph two years ago. The current schedule for the 343-mile trip is 3 hours and 10 minutes, an average speed of 108 mph. Even still, the photographs I've seen of the bullet train interiors suggest that in terms of pure style and creature comfort, the *Settebello* remains hard to beat.

Florence's Santa Maria Novella station is an exceptionally fine modern design, too, yet as we're stopped here for just five minutes, there's no time to reacquaint myself with Giovanni Michelucci's architecture. His station replaced the original, built by Isambard Kingdom Brunel. We pull out ahead of a Rome express waiting in the platform opposite ours. This is the 1648 from Milan. We have caught up and overtaken it.

Finishing our meal, we withdraw to the rear observation saloon, empty now that we're running in the dark. A steward lights a cigarette for Benedetta. Giancarlo orders an espresso. I ask for a J&B. With three hours to go to Rome, we have plenty of time to discuss our meeting tomorrow with the Experimental Flight Department at what we know as Pratica di Mare, Italy's principal military air base at Pomezia, south of Rome. Since 1959, it's been known officially as Colonel Mario de Bernardi airport. Bernardi, who died in '59, was a First War fighter ace. In fact, he was the first Italian pilot to shoot down an enemy aircraft. He went on to compete in the Schneider Trophy, take airspeed records and test Italy's first jet, the Caproni Campini N.1, in August 1940.

I land my bombshell. Our meeting's at 8 a.m., but I plan to leave the hotel just after six to see a building that we might all find interesting and useful. 'It's part of a sulphur extraction plant,' I explain. 'A lightweight demountable structure that might just make a very good hangar for jets parked in secret and fast-moving front-line locations.'

'Who's designed it?' asks Benedetta.

'A young Genoese architect called Renzo Piano.'

'Never heard of him,' says Benedetta. 'But you go and look if you must. The train doesn't get in to Termini until nearly midnight. I plan to get some proper sleep and leave for Pomezia at seven. In any case, we'll have a car waiting for us then.' Giancarlo signals his assent to Benedetta's proposal.

'In that case,' I say, 'I need to ring someone who might just help.'

I get up and make my way to the guard's office and the radio-telephone. My air force friend Colonnello Matteo Lombardi said he would be in Rome until tomorrow. I put a call through to his apartment. Matteo is happy to pick me up on his way to Pratica di Mare tomorrow morning. I re-join my colleagues and we return to our blue saloon, where we read quietly until we feel the gentle if insistent pull of the train's brakes. We're approaching Rome. Announcements over the train's PA system – in Italian, French, English and German – confirm it. We're on time, as the *Settebello* always is. It's 2348 hours.

Walking along past the humming train into the polished concourse, it's easy to see that Termini's architecture is contemporary with the design of the *Settebello*. I refrain from mentioning this as we exit from the station's swooping early

Fifties canopy, and head to the Albergo Mediterraneo just minutes away. My colleagues vanish between busts of Roman emperors and glistening marble vastness towards lifts, rooms and sleep. I decide to stay up for a little longer and to see if the night porter knows anything about its history. He certainly does.

Yes, it's a big hotel all right. Ten storeys and 245 rooms. It was designed by the architect Mario Loreti and built in 1936 for Maurizio Bettoja. The idea was to have a grand and spacious hotel close by Termini station, ready for foreign visitors to the world's fair scheduled to take place in Rome in 1942. So the style of the hotel is very much in keeping with the Mussolini era. The mosaic floor I'm standing on tells the story of Ulysses. At half-twelve and unprepared for a guided tour, I make my excuses and find my room.

At six in the morning, Matteo is waiting. We dart out of the hotel, where his car, a brand-new Lancia Fulvia S1 Coupé, is parked by the kerb on Via Cavour. 'Pretty car,' I say. It is. A trim, lightweight sports car, painted grey with cream leather seats. We crackle away, threading past early-morning trams, ticking off famous monument after famous monument, and within minutes we are buzzing through EUR, Mussolini's monumental extension of Rome to the south of the city centre planned for that world expo that never happened.

Building work proceeded apace after the Duce and his mistress Claretta Petacci had been shot to death in a village on Lake Como; their defaced bodies were strung up by meat hooks from a girder over a half-built Esso petrol station, in Piazzale Loreto near Milan's Centrale station. 'A lot of what

Mussolini planned has been completed by some of the original architects,' says Matteo. 'But not Giuseppe Pagano. He died in Mauthausen.'

'His name came up on the *Settebello* yesterday. He styled the ETR 200 trains.'

'Yes, of course, but with Marcello Piacentini he was also the planner of EUR, where we are now.' The buildings and these imperious streets seem a little less imperious with Nancy Sinatra's hit song 'These Boots Are Made for Walkin'' popping from the Lancia's radio, but when she sings about boots walking all over you, it sounds a bit too close to the days of the Duce for comfort. A strange and somehow empty place, EUR is icily beautiful yet soulless, too. Michelangelo Antonioni caught this feeling well, I think, in his 1962 film *L'Eclisse* starring Monica Vitti and Alain Delon.

We zip out into the wooded hills south of EUR, where if Matteo would slow down for a moment we might well catch sight of wild boar, fallow deer, hares and foxes. Turning towards Pomezia, we find rivers and brooks bubbling with sulphur. Sometimes the water appears to be red. 'Must be the communists doing something to it,' says Matteo. He's joking, I think.

After some wrong tracks, we find the Renzo Piano building. Matteo stops the Lancia. There is no one at work here yet. It's still too early, the sun low in the sky. I walk gingerly across uncertain ground and take photographs of this interesting GRP (glass reinforced plastic) structure with my Leica M3. I still have no idea who owns it or how to find its architect, but Matteo assures me that someone at Pratica di Mare will know something.

We drive into Pomezia, a Mussolini new town built just before the war on reclaimed marshland. The town hall, with its bullish tower and chilly arcade, is like a miniature version of the muscular Neo-Classical monuments of EUR. Then Matteo guns the responsive Lancia towards the air base, from where Mussolini was flown to Vienna in a Heinkel He 111 in September 1943, after his dramatic rescue by German commandoes from the Albergo di Campo Imperatore on Monte Portella, high in the Apennines.

And so to the 8 a.m. meeting. This goes well, and it seems right that Benedetta, Gianfranco and I should celebrate over a good lunch. We certainly know where to go for this. Our car, a gunmetal Fiat 2300 styled by Dante Giacosa, of Fiat Cinquecento fame, purrs us back to Rome and to Termini station. We are in good time to board the 1044 to Milan. This is, of course, the northbound *Il Settebello*, a modern Italian restaurant on rails.

*

Il Settebello last ran as a Trans-Europe Express between Milan and Rome on 2nd June 1984. From 1970, the journey time between the two cities had been cut to 5 hours and 35 minutes, an average speed of 70 mph. The trains continued running to Venice until 1992. After lingering in sidings for 10 years, two of the three were scrapped. The Fondazione FS Italiane, a heritage arm of the Italian State Railways formed in 2013, has since rescued ETR 302 from a yard at Falconara Marittima. Vandalized and caked in graffiti, the train is to be restored at Voghera to its original condition – except for two of its seven coaches, which will be remodelled internally in radical twenty-first-century styles by young Italian designers. ETR 302 will then return to the main line as a luxury train for hire – complete, of course, with fine Italian dining. The ETR 200s, rebuilt in 1960, ran until 1993.

Renzo Piano's sulphur extraction plant at Pomezia has long gone. The architect became world-famous for the design and construction of the Pompidou Centre, Paris in the 1970s (with Richard Rogers and Peter Rice). The monumental Albergo Mediterraneo is much as it was.

New high-speed *Frecciarossa* trains running on new tracks sprint from Milan to Rome non-stop in under three hours, or just over three and a half hours with stops at Bologna and Florence. The latest trains feature interiors by the architect Aldo Cingolani of Bertone Design, well known in the past for styling cars for, among others, Fiat, Ferrari and Lancia. The 1966 Lancia Fulvia Coupé, a prized classic car today, was designed in-house by Piero Castagnero. The world's longest railway tunnel is now the Gotthard Base Tunnel through the Swiss Alps. Opened in June 2016, it is 35½ miles long.

In Milan, you can lunch at an unchanged Baguta restaurant in the company of newspaper journalists, while Centrale station is well maintained and as dauntingly impressive as ever. Piazzale Loreto is unrecognizable from the way it was in 1945. On 18th April 2002, a Rockwell Commander 112 aircraft flew into the Pirelli Tower. It was an accident. The pilot and two people inside the tower were killed. The building has been restored, but Pirelli has gone, the company's presence replaced by commercial office space. Type 1500 trams are still busy at work.

FIFTEEN

The Black Mountains and Elan Valley: Jaguar Mk 2

8th–10th June 1993

Our emotional maps of the world coincide with those shown in atlases or lit up on computer screens. They diverge far from them, too. Things of diversions and elision, of sudden close focus, of lucent fragments and elusive distances, they can never be set down and laid out in a rational manner.

The Stokenchurch Gap, where the M40, bounding west after the climb to High Wycombe, scythes through a high chalk cutting, is a deep wound in the Chilterns landscape. And yet how I revel in the way it squeezes and narrows the focus of an enticing sun-laced evening view of Oxfordshire between its white flanks. It seems natural to nudge another few hundred revs from my lithe Jaguar and to feel the big-hearted car bound towards a landscape spelling both familiarity and freedom.

And how the car leaps along the roaring concrete. Of course she should. I have invested hard-earned money, emotions, dreams and considerable patience in reversing an ageing process so that, no longer an oil-dribbling mechanical dotard, 64 UAR has become a sleek gunmetal express belying its 30 years.

This 3.8-litre Mk 2 Jaguar is for driving – quarter-lights open, 'overdrive' signed in lit green letters above the thin steering wheel, a purposeful growl from the stainless-steel exhaust pipes, and the deep purr of her six-cylinder twin-cam engine, a motor that in lighter, wind-cheating sports-racing cars led Jaguar to victory at Le Mans three times in succession in the 1950s.

No power steering, no electric windows, no air con. No need for music. The car's mechanical soundtrack is its own ode to joy. We – the Jag and I – sweep down into Oxfordshire, bypassing the city, skirting dearly remembered Otmoor villages and ambling through honey-coloured Woodstock, and ride out onto the kind of road she was built for, even more than early motorways.

This is the A44, with its fast sections, slow bits, and hints of soulful houses and dreamy gardens – Chastleton, Sezincote, Snowshill, Hidcote; its snaking drop and climb to Broadway, demanding fourth gear rather than overdrive and even a brush on the firm brake pedal; and the dash down through the Vale of Evesham to Worcester's game of roundabouts. Soil reddening, we're on to Hereford. A nod to the cathedral and out through Clehonger and Vowchurch to a sunset Golden Valley following the River Dore. The Normans mistook the Welsh *dwr* ('water') for *d'or* ('gold').

In years gone by, I would have turned at Dorstone for Cusop, where Penelope Betjeman lived at New House – which was anything but – with Bracken the donkey in the clovery meadow behind, but in 1986 she went up a mountain in Himachal Pradesh leading a tour and died. So I nudge the Jaguar on to

Hay-on-Wye and into the car park at the back of The Old Black Lion, an inn where Cromwell really did sleep. I drink a pint of beer before sinking into a bath.

Before breakfast, I do those things you must do daily with a Jag of a certain age. Lift the bonnet. Check the coolant, oil and tyre pressures. Plan on refuelling. If I have one beef with this glorious car, it's the 12-gallon fuel tank. She's done well to get from London to Hay without running dry. I imagine Penelope joining me and, talking non-stop, diverting my attention from mechanical matters. Who would want her to stop? Penelope was enormous fun, her spirit as young and playful as it had been in the 1930s. What she took me to see one weekend in the early 1980s has stayed with me ever since. The Elan Valley. I hadn't known it before, and this, for Penelope, was thrilling.

We were going to drive in the Jag, but this was before she was restored. While she made it to Hay, she blew not one but two tyres in and around Cusop. I would have had to wait for a spare. So we headed north in a small car driven by one of Penelope's 'old ladies', the sort who thought nothing of walking halfway across the Himalayas to take in an obscure temple or two with Penelope as their guide. We had barely got on to the road towards Builth Wells when Penelope said how hungry she was. 'Can we stop for some chocklit?' And, when we got to Llandrindod Wells, we were forced to try the revolting rotten-egg spa water while Penelope laughed like a donkey between mouthfuls of 'chocklit eclairs'.

Today, I drive quietly, taking a backwater road, the B4567, and negotiating wandering lambs, ferns, heather, bracken and

– I was going to say cattle grids, but these must be for sheep. There is no traffic and just the whisper of a breeze insinuating its way through the quarter-lights; well, that and the raucous call of morning crows. I stop in Victorian Llandrindod Wells – a town that feels as if it has been shipped lock, stock and timber gable from the North Wales coast – neither to take the water nor to eat eclairs, but to find out what treatments were on offer here in the spa's heyday between the coming of the railway in the 1860s, with its connections to Swansea in the south and Shrewsbury across the border to the north, and the First World War. It was these treatments that brought so many Victorians and Edwardians to this remote town and gave Llandrindod Wells its special character.

In 1900, you could visit the High Street baths for a spinal sulphur douche, a carbonic acid bath, a Tribune Scotch douche or even a Fango radioactive mud treatment. They must have been made of stern stuff a century ago. I think I'd prefer a chocolate eclair.

Just north of Llandrindod Wells, there is a sign to the Elan Valley. What I hadn't known the first time I came here is that my then 'unknown' valley has long been a huge draw for holidaymakers; not from London I suspect, but – more likely – from the metal-bashing Midlands. I say this because the 70-square-mile Elan Valley is one great water supply for Birmingham.

This sounds strange at first and then more than a little unfair. Did the Welsh really give up what I think is 45,000 acres of rural splendour to slake the thirst of and wash Brummies living five counties and 70 miles away? They did, although they had no choice in the matter. And yet, what might seem like an outrage has served central Wales well ever since. The landscape, which I adore and find solace in, is preserved *because* it is one giant water supply for Birmingham. Yes, there are tens of thousands of sheep here spread across a landscape as seemingly remote as the Russian steppes or the great Mongolian plains. There are red kites overhead, as there have been since 1989, when several were released over the Stokenchurch Gap. Kestrels, merlins and peregrines, too. Some 27 species of butterfly, 17 kinds of dragonflies and damselflies, eight species of orchid, and ferns, heather, gorse, bracken and mosses as far as the eye can see. But very few people.

Once, Elan Village teemed with people. This was during the period of the mighty construction work undertaken here between 1893 and 1904 (when King Edward VII and Queen Alexandra declared the scheme open), and millions of gallons of soft Welsh water flowed slowly by gravity from four new dams and through an ambitious aqueduct all the way to a reservoir on the edge of Birmingham, a city whose population was growing at a prodigious and thirsty rate. There are those who have never forgiven Birmingham.

The flooding of the Elan Valley meant the death by drowning of eighteen farms, a school, a church – they say that on a quiet day you can hear the bells ring – and three manor houses.

Since my first visit, I've read – in Birmingham's central library, a characterful concrete brute of a building – that the poet Percy Bysshe Shelley wanted to rent his Uncle Thomas's handsome home, Cwm Elan; and, when he was refused, he tried to rent another fine house, Nantgwyllt. This was to become home for George Yourdi, the engineer in charge of constructing the Elan Valley dams. It was demolished when the Caban Coch dam was nearing completion. Shelley, of course, drowned in the Gulf of La Spezia shortly before his 30th birthday.

This is all a bit sad, so it's time to slip behind the wheel of the Jag and purr gently around the Edwardian road that links one dam to the next. The first is Caban Coch, looking for all of Wales like some perfectly controlled waterfall. The sound is exhilarating. Caban Coch, though, is simply an introduction to the glories that lie higher up the valley. Here's Garreg Ddu, a dam attended by the Foel Tower, with echoes of Nicholas Hawksmoor's circular mausoleum at Castle Howard. This is the tower that controls the flow of water into the Elan aqueduct. What I see of it, though – as with the dam wall – is just the top of a structure that, elegant throughout, is rooted deep below the surface.

Up again to Pen y Garreg, a stone-faced dam crowned with what appears to be either a medieval knight's helmet or, as I draw closer, a small rotunda in the Birmingham Baroque style, representing the manufacturing city at its Edwardian best. I stop and get out of the car. It might be June, but I know that, on average, rain falls over the Elan Valley 275 days each year. I look and listen to the cascade of water pounding over the dam wall. This is very much by design. James Mansergh was the inspired Birmingham city engineer who made this enormous scheme possible. He wanted to shape something that was beautiful as well as efficient. The dams were to enhance the landscape, not to destroy it. And how Mansergh and his team succeeded.

The dams are powerful and poetic, abounding in latent and expressed energy. The valley is viscerally beautiful, life-enhancing. And there's still the top dam to come, Craig Goch, its largely sunken wall supporting a great curved arcade; on top of this, the road runs, and below it the water unleashes a cavalry charge of H2O. I walk out and up from the narrow winding road, to eat a picnic lunch and let the landscape do all the talking I need. The high-pitched screams of patrolling kites and the rush of water, softened at this height, are nature's conversation. Very often, this makes more sense than the things people say, with all their guiles and reckless play.

I drive on, eager to find the mountain road leading from the Elan Valley to Devil's Bridge once again. This is surely one of Britain's great roads... Wild. Chased by fast black water – the blackness from slate channels rather than Dylan Thomas's Bible. There are no chapels near, or haven't been for a very long time. There is evidence, of course, of lead mining at Cwmystwyth. This, presumably, is why this unlikely road was built. I like its sudden twists, dips and the uncertain cambers around steep ledges. The Jag must be nursed along. Her steering is not the quickest, while her tail can easily hang out on slippery roads. But what fun to drive in old-fashioned style, knowing that the engine will never run out of puff and that Dunlop discs, should I need them, are exactly as they should be, strong and progressive. Much as I love walking, this is a road better driven. The landscape is big and unyielding. There is nowhere to hide from either the year-round rain or long bursts of summer sun.

After 25 miles, I come to Devil's Bridge, where I drink tea at the Hafod Hotel, an enormous 'Swiss cottage' and a fascinating example of an early-nineteenth-century hotel for tourists in search of the sublime – if not the devil whose name is attached to any number of venerable bridges across Europe. The stories underpinning these tend to end with a poor dog going to hell instead of some baggage who tricks Lucifer. While I'd like to scuttle down the 600 or so devilish slate steps by the side of the bridge – and back up again, to stand at the foot of a vertiginous waterfall – I'm after something else here. I can't resist the allure of steam, and minutes from the hotel is the inland terminus of the Vale of Rheidol Railway.

The last train of the day is leaving for Aberystwyth and the Irish Sea. A mix of seven open-sided and enclosed chocolate and cream carriages huddle behind No. 7 *Owain Glyndwr*, one of the line's sturdy 2-6-2 tank locomotives, three of which were built by the Great Western Railway's Swindon works in the early 1920s. Although the gauge of the track is just 1 foot, 11¾ inches, *Owain Glyndwr* is 8 feet wide, so she has a powerful, broad-shouldered appearance true to her doughty abilities. I won't go down by train to Aberystwyth today, as there would be no easy way back. I have no interest in sitting in the back of a minicab – and, in any case, the joy of this narrow-gauge railway is that it runs through a landscape, clinging to a ledge for much of the run, along a valley where roads are invisible.

I have come back the other way by train, though. The beauty of the landscape and the beat of the locomotive as it commands the long 1-in-50 gradient from the water stop at Aberffrwd all the way up to Devil's Bridge are unalloyed joys. It could hardly be further from the cares of London, and yet the railway – opened in 1902 to fetch and carry felled timber, lead ore and tourists, too – was engineered by James Weeks Szlumper. He worked for many railways, including the Great Northern, Piccadilly and Brompton (London Transport's Piccadilly Line), while busy here in the Rheidol Valley.

I watch the train steam sure-footedly down the incline west from Devil's Bridge before firing up the Jag. Cantering back to Rhayader at the foot of the Elan Valley, the evening sun casts an elongated shadow of the curvaceous car far in front of her leaping Jaguar mascot. On through Builth Wells I come to Clyro, where I pull up outside the Church of St Michael and All Angels.

This was Francis Kilvert's haunt. The Victorian diarist was curate here. The small church was rebuilt top-to-toe in the early 1850s, in a vague Decorated Gothic style. Thomas Nicholson, diocese architect of Hereford, was in charge. He did much of the planning of Llandrindod Wells. Inside, Nicholson has left the Georgian box pews. In winter, these must have been a comfort to Kilvert's poor parishioners. And here on a wall is the curate himself, an old photograph of a young man, and beside it a plaque dedicated, in indifferent lettering, to 'THE REV. R. F. KILVERT, M.A. THE DIARIST CURATE OF THIS PARISH 1865–1872'.

Poor Kilvert. He fell in love with Frances Thomas, whose father, the vicar of nearby Llanigon, felt the curate insufficiently rich. He wasn't rich in the slightest. 'On this day', he wrote, 'when I proposed for the girl who will I trust one day be my wife I had only one sovereign in the world, and I owed that.' After being rejected, he made this entry in his diary: 'The sun seemed to have gone out of the sky.' Much as he cared for his parishioners and loved this part of the world, he left and never came back. Years later he did marry, but died of peritonitis ten days after the wedding.

'Fond of local history, then?' asks an elderly man in a beige windcheater, beige slacks, and beige shoes fastened by Velcro. I hadn't been aware of him. 'It's not just Kilvert in Clyro, you see. We had Sherlock Holmes, too, you know.'

'Conan Doyle?'

'Same fellow, isn't it? He used to stay at Clyro Court on the Baskerville estate. That's how he came up with *The Hound of the Baskervilles*.'

'I see.'

'It's a fine old place, but they have the disco there now. It's a hotel, you see.'

'A disco?'

'Call it a rave, they do, you see. It would scare the life out of any hound this side of hell.'

I make my excuses. Clyro, with its rave and disco, seems suddenly ordinary and – for that beige, windcheating moment – as if it is hard to escape thumping, whooping metropolitan noise. I suppose that local people didn't like the noise of Lancaster bombers, either, as they roared perilously low over Nant y Gro dam in preparation for Operation Chastise, the attack on the Ruhr dams by No. 617 Squadron in May 1943 using Barnes Wallis's bouncing bombs.

In the morning, with the Jag's two-inch SU carburettors hissing as she warms to the climb, I go up from Hay and then down past Hay Bluff into the Gospel Pass. I first came this way with my school friend Bernard Johnson. We stayed at The Old Black Lion and found it funny that they served us a London bistro meal – *bœuf bourguignon* – rather than something Welsh, which I suppose we had been hoping to find. The next day, we walked 25 miles to Abergavenny on the edge of the Black Mountains. We were in search of Capel-y-ffin, the abandoned Victorian monastery that was home to Eric Gill and his community of craft workers in the 1920s. This was some years before Fiona MacCarthy published her sensational 1989 biography of Gill, reintroducing the stone carver and letterer as a sexual predator, paedophile and all-round pervert. No one was safe, it seemed, when this priapic monster was at large, not even, as MacCarthy revealed, the family dog.

I had known Gill's work and even his name from childhood, without knowing anything about him – from his Stations of the Cross in Westminster Cathedral and from the Gill Sans lettering and numerals used by the London and North Eastern Railway and, in my own time, by British Railways. I could say 'Gill Sans' as I could 'Johnston' without being able to put a face or even the most basic biography to the name. Fond of railways before I could speak, I remember being amused and feeling guilty in equal measure for thinking of King's Cross and Gresley A4s or Waterloo and Bulleid Pacifics rather than holy things when priests, acolytes, incense, the *Stabat Mater* and the colour purple conspired to lament the sufferings of Christ during long weekly Stations of the Cross during Lent. 'The next station...' the celebrant would intone, '... is Clapham Junction, change for Purgatory,' I'd think. And while I never noted down or under-scored locomotive numbers, I liked looking at the numerals themselves. Their names, too.

During boring meetings, I still find myself doodling numbers in approximations to Johnston and Gill Sans. These conjure names – *Prince Palatine, City of London, Drysllywn Castle, French Line CGT, Meg Merrilies* – that in turn spark flutters of unrelated and inconsequential memories. *Drysllywn Castle* flashing from Bristol to London in 93 minutes and at over 100 mph. *French Line CGT* and SS *Normandie*, an ocean liner I can only dream of travelling on, and *Meg Merrilies*:

> *But every morn of woodbine fresh*
> *She made her garlanding,*
> *And every night the dark glen Yew*
> *She wove, and she would sing.*

And, Keats, in turn, leads me on to yearn for a glass of vintage:

> *... that hath been*
> *Cool'd a long age in the deep-delvèd earth,*
> *Tasting of Flora and the country green,*
> *Dance and Provençal song, and sunburnt mirth!*

Even then, as I drop down to fourth from overdrive to climb close by Lord Hereford's Knob, I feel shifty for entertaining the silly schoolboy thought that wine tasting of Flora – marge, not butter – could have been worth a line of Keats's exquisite verse.

Driving alone, it's easy to drift like this, and a good thing, too, allowing time away from more pressing thoughts. Here's

Capel-y-ffin, the monastery, with its white rendered walls, slate roofs and lancet windows. Tainted, perhaps, because of Fiona MacCarthy's exposé, and yet the country here is special and the monastery sits serenely within this deep glaciated valley adorned with trees: now in sun, now in shadow, and suggesting – more than retreat – spiritual as well as physical freedom.

Leaving the Jag, I walk down to the Church of St Mary, built in the mid-eighteenth century from the foundations of an earlier structure. The Virgin Mary has been busy here over the centuries, appearing in a burning bush, in a red gown and even running across a field. Her church at Capel-y-ffin is a tiny affair but is silent and near numinous today, the only sound a raven clearing its throat and a clacking of jackdaws. Inside, my eye is drawn, as it has been before, to the clear west window. Gill has engraved these words: 'I will lift up mine eyes unto the hills from whence cometh my help'. And the view through the window is of the hills. Time to head upwards to find, if not salvation, then inspiration, perhaps.

A steep bridle path leads up from behind the nineteenth-century farmhouse beyond the monastery and its ruined Victorian abbey church. The farm is a pony-trekking centre, but I'm light on my feet and can manage happily on just the two of them. On a ridge, a path leads inexorably south, and this, I think, will take me to Llanthony Priory. There is, though, a second path, pointing higher up the Black Mountains. The day is fine. Accompanied by occasional ravens and raucous crows, I keep on going. And, what a discovery. No one had told me there was a reservoir up here, and that can only be a dam in the distance.

It is a brooding, stone-faced dam, cousin by the look of it to the Elan Valley wonders, complete with a roundhouse – plainer than Penn y Garreg or Craig Goch; not quite Baroque – and a path leading to it. It's so strange. Water gushes down to rocks far below, and yet from the other side of the ridge silence reigns. Stranger still is the fact that the dam and reservoir appear to be neglected. Has this fairy-tale place been forgotten? Am I dreaming?

No, it's real enough. I lean on the railings that seem secure and take in immense and unfamiliar views. Who built this, and why? Where does the water from the reservoir go? I have no idea, but aim to find out. I'm not thinking about time, but I am getting hungry. Back to the lower ridge I walk, speeding up as I go, for two hours with the ruins of Llanthony beyond, below and now firmly in view. I love this feeling of walking briskly across high ground. For a moment I'm footloose in the foothills of the Himalayas. No wonder Penelope lived among the Black Mountains.

Down across dark shallow streams, over stiles and through sheep fields, saying hello to a pair of collies and on to the road at Llanthony. The Half Moon is closed. Open at six. I try the Priory Hotel, shoehorned into the medieval ruins. A lady with a mop listens to my predicament. Ten minutes later, a cup of tea and a cheese sandwich appear. 'You've been here before, haven't you?' she says. 'With the fancy cars.' She's quite right.

For a spell in the 1980s, I was motoring correspondent for *Tatler*. Mark Boxer hired me. Jonathan Meades and Alexandra Shulman were features editors. It was, to say the least, great fun. Not just the writing, but the invitations, parties and general play. And I could borrow pretty much any new car I wanted to. Which is why I came this way in a succession of cars I would never dream of owning, even if I could have afforded to. A 200-mph Ferrari F40. An imperious Bentley Turbo R. A wildly sculptural Lamborghini Countach LP5000 QV, which I had to back down a narrow lane leaning on the door sill with the suicidal driver's door open at a crazy angle – the rear view was all but non-existent – as an unyielding farmer on a big green tractor and with livid eyes inched towards me. He would have saved himself a lot of time if he'd backed into an opening mere yards behind him, but that wasn't the point. How could I tell him that this operatic machine wasn't mine and that, in any case, I wouldn't buy one for all the water in the Elan Valley.

It's a local farmer, though, who gives me a lift back to Capel-y-ffin in a dusty grey Land Rover with the two boisterous collies I met earlier. I ask about the dam. 'Grwyne Fawr. One of the wife's great uncles worked on it, see? I think it opened in 1928, or was it '32? They built a village for the workers and there was a little railway that ran from the main line at Llanvihangel all the way up.'

'They should have kept it.'

'But there're not many people here, except in the summer holidays when you get walkers like yourself and campers and the Dutch people in the motor homes. They make it impossible to get through the valley. Should be illegal.'

'But where does the water go?'

'It's not for drinking anymore. They've let it go. A great pity. But it was for the Valleys, you see, for the miners and steelworkers. All gone or on the way out.'

Mention of Llanvihangel reminds me that Eric Gill lived in the Black Mountains for just a short while because, although the isolation suited him and the hills are hauntingly beautiful, he needed to ship sculptures to clients in London and the trek to the Great Western station, closed thirty-five years ago, proved impractical. He resettled near High Wycombe.

At Capel-y-ffin, I make my thanks to farmer and dogs, and slide back into the Jag. Fuel on. Choke on. Window wound down. Turn the key. Press the starter button. Hiss. *Whoomph.* Engage second gear. Drop the fly-off handbrake. Feed the wheel slowly through my hands, and so back to Llanthony, where I stay tonight in the room at the top of the tower. Alone and out of season, yet in a familiar landscape that somehow wants to give me wings. I soar to sleep with a kaleidoscope of images playing through my mind's eye: of cascading water, high mountain tracks, Indian temples, engineering magnificence, twisting roads, wayside chapels, enfolding valleys and choco-late eclairs.

*

Penelope Betjeman died in Himachal Pradesh in 1986. Since then, New House has been 'sympathetically renovated' and extended, so it is nothing like it was in Penelope and Bracken's day. Bracken went to live with Penelope's much-loved and delightfully funny daughter, Candida, in rural Berkshire. Candida died, far too early, in 2014. Mark Boxer, founding editor of the *Sunday Times* colour supplement in 1962, was a witty and charming editor. He died in 1988, aged just 57, from a brain tumour.

Llanthony Priory Hotel thrives, smarter than it was in 1993, yet still full of character. The top room remains, although some guests complain of having to climb sixty steps around a spiral stair to reach it. And of having to climb back down – though not all the way – to the lavatory at night.

The remote Grwyne Fawr dam seems more neglected than ever, but – 20 years in the making – its structure is, hopefully, strong and resilient. A great-granddaughter of Eric Gill owns and runs the Grange Trekking Centre at Capel-y-ffin. Accommodation is not exactly five-star, but the rides are unforgettable. The monastery has been divided into self-catering holiday flats. Eric Gill's reputation has never really recovered from Fiona MacCarthy's biography.

Bernard Johnson is a talented stone carver and letter cutter based in a former pigsty in Oxfordshire. Clyro Court is still home to discos. The first part of British Railways to have been privatized, the Vale of Rheidol steams on. *Owain Glyndwr* is 95 years young.

The Elan Valley remains magnificent, at its romantic best out of season. Llandrindod Wells is despoiled by some horrid new housing today. It deserves better. The Stokenchurch Gap – once white – is almost green.

SIXTEEN

London to Fort William:
West Highlander

8th–9th March 1995

The BBC's Michael Fish promises rain, snow, ice, wide-spread frost and strong gales, especially in Scotland. Judging by the bite in the wind as I walk towards Euston station this evening, I have a feeling that, this time, the moustachioed weatherman might just be right. For the railways, these are certainly stormy times. John Major's government is mustard keen on their messy privatization, while there is no indication from Labour's new leader, Tony Blair, that the party – if it comes to power, as the opinion polls strongly suggest it will at the next election – is prepared to fight this idiocy.

I'm here this evening, though, because British Rail – evidently no guarantor of a national railway in public service – has announced plans to kill off the *West Highlander*, the portion of the *Royal Highlander* sleeping-car and motorail express that detaches north of the border for Fort William, while the principal section braves the gale-blasted heights of Drumochter (1,454 feet) for Aviemore and Inverness. My plan is to ride the sleeper from Euston to Fort William and write the story for the *Independent*, where I'm a features writer, architecture and design editor, comment page writer, and jack of all trades short of cleaning the carpets and manning the canteen – both of which I'd be happy to do, given more hours in the day, to keep this truly independent national paper on the go and true to its principles. I'm sure many of my highly likeable colleagues feel much the same way.

When I was asked eight years ago by Andreas Whittam Smith, the *Independent*'s founding editor, if I'd like to come for a chat with him at the paper's City Road office, I took my dog, William – a beautiful, curly-haired mongrel – with me. William jumped up on Andreas's black leather sofa and fell asleep. Deciding it was the best policy to let a sleeping dog lie, the editor wheeled in a swivel chair. After some minutes of polite conversation, he looked at his watch and said, 'Goodness, it's... ten to five. Would you like a whisky?' His parting shot when he left to 'put the paper to bed', a task that sounded so nursery-snug, was: 'If you'd like to join us, I would add that there's just one thing you must bear in mind. I'll want you to write to your enthusiasms.'

Which is why I've boarded the sleeper berthed at Euston's platform 15 and settled myself – dogless tonight but with a single malt to hand – on a black leather sofa that is very much like my editor's was at City Road. Times, though, have changed. Today, the *'Indie'* is slotted into the 18th floor of the soulless, stainless steel–clad Canary Wharf Tower and we're on to our second editor, Ian Hargreaves, whose features editor Charlie Leadbeater has just launched a clever and funny new column, 'The Diary of Bridget Jones' by Helen Fielding.

Somehow, I think Bridget Jones marks the real end of the Eighties, as has the collapse, a fortnight ago, of Barings Bank, a venerable and seemingly rock-solid City institution blown down like a house of cards by Nick Leeson, a rogue trader. I can't help feeling, as at 8.25 p.m. we pull out of Euston, that the brave new world of privatized everything – what next, public parks, the Royal Mail, the air we breathe? – will be something like the spectacle of Barings but splashed dodgily across an even bigger canvas.

I move to one of the tables in the lounge car as the polite skirmish for these begins. I order a half-bottle of Rioja and try to decide between two curious Scottish dainties, chicken tikka masala and rice (£3.99) and Thai-style vegetables (£3.45). The curry wins as I open my notebook and realize that in my 'Fleet Street' rush to get to the train, I haven't been able to check the identity of the locomotive at the head of our heavyweight, 16-coach, air-conditioned express. I'm pretty sure it'll be one of the 36 5,000-hp class 87 electrics built by British Rail at Crewe 20 years ago. Though veritable boxes on wheels, unnamed and with no concessions to styling, they are powerful, fast and reliable machines. I like the story Colonel Hugh Rogers, author of several fine books on British and French steam locomotives, told of 'Robin' Riddles, who had been appointed the Railway Executive member for mechanical and electrical engineering on the formation of the new state-owned British Railways in 1948. Riddles was offered a ride in the cab of a new class 87 shortly after the completion of the electrification of the West Coast Main Line I'm riding now all the way from Euston to Glasgow. Rogers asked Riddles what the electric was like. 'I didn't really notice,' Riddles replied, 'the driver was an old steam man and we talked about steam engines all the time.'

I ask the Glaswegian steward if he might know what the engine is. 'I shouldn't say,' he confides as he uncorks my wine bottle and fills my glass, 'but I'm a secret railway enthusiast. The management would sack me if they knew. It's all about business today, not trains. But yes, it's an '87. The loco I mean' – he adds with a grin – 'not the wine.'

The lounge car is full now. Highland ramblers and would-be Eddie the (golden) Eagles clad in multicoloured mountain jackets mix with a group of Italian students – I know they must be Italians even before I hear them speak, because one is wearing a red jester's hat, compulsory headgear (or so it seems) on campuses from Turin to Taranto. Also on board are a self-consciousness of prime City bankers shoehorned into brand-new tweeds and creaseless brogues – presumably on their way north to blast away at fallow bucks and roe does at the tail end of the season – working men in heavy shoes and lumberjack shirts, two country ladies, and a man in a well-worn if well-cut suit and cape who asks if he might join me at my chrome-legged table for two.

I pour him a glass of Rioja. 'Thank you. I'll order another bottle. On your way to Fort William?'

'I am. Writing up the story of the threat to the sleeper.'

'For whom, if you don't mind me asking?'

'The *Independent*.'

'I see. Well, that's all to the good.'

My companion, a genuine Highland laird, though lacking a Sherlock Holmes hat – the combined *Royal* and *West Highlander* is nicknamed the 'Deerstalker Express' – tells me about the torchlight parade held in Fort William a fortnight ago in protest against the threatened withdrawal of the *West Highlander*.

He was in town to attend a meeting of the newly constituted Friends of the West Highland Line. The group has friends, he says, in high places, and disputes the government's figure – leaked to the press by the Office of Passenger Rail Franchising – of a £453-per-head deficit. The real figure is more like £43. But, in any case, the line has never made money. When it opened on 7th August 1894, a reporter for the *Glasgow Evening News* wrote, 'for mile upon mile of its length, not a single vestige of human life is to be seen. Its very stations are simply names – oases in barren moorland. A paying traffic must be a matter of slow growth.'

I have this quote written down in my notebook, along with the words of Alan Kirk, a Fort William restaurateur and unpaid head of the Fort William tourist board. I relay them to my companion. Putting down the *West Highlander*, Mr Kirk says, is the thin edge of a wedge that will lead to the closure of the line. The next thing will be a reduction in daytime trains – currently three daily in each direction, as there have been since 1894. 'The fewer the services, the higher the marginal cost of each surviving train, the greater the subsidy needed and the more ruinous-looking the account for the line.'

While it is easy to see, as we rumble through the blind depths of Kilsby Tunnel south of Rugby, why some future private railway company would be only too happy to get shot of the West Highland – a public service since day one – it is equally difficult to understand why the line has been so little marketed. It serves one of the most sublime landscapes, not just of Scotland or of the British Isles, but of Europe and perhaps even the world. Every year, legions of visitors head this way to walk the glens, to climb Ben Nevis and its attendant peaks, and to take bonny boats over the sea to Skye and a rosary of other enticing west-coast islands. They come to shoot and ski and to revel in a natural world like no other. There is no airport here, and roads – slippery and even impassable in winter – are slow. The one sure and comforting way to reach the West Highlands is by train, which ferries cars too, for those unwilling to face the long and sometimes grumpy motorway grind from southern England to the Scottish Lowlands.

There are people who make their way to Fort William simply to ride the summer steam trains that, revived in 1984, take passengers up and down steep gradients, and around severe twists and improbable bends, and over the curving Glenfinnan Viaduct overlooking the length of Loch Shiel, to the port of Mallaig, and so to Skye, 42 miles north-west. This extension of the West Highland Railway, a triumph of civil engineering making considerable use of concrete, opened in 1901.

It was at Glen Shiel, some miles north of Mallaig, that Dr Samuel Johnson, making his way to Skye in the early autumn of 1773, decided that his adventure by carriage, horseback and boat in company with James Boswell – his amanuensis and future biographer – must be written up in the form of a book. Published two years later, Dr Johnson's *A Journey to the Western Islands of Scotland* sold well, as did Boswell's *A Journal of a Tour to the Hebrides*, published soon after his friend's death in 1784.

Both books are in my overnight bag. Together, they did

much to promote travel – or 'to make journeys of curiosity', according to Johnson's famous dictionary published in 1755 – in the Highlands. Up until the arrival of the West Highland line, operated and owned from 1908 by the North British Railway, the landscape and, to a remarkable extent, the way of life were little changed from Johnson's day, although by then the view of the region had been romanticized by the popular novels of Walter Scott and the sentiments of Victorians – not least, of course, the long-lived Queen herself.

Johnson's view of the Highlands was ebullient and damning in consecutive sentences. The landscape was at once beautiful and sublime. The inhabitants of Iona, though, were 'remarkably gross'. Gaelic was the language of 'a barbaric people who had few thoughts to express', and oats something the 'Scotch' ate and the English fed to their horses. Boswell encountered people as 'black and wild' as 'American savages'. Or, as Johnson wrote of Highlanders:

> Till the Union [between Scotland and England that took effect in 1707, two years before Johnson's birth] made them acquainted with English manners, the culture of their lands was unskilful, and their domestic life unformed; their tables were coarse as the feasts of Eskimeaux, and their houses filthy as the cottages of Hottentots.

Long days in the saddle over difficult terrain might have strained Johnson's humour. He was then in his sixties, and far from being in good health. And how else might his mood be when he rode down to Glenelg after a long day high in the hills and put up at the local inn? Its beds were filthy, and because there was nothing else on offer, Johnson 'had a lemon and a piece of bread, which supplied me with my supper'.

I have been daydreaming while my lairdly companion has gone to his berth to make a call on his mobile phone. I wonder if I will yet feel pressed to rent one? My companion's seat has been temporarily occupied by a Scotsman with straggling hair and a brown and orange ribbed jumper who appears to have swayed straight out of the pages of Boswell and Johnson. As we slow for Crewe he makes it whisky-clear that he's heard enough this evening about the virtues of the sleeper.

'I can do this journey much quicker by car,' he says, challenging me and a steward preparing meals in the galley kitchen behind me. 'What's so special about the train, then?' The steward asks why he's on the train tonight and not in his car. Ordering another wee bottle he explains, 'Aw, ye don't understand,' then gets up and reels away in a haze of alcohol that might just power a diesel locomotive.

'You must meet some characters,' I suggest to Ken Lightfoot, the chief steward tonight, as he bustles amiably through the car.

'Tell me about it,' he says. 'The times I've been asked to write a book about it, I can't tell you.' He doesn't tell me.

It seems a good time to retire to my berth. It's well past 11 and, before things get too hazy, I'd like to finish Boswell and Johnson and read more of the history of the West Highland line.

Tonight the train is busy, so I'm braving a shared berth. The lower bunk barely contains the frame of a brawny man who looks up for a moment and says hello in an accent that conjures Connemara. He's a builder, he tells me, on his way to work on a project near Fort William. Been using the sleeper for four years. 'Four vodkas and a good night's kip – that's the way. You can't do that on a plane or in a car, can you?'

But even before I've replied from the crush of my top berth, he's miles away. I've hung up my jacket, scarf and coat, and placed my shoes by the *funny little basin you're supposed to wash your face in*'; although, this being an air-conditioned coach, there's no *'crank to shut the window if you sneeze'*, nor any sign of Skimbleshanks, T.S. Eliot's railway cat. I have, though, brushed past four dogs in the corridors.

Fiddling with a set of brushed-aluminium rocker switches, I leave myself just enough light to read by – that and the soft blue gaze of a night light set high in one anodyne wall. Unlike Dr Johnson's eighteenth-century Highland inn, my cabin is clean enough – although almost wilfully spartan, down to a drab brown apology of a blanket. The featureless grey-beige decor seems the perfect match for the antiseptic, air terminal–style architecture of Euston station some 250 miles south.

Beyond the confines of this mobile cell, however, and wholly invisible, the Lake District broods in dark magnificence. With no real sensation of speed, we might either be climbing Shap or else dropping down from there to Carlisle and the Scottish border. How I long for a sliding window ventilator and the childhood sound of a sovereign four-cylinder Pacific calling across ice-dark moors to the silhouettes of Lake District peaks under low clouds pregnant with snow.

Five thousand men just like the Irish builder snoring gently below me laid tracks in all weathers – from Craigendoran across the bogs of remote Rannoch Moor, then over 350 viaducts and underbridges and 50 overbridges built by the sons of 'Concrete Bob' McAlpine – to gain Fort William. Stations were designed in the guise of Swiss chalets. Trains, restricted at first to a top speed of just 25 mph – it's 40 mph today – battled rainstorms, blizzards and winds that made challenging marks on the Beaufort scale. Militant Sabbatarianism meant that for many years there were to be no trains on Sundays, while the luxury homes that directors of the North British Railway imagined would spring up along the banks of Loch Long and Loch Lomond, enticing wealthy businessmen to and from industrial Glasgow, failed to materialize. The line did, though, bring fresh fish to Billingsgate and hikers to Ben Nevis, while fetching and carrying schoolchildren, wood pulp, forestry equipment and the Royal Mail. It even gave a free ride to a golden eagle that settled one day on the buffer beam of a North British 'Glen' class 4-4-0. A baby was born on a Glasgow-bound train one day in 1935, and yes, there was a doctor on board.

Fully dressed, I fall asleep, waking momentarily as the carriage shakes and groans somewhere in the depths of the night and the *Royal Highlander* and the *West Highlander* part company.

A slither of light under the window blind is enough to wake me again. It's very nearly 7 a.m. I step down as quietly as possible from my bunk and walk the silent corridor to the lavatory, big and clean enough to wash and shave in. The train is rumbling at a steady jog alongside a wall of snow. When I look out from the window of the carriage door on the other side, it's as if a miracle has occurred.

Can this really be the same train that departed subterranean Euston in a blaze of harsh fluorescence last night? Not quite. Leaning out of the window of the carriage door, my lungs filling with cold, moist Highland air, I can see that our train is now just five coaches long, and at its head is a growling three-tone grey Type 37 diesel-electric. But if the train has mutated, the scenery has been transformed out of all time and recognition. I slip back in socks to my cabin to fetch my camera, a black Canon A-1 that has travelled the world with me, and load it with a roll of Ilford HP4. With a 135mm lens I can read the number and name of the deep-throated diesel locomotive nosing towards the Monessie Gorge. She is 37 428 *David Lloyd George*, a 100-ton, 1,750-hp, 30-year-old Welsh interloper.

At 7.45, we curve into the gorge – a haunting ravine, dressed in white this morning, of jutting rocks, rushing water, drifting snow. A watchful stag and black-faced sheep are woken by our encroaching diesel alarm. This is un-distilled Highland sorcery and the very reason why – even though the design of my train is dull – sleeping-car and motorail expresses must surely continue for the sake of future generations. I pop my head back in and make my way to the lounge car for tea and toast and butter. Soon enough, the driver checks the loudly chattering engine of *David Lloyd George* as air brakes slow the *West Highlander* to walking pace. We draw into Fort William, 525 miles and – on time to the minute – 12 hours from Euston.

I fetch my bag, ready to take a utilitarian two-coach diesel multiple unit on to Mallaig and a prearranged speedboat from there to Dr Johnson's inn at Glenelg, before returning to Fort William and the sleeper, with a berth of my own, and so back to Euston and Canary Wharf to write up my story. The Irish builder who has been asleep the whole while sticks his head out of his blanket. 'Jesus, are we there?'

'We are. Time to get up.'

'It's been a pleasure sleeping with you,' he says.

*

The *West Highlander* survived. Politicians and Scottish grandees were regular passengers. With support from the Highland Regional Council and the Scottish Court of Session, they made the case for the train's future vociferously and well. The day my article appeared in the '*Indie*', Lord Gray rose in the House of Lords to ask Her Majesty's Government whether they would advise the director of rail franchising to maintain the West Highland sleeper. Impeccably dressed for the journey, Angus Campbell-Gray, 22nd Lord Gray, was a regular and genial passenger on board Anglo-Scottish expresses. A one-time advertising man, he had designed HP Sauce labels and dreamt up slogans for Fyffes bananas. He served motorists at his own petrol station at Taynuilt on the edge of his Airds Bay estate. A well-known story about how he came to serve fellow passengers breakfast on board the sleeper to Euston did not escape the attention of the *Daily Telegraph*'s obituary desk. Celebrating his imminent retirement, Lord Gray's sleeping-car attendant was 'desperately hungover'. Offering the sozzled attendant his bed, Lord Gray took over the man's duties.

Since 1995, north of Edinburgh the overnight London to Fort William train has been a two-coach section of the *Caledonian Sleeper*, a 16-coach circus departing Euston six days a week at 2115 on weekdays, arriving in Fort William at 0957. A second *Caledonian Sleeper* leaves later on for Glasgow and Edinburgh. In 2019, the 1980s Mk IIIs I rode in 1995 were replaced by Spanish-built Mk V coaches designed, inside, to a hotel-like specification with *Wallpaper** magazine–style decor. Although neither as stylish nor as glamorous as the New York Central's *20th Century Limited* in 1940, the new-look *Caledonian Sleeper* proffers 'Suites with double beds, lavatories and showers as well as "Classic Rooms", or traditional single or twin berth cabins'.

Living for a year in the Scottish Highlands, an hour's drive north of Inverness, I made return journeys on the *Caledonian Sleeper* a dozen times. The trains seemed a little tired, but the Scottish stewards were mostly friendly, and the 1980s-style lounge car was enjoyable for its haggis, wines and whisky, and its period-piece decor complete with leather sofas. It was also a delight to be able to read in bed as the train thrummed north and to wake up, release the blind and see wild landscapes that made up for the glumness of the departure platform at Euston.

One great advantage of sleeping through England is that passengers, known as 'guests' in the latest management jargon, can avoid the sorry sight of wilfully horrid, cheapjack new housing being rolled across the landscape and the motorways that scar it.

There was something both majestic and poetic about the sight of a pair of Stanier Black Five 4-6-0s storming up Drumochter in morning light at the head of the *Royal Highlander* sleeper from Euston, the thunderous train and epic landscape in empathetic embrace. Still, the *Caledonian Sleeper* offers a glimpse of romance on Britain's intensely occupied and increasingly homogeneous railways. This side of the *Night Riviera* running from Paddington to Penzance, the *Caledonian Sleeper* is the last of its kind in Britain. And the investment made in the new Spanish Mk V carriages means that the Inverness and Fort William sleeper should run for many more years. Since 2014, the train has been run by Serco, a private sector 'provider of public services' – from prisons to hospital employees – with a name that sounds like a brand of washing powder.

David Lloyd George, the 1,750-hp class 37 diesel-electric locomotive, built by English Electric at its Vulcan works at Newton-le-Willows in Lancashire, was withdrawn in May 2012 and scrapped in Rotherham, Yorkshire, the following March. The works has been replaced by a sprawl of indifferent new housing. One disappointing feature of the West Highland line is the dismal Fort William station, built in 1975 as a replacement for James Miller's romantic terminus of 1904 and its deep-eaves, double entrance arches, Arts and Crafts details and fort-like tower that allowed train engines to stand close to the pier on Loch Linnhe, buffer-by-bumper with taxis and MacBraynes buses. Miller's station, of which not a trace remains today, was demolished to make way for the A82 dual carriageway that thunders through the town as if cars were more important than civility, and HGVs more vital than the Highlands. And yet Fort William itself, first built in timber by Cromwell and rebuilt in stone in 1690, was knocked down at the beginning of the twentieth century to make way for the station yard.

What does remain largely unchanged since 1995 is the glorious West Highland landscape.

SEVENTEEN

Tongliao to Hadashan: QJ

8th–12th January 2001

I s it true? Have the Chinese really built a brand-new, 600-mile-long steam railway through Inner Mongolia? I first heard this surprising news in late 1993. Improbable perhaps, and yet on second thoughts there were perfectly good reasons why the Chinese might be doing just this. A line across the steppes and mountains from Tongliao in the east to Jining in the west would link major national and international rail hubs, including the Trans-Mongolian and Trans-Siberian railways, while opening up a remote and sparsely populated region of northern China to economic development.

Given that much of the route was through wild landscapes – bitterly cold and snow-blasted in the depths of winter – and that it sat on rich seams of coal, steam was a good idea after all. Steam railways can be simple, practical, reliable, all but weatherproof, and easy to maintain. Steam locomotives are not afraid of the 'wrong' type of snow, which when it falls in Britain brings fey diesel and fragile electric trains to a halt.

Equally, as China's state railway has modernized, it must

surely have many surplus steam locomotives on its books. The fact that powerful long-distance 2-10-2 freight locomotives were built at the rate of up to 350 a year as late as 1988 at Datong works, 80 miles south of Jining, means there will have been a fleet of next-to-new locomotives on tap that could be thrashed across this wild landscape. Even if they were to expire through overwork, misuse and lack of maintenance, there would be plenty more where they came from. Yes, I can believe in China's brand-new 600-mile-long steam railway.

To ride the railway solo, however, is easier said than done. I'm free to travel in January, a month promising blizzards and Captain Scott temperatures. I like cold climates, so this is fine, and – knowing my steam locomotives and something of China's can-do ethic – the 'Jitong' line is sure to be running as normal. But, as I looked at the map before I set out, I did wonder how I could get to either end of the line. Would I need internal visas? Would I be allowed to travel by myself? Language, at least, isn't a particular concern as, although I speak neither Mandarin nor Mongolian, I have always enjoyed meeting people with whom, one way or another, I have had to learn to communicate.

Some years ago, I much enjoyed travelling through Hungary by train in winter with the architect Imre Makovecz, who designed haunting, wholly original, tree-like buildings mostly in wood. Neither of us could speak the other's language, so we talked in our own, filling the pages of a notebook with sketches. We got to understand one another, imperfectly perhaps, and became friends. I remember, too, doing much the same thing in non-Russian on a winter train through Karelia, pounding its 40-mph way from Pitkyaranta to Olonets through the pine forests fringing Lake Ladoga. The railway engineer with whom I shared my steam-heated compartment provided the specifications of our Er class 0-10-0 in jottings and technical drawings, along with a potted guide to the line and the surrounding area.

My work has introduced me to architects and engineers worldwide. These connections have, almost unfailingly, helped me to get to places that might otherwise have been out of reach. There is a common bond between people with a passion – however it is expressed – for intelligent architecture and engineering, as there is, of course, between those whose overriding interest is in astronomy, scuba diving, music, stamp collecting or horses. Those who share enthusiasms will often go to great lengths to help one another. My vague architectural connections with the Beijing University of Civil Engineering and Architecture will hopefully prove to be invaluable. I will need them on this trip, as I'm flying from Heathrow on a wing and a prayer aiming to get to the Jitong steam railway and its QJ 2-10-2s by hook, crook or coupling rod.

We touch down in Beijing just after 9.30 a.m. A taxi takes me through light snow and sliding traffic to Zizhuyuan residential district, where for some reason the driver insists on taking me to the zoo rather than the engineering and architecture school. Perhaps the word 'architect' in Mandarin is similar to that of 'animal'. I have no idea, but accept his decision, pay up and clamber out of the cab. I know I can't be far, yet with streets and buildings white with snow, I don't want to head off in the wrong direction.

A group of students greets me. I say hello in English because it's the first word that comes out of my mouth and because 'Nǐ hǎo', which I had remembered on the plane, proves elusive on the bitterly cold street. 'Hello,' they chorus. They take me to the University of Civil Engineering and Architecture, where they're studying, and make sure someone comes and sees me before they vanish. Another student arrives. She takes me up in a bare metal lift to a sixth-floor room where what appears to be the entire teaching staff is holding a meeting.

Tea arrives, as it always does in China, while English-speaking tutors cluster around. The magic words 'Architectural Review', where I worked as a young assistant editor, though not 'Guardian' or 'Independent' – words that mean nothing to them – place me on their map. I have already clocked a chart on one of the walls of the school's reception lobby showing China as the centre of the world. When you live in a country as big as this and nearly everyone you see day-to-day is Han Chinese, perhaps it is. The upshot is – aside from maps of places and buildings to see in Inner Mongolia, and a promise of a tour of Beijing architecture ancient and modern on my return from the north – I get the practical help I need to make it to Tongliao, and from there across to Jining.

A super-efficient member of staff is on the phone, speaking loudly now with this person, then with the next. 'Now we can go,' she says. We drive to the old Beijing South station, where in an over-lit office I pay not very much money in exchange – as my documents are checked, rechecked and their details typed up – for a wallet of chits and tickets, all in Mandarin. I can barely express my gratitude. What I have in my hand is a ticket for the Tongliao sleeper leaving in four hours, return tickets for the length of the Jitong line, and a voucher for a hostel in Daban, halfway along the route, where I hope to break my journey both because the main Jitong engine shed is there and because the scenery and civil engineering around Daban are meant to be dramatic.

Alone again, I eat noodles and chicken broth in the noisy station restaurant, half trying, half pretending to read. Boarding the sleeper comes as a relief. Two attendants hold a loud discussion before I'm ushered further up the train. 'Super deluxe,' one says, unlocking a door, and thank Confucius – and my jacket and tie – for this. The heavy green train is busy, and the noise from the six-berth and four-berth compartments is already hard to bear. I still have no idea why people shout when they can talk. This is not a phenomenon confined to China. The loudest train – in terms of shouting – I have yet ridden was from Barcelona to Santa Coloma de Cervelló, to see Gaudí's Church of Colònia Güell. It wasn't a long ride and the women in my carriage were holding, in their terms, a normal if highly animated conversation. How they understood one another given that they all spoke non-stop, without pause for breath, was quite beyond me. Since then, mobile phones have conquered the world and everyone everywhere shouts, especially on trains.

My 'super deluxe' berth is a true haven. I have it to myself, but then who in the People's Republic would want to share with a 'ghost person'? And, happily, I have my own lavatory and shower. I sleep the sleep of an unexcavated terracotta warrior.

I wake in a morning half-light – it's snowing – to stare at a mountainous landscape between long tunnels. An attendant brings tea and egg buns. I shower and read *David Copperfield* with more than half an eye on the passing scenery.

Approaching Tongliao, I'm raring to go. Here in one of the station yards is what I've come to see, a pair of muscular black 2-10-2s simmering at the head of long train of snow-covered logs. At the station, which is a curiously bland building realized in some vague traditional Chinese style and yet four-square and functional inside, I thank my stewards, check to find out what the locomotive was that brought me to Tongliao – a dark green DF4 diesel-electric – and walk to the end of the platform. I can make out more 2-10-2s in the yard beyond the station.

As I watch, two Germans come to stand alongside me. They look like bikers, but have flown, they say as we fall into conversation, from Munich. They have been on the same sleeper and, as if there were any doubt, are in search of steam. Both Stefan and Jürgen work in Alpine hydroelectricity plants. They have known each other since high school, when they made trips together to East Germany to ride the Pacific steam-hauled expresses of the Deutsche Reichsbahn between Dresden and Berlin. After their weddings, they say, they agreed a plan with their wives. Husbands take an early January break together one year, wives the next. Year three, they take husband-and-wife holidays or everyone stays at home.

Stefan and Jürgen prove to be good fun. They have their wits about them, too. Although I've long been happy to travel the world alone, I'm glad of their company. They were here three years ago and have an itinerary I'm happy to fall in with. The most impressive stretch of the route, they say, is up in the mountains between Shangdian and Jingpeng, two hours or so west of Daban. Yes, Daban is where many of the 100 or so QJ 2-10-2s working the line are based, but we will do best to take the train to Hadashan, where they know a farmer who will put us up in a house. More of a hut than a house, but not so bad. The reason to stay there is that the village is right by the spectacular loops the trains negotiate on curving viaducts and around cliff edges on steeply rising gradients.

It sounds perfect. We go for a warm drink of curdled something or other that everyone else is drinking and tuck into mid-morning dumplings. Stefan explains that if I had planned to go all the way to Jining on the same train, I would miss a lot of the scenery as the journey takes 24 hours and, especially in winter, many of the most dramatic stretches of the line would be in the dark. Also, there are no sleeping cars and the seats are quite hard. The trains shouldn't be too busy this time of year so you might be able to stretch out on a seat, but you never know.

At midday, a chime whistle followed by the blast of an air horn announces the arrival of the empty stock of train 6052, the 1220 Tongliao to Jining. We move quickly to catch up with its locomotive, QJ 6992, a tall, rugged, well-polished locomotive, black with red wheels; shafts of white steam shoot clear from her big 26 by 31½ inch cylinders, the safety valves on the verge of lifting. With just hints of ice and sludge around her frames, she must have been steam-cleaned this morning. I'm pleased to see our eight-coach train is green. 'They call them green-skinned trains,' says Stefan. 'Like they were a snake.'

'Or a dragon.'

'Yes, of course, dragon. What else can a steam train be in China!'

I've seen photographs of Jitong trains in a pale blue and grey livery, a sort of intercity look that must surely be out of place on the Mongolian plains. We climb on board. The interior of the carriages, which date from any time between 1959 and 1994 – the Chinese built 270,000 of them – is resolutely spartan. Upright two-tone blue plastic leatherette seats and, everywhere, the hardest of hard surfaces.

A member of the platform staff finds Jürgen and hands him several brown paper bags. 'Food,' says my new friend. 'You cannot be sure of eating on the train. Sometimes there are food sellers at stations on the way, but in this weather I wouldn't be too sure.'

It's snowing hard now. Stefan checks his impressive Swiss watch. The temperature, he says, is minus 2 degrees Celsius. Several families carrying heavy laundry bags – or at least that's what they look like – and men in snow caps and leather jackets have joined our carriage. Two of the men lean on steamed-up windows and fall asleep even before we've moved.

Move though we do, the big 2-10-2 accelerating rapidly away from Tongliao. We pass a pair of QJs at the head of a long train of oil tankers. 'It will follow us,' says Jürgen. Although Tongliao is clearly expanding, with high-rise buildings under construction on all sides, almost as soon as we've cleared the usual urban detritus of warehouses and depots, half-built concrete structures, lorry parks and junk yards, and switched on to the Jitong line itself, the landscape opens up. On either side lie boundless stretches of Mongolian plain, carpeted in snow, and high hills merge with low clouds in the far distance.

While we bowl along at what must be 50 mph, families dip into bags in search of lunch. Our heavy green carriage rides comfortably and, with steam heating, is cosy, although now and then we do need to wipe the windows to see out. We call at 10 stations, always on time, before the scenery changes. Out from Fuxingdi, 106 miles and 3¾ hours from Tongliao, the plains yield to an imposing backdrop of sculpted hills on both sides of the train. Half an hour later, we call at Chabuga and hop off to watch as QJ 6356 replaces QJ 6992, her extremities laced with icicles, her smokebox adorned with a stentorian red and yellow slogan that, says Stefan, means something like 'prosperity through progress'.

'Do you speak some Mandarin?'

'No. I try to copy the Chinese characters into notebooks and then show them to a friend in Munich who translates them. It's too cold for writing without gloves today, but I've seen this one before. Anyway, they all mean much the same thing.' Stefan also explains why we're changing engines less than 120 miles from Tongliao. 'Because the line is worked in sections. So 6992 and the crew will take a return train to Tongliao. If we were to go all the way to Jining, we'd have five different locos.'

A pair of QJs pull alongside in the opposite direction, at the head of a heavy goods train composed of flat wagons, containers, boxcars and, at the back, an American-style caboose, its chimney smoking contentedly. The line, I learn, is single track for most of the way, so trains wait to pass one another at stations. With our new engine blowing off steam and the semaphore signal raised – yes, 1990s vintage semaphore signals – to give us the road ahead, we retreat to the warmth of our carriage. Jürgen has bought flasks of hot tea. 'I even have milk for our Englishman. Don't ask me which animal.'

With a scattering of new passengers, including men and women brandishing briefcases – on their way home from work, perhaps – we accelerate briskly forward into a wild prairie landscape. Although once up to speed it is hard to detect the beat of the locomotive, because with an eight-coach load she is running under easy steam, we do hear her haunting chime whistle and long blasts from her air horn on the approach to road crossings. There are 252 of these between Tongliao and Jining.

It's a quarter to six and almost dark when we stop to take water at Lindong. Despite the failing light, work in this developing region clearly never stops. A long queue of coal lorries inch forward as their loads are transferred to the wagons of an equally long train. A further 30 minutes brings us to a stop at Gulumanhan. Stefan and Jürgen say we have some time here. Outside, it's a bit colder still, but the snow has stopped falling. We're waiting here for the fast train from Tongliao to overtake. Fast train? Yes, says Jürgen. Since last year, there's been a semi-fast air-conditioned diesel train, the first of its kind on the line. It left Tongliao two hours after we did and will be in Jining at six in the morning. Our train will be there just after midday. The new train makes many fewer stops and is a sign of the times. For its first five years, the Jitong railway was 100 per cent steam. Now, it's 95 per cent. Not so bad, perhaps, and yet that 100 per cent had been very special indeed.

A distant headlamp, the growl of a diesel engine, and a dark green DF4 blares past with its brightly lit train of air-conditioned carriages. Back on board we discuss the future of the line. We can expect steam to hold out here, it seems, for the next five years. The whole point of the railway is that it can be upgraded easily. The semaphore signals will be replaced one day by colour-light signals and who knows what else. And yet this is such a wild and distant landscape that keeping things simple seems wise.

In the darkness we climb to Daban where, under arc lamps, we see row after row of QJs, many in steam awaiting their next turns of duty. At the station, we get out to see QJ 6356 make way for QJ 7041. It's 8.40 p.m. as we roll west. 'Just another three hours to Hadashan,' says Stefan encouragingly. 'But now our loco will have to work.'

An hour out from Daban, she really does. From our carriage we can hear her barking ever more loudly as she tackles the steep, twisting grades up towards the mountain passes that we plan to ogle over the next couple of days. Although it's dark, I can see QJ 7041 from time to time as she writhes around improbable loops, her firebox flickering and her powerful electric headlamp lighting up the road ahead. Our speed is in the low 20s as engine and track guide us ever higher across what must be, from the sound of the hollow rumbling, high bridges and long viaducts.

At a quarter to midnight we stop in what seems like the middle of nowhere. If you live in New York, Paris or London, it is the middle of nowhere; as it is for those living in Beijing and provincial Tongliao. We step down into a biting wind, yet under intensely bright stars twinkling between fast-moving clouds. Only minus 18, says Stefan. Here, though, our farmer is waiting in what looks like a military Jeep. He makes a sign to say 'come, come and quickly'. We don't hesitate. Only inside the 'Jeep' – it's a mid-70s Russian UAZ-469 – do we stop to watch our train blasting away ever higher into the mountains on its 12-hour run from here to Jining.

Negotiating an uncertain track, we drop to a huddle of brick cottages. This is Hadashan in the heart of the Jingpeng Pass, the newfound Mecca for steam enthusiasts from around the world. Our cottage is rudimentary but comforting neverthe-less. Jürgen and Stefan share one room, I have another. There is a stove in a third room, which doubles up as a kitchen. A door leads into a tiny walled yard where we'll find an earth closet and a water pump. Soup is served, along with schnapps. I force myself to brush my teeth at the pump and fall asleep fully dressed.

Thundering steam trains haunt my dreams for good reason. During the night steam trains ride above us. But it's the raucous trumpeting of cockerels that wakes me up, rather than chime whistles, air horns, deep rhythmic exhausts and the low rumble of goods wagons. Slowly a low red sun helps me to remember where I am. After washing as best I can, I go outside and see the railway above Hadashan. It really is an engineering marvel.

The next two days pass, between warming meals, in a blur of steam and snow. Either our farmer friend or one of the villagers takes us up in the UAZ to vantage points where, with tea and schnapps to gloved hand, we revel in the snowy spectacle of steam locomotives working very close to their limit around 360-degree loops over and around rivers and ravines. A Chinese winter rather than an Indian summer for steam – can it get any better than this?

Yes, it can. On the third day, we're driven the 70 miles to Daban, where, for a payment of 200 *renminbi* each – something like £15, I think, a lot of money here – we are allowed to walk freely among the QJs and their busy fitters and crews. This panorama of steam, ice, fire and snow is painterly and moving. This is an alternative twenty-first-century landscape, and we get to see it in forensic and truly sensational detail when offered a footplate ride back to Hadashan, on a pair of QJs working a midday goods train to Jining. Stefan and Jürgen climb up to the footplate of the lead engine. I choose the train engine. This allows me to see and hear both locomotives in action.

The Mongolian crew, driver and two firemen are all smiles and very direct. The driver points to where I should sit, or stand, on the right-hand side of the cab. The firemen will take it in turns, 20 minutes at a time, to feed the QJ's capacious and hungry grate. The footplate feels happily familiar. Whistles and air horns chiming and blasting, we set out, sure-footedly, onto the single-track main line, the exhaust of the engines now in, now out of harmony until, as they get into their stride, they sing – basso profundo – together. I know from Stefan and Jürgen that the QJs were fitted with mechanical stokers but that these have not worn well, which is why the locomotives need to be fed by hand.

As it climbs ever harder towards the Jingpeng Pass, our train becomes increasingly at one with the elements, a storm within a snowstorm. And when the snow stops and a weak sun lights up the track, train and mountains, we seem a natural part of this sublime landscape. The loops around and through the pass are terrific. An exultation of engineering, nature and steam. For all the cacophony, I feel wholly at peace.

*

Scheduled steam on the Jitong railway ended on 8th December 2005. Steam locomotives were replaced by DF4 diesel-electrics. Since 2018, a new high-speed line has been in the offing, spearing through the Mongolian mountains in tunnels. If and when it goes ahead – things usually do in China – the Jingpeng Pass may become a tourist attraction rather than being the busy, if highly scenic, section of a workaday long-distance main-line railway that it has been since it opened in December 1995. Perhaps it will become the stamping ground once more of QJ 2-10-2s, for these are what most foreign visitors will want to see. Some 4,700 of these impressive machines were built between 1956 and 1988 at Datong. The design was updated in the mid-1960s, and the majority of the locomotives date from then. At first they were coded HP (for *hé píng*, meaning 'peace'), but during the savagely destructive years of Mao Zedong's Cultural Revolution they were transformed into heroic members of the proletarian FD class (*fan di* or anti-imperialist). In 1971, when the political heat was a little less intense, they were re-designated QJ (*qián jìn*, to 'go forward' or 'march on').

Based on the Soviet Railways' LV class 2-10-2 of 1954, the QJs were rugged and highly capable machines. Designed for a maximum speed of 50 mph, they were rated at 2,980 ihp. On test they developed up to 3,580 ihp. With their small 4-foot, 11-inch driving wheels and tractive effort of 63,235 pounds, they worked away at the head of heavy goods trains with ease. In the mid-1980s, the British steam engineer David Wardale worked at Datong in an attempt to improve the performance

330

and thermal efficiency of the class. But as the Chinese authorities wavered between extending the life of steam or replacing it with diesels and electrics, the project hit the buffers. How glorious, though, is even the thought of 5,000-ihp QJs at work high in those far-distant and unforgettable Mongolian mountains.

EIGHTEEN

Baghdad to Basra: Toyota Land Cruiser and Chevrolet Suburban

3rd–7th May 2002

On 2nd April, Admiral Lord Boyce, Chief of the Defence Staff, went to see Tony Blair at Chequers, the prime minister's country residence. The meeting was vague – something to do with Blair's intentions towards Iraq – and Lord Boyce left feeling none the wiser. Three days later, Blair was at Prairie Chapel Ranch in Crawford, Texas. It appears that, here, he and the US president decided to invade Iraq and overthrow its dictator Saddam Hussein.

A month later and I am here in Iraq. I'm a journalist with the *Guardian* but not an accredited foreign correspondent. Intuition – along with discussions with fellow journalists, film-makers, diplomats, military historians and museum curators specializing in this ancient land – has told me that there is precious little time to explore Iraq's ancient heritage, something I have wanted to do since my childhood meanderings through the Assyrian and Mesopotamian galleries of the British Museum. More than this, though, a war of aggression with a sovereign country, no matter how nasty President

Saddam might be, is illegal; and given the febrile social, tribal, religious, economic and political history of the region – ancient, middling and modern – invasion and a regime change can only stir a hornet's nest.

Saddam is not Tito, yet like the Yugoslavian dictator he keeps Iraq under tight control. Initially, this was through the fruits of a booming economy as well as an iron fist, but after the draconian sanctions that were imposed on the country by the United States after the Gulf War a decade ago, it is now by brutal methods alone. And yet, aside from finding a legitimate excuse to go to war, if any foreign government wishes to topple Saddam and his Ba'athist regime they need a plan in place for Iraq's future. This is known and all but crystal clear, except in the befuddled or wilful minds of supine British and American politicians – and, distressingly, of gung-ho journalists who should know better. Politicians and the public elsewhere in the world appear to have more than an inkling of what brothers Bush and Blair are up to. In his own words, Bush clearly wants to 'kick ass', while Blair, in awe of the gun-slinging US president, wants – what – glory?

Will people back home in Britain protest against the idea of going to war with Iraq before the dog (Bush) and the poodle (Blair) of war are let loose on the country? Perhaps they will. It has certainly been hard to get an honest answer from a slippery British government about its intentions. When I called 10 Downing Street's press office to ask the simple question 'Are we going to war with Iraq?', the answer was 'no'. And yet there is talk of Saddam possessing weapons of mass destruction that, unless checked, the Iraqi dictator may yet unleash on us. It does seem odd that only a few years ago Saddam was America's 'strongman' in the Middle East, seen shaking hands in American newspapers with beaming US visitors, among them Donald Rumsfeld, US Secretary of Defense.

The idea that Saddam has 'weapons of mass destruction' at his disposal is patent nonsense, but where there is a will to go to war, any excuse will do as long as enough people – and especially the media – are willing to suspend their disbelief and curiosity. There has been, though, something else that has made me want to come to Iraq. What do Iraqis themselves feel about the idea of their country being ploughed into the mother of all battlefields, just 11 years after the last invasion and during the latest round of sanctions that together have caused large numbers of deaths among the country's poor? 'We think it's worth it,' says the self-righteous US Secretary of State Madeleine Albright.

Really? Here is a land not just of Sunni and Shia Muslims, but of Sufis, Copts, Roman Catholics, Yazidis, Turkomans, and a few remaining Jews and Assyrians, too; of people as different as the surviving Marsh Arabs are from millionaire traders in Baghdad, or as far apart as Kurds in the north of the country yearning for their own independent state are from young recruits in Saddam's army aiming, against the odds, to live worthwhile and decent lives.

To get to Iraq hasn't been easy. I've been helped on the way, as have others, by 'Gorgeous' George Galloway, the controversial Labour MP, a welcome figure for whatever reason in Iraqi political circles. Perhaps, though, my genuine interest in Iraq's ancient history, monuments and cities was my trump card in getting an impressive visa – after a long wait – with its stamps, forbidding eagle and a handwritten note in Arabic that reads 'Give this man every assistance'.

I've had time to think these thoughts on the 600-mile night drive from Amman airport in the back of a Chevrolet Suburban, at first on the perilous road etched across the Jordanian desert littered with wayward oil tankers, and now along a sweeping concrete Iraqi autobahn at a steady 100 mph. Here we are at last, in time for breakfast, lumbering up the driveway of the Al-Rashid Hotel, a severe 18-storey concrete pile, dating from the 1970s and looking more like a Ministry of Truth than a place anyone would dream of paying to stay.

The interior is shiny – lots of marble – yet strangely glum. George Galloway, puffing sybaritically on a cigar, seems to know everyone in the bar, so I hang on for a while to find out who they are. Bright-eyed and friendly young foreign correspondents from, among others, the *Daily Telegraph* and *The Times*, and an assortment of European politicians, that's who. One is Jörg Heider, who until 2000 was leader of the right-wing Freedom Party of Austria. One of the foreign correspondents points him out to me. Saddam, of course, is a big fan of Adolf Hitler.

This is absurdist stuff, almost straight out of Evelyn Waugh's *Scoop*, which I've brought with me to read, again. Here is a pack of foreign correspondents cooped up in a hotel in a hot country in pursuit of a promising war, and raring to race off together at the first hint of it. Here, as in *Scoop* – set in fictional Ishmaelia, a flyblown country, and based on Waugh's experience of Abyssinia while working as a correspondent for the *Daily Mail* at the time of the Italian invasion of the country – the government appears to be unhelpful and manipulative, while friends and colleagues are also rivals in search of exclusives. The British government, of course, is even more unhelpful than Iraq's.

The foreign correspondents enjoy telling me that every room in the Al-Rashid is bugged – I'm sure they are – that the food is filthy – it does seem to be – and that all I'll find in my minibar will be cans of Pepsi and 7 Up and perhaps a chocolate bar best eaten ten years ago. More disturbingly, they say that it is very difficult to travel outside Baghdad and that the Al-Rashid is the only place in town we're allowed to stay.

I go up to my room. Looking out from the heavily draped and sealed windows of this tepid cell – sofa covered in cheap-looking black leather; brown fitted carpet; nylon bed sheets – the Al-Rashid is evidently as much a prison as a hotel. Closely watched, it stands ominously alone. The city, as I can see from my eighth-floor window, is on the far side of the Tigris. I decide to leave in the morning. I have come to explore Iraq, not to while away truly precious time in a hermetic building planned in every which way to keep visitors at a distance from the country itself. In any case, the Al-Rashid is ugly and my room has an unpleasant smell. I never stay in hotels like this through choice.

After a sip of foul coffee and a bite of what might once have been a shrink-wrapped and deep-frozen croissant, I make my move. I go to the reception desk and say, 'Good morning. May I check out please?' I check out, tread dutifully over the mosaic of George Bush senior sporting the legend 'Bush is a criminal', and walk purposefully to the hotel gates. It is 9 a.m. and already very hot.

An armoured car and a small troop of moustachioed soldiers outside the gates seem peaceful enough. I say 'good morning' to the strapping sergeant in charge, who asks where I'm going. 'Into town to find another hotel.' The sergeant smiles. I don't look back while walking slowly along Yafa Street towards the Al-Jumariyah Bridge, but assume I'm being watched every inch of the way. Here, though, is the Tigris, a hot breeze along it, boats going about their business and the sense that a real city is getting closer by the step.

On the other side of the river, I wander for a good forty minutes. People seem friendly enough. On the corner of a long and busy street – Nidhal Street, I think – a small white hotel with balconies profuse with bougainvillea tells me to stop. This is Hotel Petra, and very much what I have hoped to find. It couldn't be more different from the Al-Rashid. In the lobby, cooled to a degree by a venerable ceiling fan, an elderly man in no hurry mops the floor.

A portly fellow perhaps in his late fifties, with a tie, straining waistcoat, ambitious moustache and a beaming smile, pops up from behind the counter like some oddball character in a Punch and Judy show. 'Mr English, welcome to our country.'

'Do you have a room, please?'

'I have many rooms for you, my dear, but you will have the best.' He makes me laugh. 'First... you must sign these documents. There are four copies. One for hotel, one for City of Baghdad, one for Immigration and, here, one for secret police.'

'So, will anyone know I'm here?'

'My dear, everyone will know you're here. Would you like something to eat or drink?'

I would. I haven't eaten properly since I left London. He shouts to the old man, whose new job is to walk me into an empty dining room where, under another eccentrically rotating fan, I'm served fresh orange juice, scrambled eggs on toast and a cappuccino that might have been made by a serious-minded barista in Milan.

My room is simple and generous. There is an immaculate bathroom. The freshly washed balcony is perfection. I shave and brush my teeth and, as I do, the veteran GPO-style phone on the table rings. 'Mr Jonathan, a gentleman for you in reception.'

The gentleman, although slim and no more than 40, is sweating and out of breath as if he's been running, and yet he manages to return my smile with a grin. His eyes twinkle. 'Mr Jonathan?'

'Yes.'

'Kerim. I'm very pleased to meet you.'

'Did I give you the run?' I'm guessing that Mr Kerim is a minder of some sort. I cannot believe for a moment, though, that he's a secret policeman.

Kerim is indeed my minder from the state press office. We need to go together to get me registered and to discuss my itinerary. When I tell Kerim where I hope to go, his brow furrows. Babylon, Ur, Eridu, the Marshes, Ctesiphon, Mosul, Nimrud, Hatra, Samarra, Nineveh...

'We'll talk to the boss.'

The boss is a serious, hard-working man with an air of efficiency about him. He listens to me politely and says I must come back tomorrow. Before I go, I meet Stuart Freedman, a

JONATHAN GLANCEY

distinguished photographer and lovely fellow who, all going
well, will travel with me through Iraq.

Next day, it's fixed. I can travel from one end of the country to
the other. The journey can be made in two parts: Baghdad and
the south, and Baghdad and the north. I want to go south first,
because more than anything else I want to find Eridu, among
the candidates for the titles 'World's First City', 'Cradle of
Civilization' and so on. I have read what I've been able to find
about this all-but-mythical proto-city on and off for years.

Kerim will be our guide and minder, and Mohammed – a
powerfully built man dressed in a high-quality black leather
jacket and pressed jeans – our driver. Our transport is a
polished black Toyota Land Cruiser. Kerim changes money
for me. For £200 I receive something like 650,000 *dinars*. The
money is handed over in bundles of notes bound up in elastic
bands. These bundles are called 'pieces', and their street value
is wholly negotiable. Kerim stashes them in a box in the back of
the SUV. His hands are now full of documents. 'Internal visas,'
he says.

We thread through late-morning traffic more orderly than
that of Paris or Rome, before accelerating out along an arrow-
straight road dotted with date palms. 'Mr Jonathan,' says
Mohammed, 'do you know how many date palms we have in
Iraq?'

'I couldn't begin to guess.'

'Twenty-two million, one for every person in the country.'
Mohammed pulls over. He turns around and says, 'Will it be
okay for me to stop at prayer times?'

'Yes, of course,' we chorus from the back.

The ride to Babylon is fun. I can't help asking, 'How many miles to Babylon?' The answer, says Mohammed, is not three score miles and ten, but '90 kilometres'. Kerim, who has a doctorate in Hispanic literature from the Universidad Nacional Autónoma de México as well as a wife and seven children – we learn all this within half an hour – is a good-humoured chatterbox. Stuart asks if all Saddam's minders are like him. 'Shh!' Kerim laughs. 'The car may be bugged.' Mohammed, a serious and quiet man, smiles as if to mean 'you never know', then wags his finger to say 'no'.

There and then, it strikes Stuart and me that Kerim is one of those very bright people doing their best to get by in a tricky world. I think we had both imagined an Iraqi state minder being like a US immigration officer. Kerim is quite the opposite. And yet – I can't help thinking – if he makes one false move he could lose everything. Stuart and I agreed over dinner last night that we wouldn't talk politics, or God, or war. I tell Kerim I'm sorry to have made him run after me.

'But why did you leave the Al-Rashid?'

'It's ugly.'

Babylon, an hour from Baghdad, comes as a surprise. Rather than ruins, we find colossal swallow-haunted courtyards realized in mud-bricks that look brand new. His Excellency, we are told by a determinedly humourless guide, has directed a rebuilding programme here since 1978. 'Look over here,' she says, pointing at bricks adorned with Arabic inscriptions that, translated for us, read 'This was built by Saddam Hussein, son of Nebuchadnezzar, to glorify Iraq'.

In the air-conditioned museum, we hear the words of Nebuchadnezzar himself. Of the vast city he built here in the sixth century BC, most likely the world's largest at the time, the Assyrian king says:

> I built it by bitumen and bricks and by shining glazed bricks decorated with serpents. I built roofs from the trunks of the huge cedar wood and its door leaves were made of cedar. I covered them with copper sheets and made its steps from bronze, and in the gates I erected huge bronze bulls and huge serpents to arouse the admiration of the people.

If Saddam is a chip off the ancient block, I can't help thinking that he might want to listen to the prophet Daniel anew, as well as to Nebuchadnezzar. Mysterious writing, the Book of Daniel tells us, appeared on the palace walls here at Babylon during a feast given by Belshazzar, descendant of Nebuchadnezzar. The prophet was able to read it for the king: 'God hath numbered thy kingdom, and finished it; thou art weighed in the balances and found wanting.'

Can Saddam hear Daniel? No. Oblivious it seems to the wills of Bush and Blair, we learn that the Iraqi president has many further plans for Babylon. He means to rebuild the long-vanished Etemenanki ziggurat, the 'temple of the foundation of heaven and earth' that was probably the inspiration for the biblical Tower of Babel. He wishes to recreate the legendary Hanging Gardens. There will also be a new palace for His Excellency in the shape of a ziggurat, and a cable car will take visitors across the site.

'Across His Excellency's palace?' I ask.

'No.'

Leaving Babylon, we stop mid-afternoon at a roadside restaurant for what proves to be the Iraqi equivalent of fish and chips or a curry: mutton, rice and salad. What I like is the way everyone coming here washes scrupulously before they eat. Unlike in Britain, roadside lavatories are nothing to fear. What is particularly noticeable, though, is the fact that the clientele is exclusively male.

Back on the road, we stop at occasional military gateways, where Kerim produces sheaves of permits stamped with fierce eagles. We head steadily south, parallel with the railway. In a country where petrol is cheaper than mineral water, it seems impossible to generate any enthusiasm for railways. Something I'd like to see in Iraq are some of the Stanier 8F 2-8-0s built at Crewe for war service here, awaiting discovery so they can be shipped home and restored. It would be even more exciting to find that one of the streamlined PC class Pacifics, built by Robert Stephenson and Hawthorns Ltd in 1940 to power the *Taurus Express* from the Syrian border at Tel Kotchek to Baghdad, has been hidden away. That train ran through to Istanbul, from where the *Orient Express* steamed on to Paris and the *Flèche d'Or* (*Golden Arrow*) took you via a Channel ferry to Victoria. Kerim has no idea what I'm trying to say.

We drive on to Nasiriyah. 'Arab or Western hotel?' asks Kerim. Guessing that a 'Western' hotel 250 miles south of Baghdad after more than a decade of sanctions is unlikely to be better than the Al-Rashid, Stuart and I opt for an 'Arab' hotel, which from Kerim and Mohammed's faces is clearly the right answer. Quite what makes our hotel an Arab hotel, I don't really know. The bathroom has a squat toilet and this seems to be about it. Anonymous, it is spotlessly clean.

I knock on Stuart's door. 'Could you murder for a cold beer?' I ask him.

'Definitely. Mass murder.' It's 45 degrees outside.

We can only dream, though, until Kerim appears. 'Do you want a cold beer?' he asks, a mind-reading minder. A plot is hatched. If I walk further into town, not too many streets from here, there is a shop that sells alcohol to foreigners.

'Does he mind being sold?' I ask.

'Who?' says Kerim.

'Al Kahol? He sounds too grand to allow himself to be sold from a back-street shop in Nasiriyah.'

'You are funny guys,' says Kerim. The truth is that Kerim would like a beer – well, three beers – but Mohammed mustn't see. No one must see. 'You bring the beers back in a plain brown bag.'

First I need a 'piece', or however many pieces will buy some cold beers. So Kerim finds an excuse to get the Toyota's key from Mohammed. Mission accomplished, I set off into streets that really do feel like the inside of an oven. And come back, walking slowly, with two brown bags full of beer, doing my best when I cross the hotel lobby to keep the bottles from clinking.

Kerim has friends here. He seems, as we discover, to have friends at every port of call. They hide away in a room and enjoy their cold beers. Mesopotamia was a land where beer was brewed from time immemorial. Its ancient cities have revealed evidence of wine-making, too. It does seem odd that Iraqis can buy all-American Pepsi and 7 Up here, but not local wine or beer.

The next morning, all of it, is spent in the regional governor's compound drinking glass bulbs of sweet tea. In the courtyard, soldiers chat around an array of armoured cars. The governor's Head of Information explains above the rattle of typewriters and the constant coming and going of people – some in uniform – in and out of his room, why we cannot go to Eridu. Because of the wolves. There are no wolves in southern Iraq, I counter. Bandits, he says.

Bandits? 'He means Shia militia,' whispers Kerim. 'They shoot at the army.'

But, after a long conversation with Kerim, the Head of Information relents. Documents are typed, signed and stamped. In the courtyard, we are ushered into a travel-worn Chevrolet Suburban along with the Head of Information and some new friends – two I presume to be from the governor's compound, and the other a retired schoolteacher and local historian with gracious manners. He hands me a brochure on local culture. The cover reads 'Yes... yes to the leader Saddam Hussein'. Something similar, I think, should have been done for Tony Blair at the time of the opening of his promiscuously expensive Millennium Dome.

As we pull out from the courtyard, an armoured car of soldiers follows. The Head of Information, it seems, is happy for us to see the ancient city of Ur, not far into the desert from Nasiriyah, and yet Eridu, further on and wholly isolated, is in a military zone and might well be dangerous.

Ur, as I'd expected it to be, is utterly thrilling. We climb to the top of the Great Ziggurat, an eerie desert sentinel today. It was commissioned by Ur-Nammu, a king we ought to know for creating the world's first legal code more than 4,000 years ago, as well as for this monolithic structure. The local historian explains that Ur-Nammu was a great builder of roads as well as palaces and temples. On one side below us is evidence of a major archaeological dig abandoned at the time of the 1991 war. I see streets and the outlines of houses and other buildings. This, says the historian, is where the prophet Abraham lived. The thought sends shivers up my spine.

'His Excellency Saddam Hussein rebuilt the ziggurat. It was much ruined before him,' the historian continues. And yes, we find Saddam's name inscribed into recent brickwork. We also find bricks with the names of Nabonidus, father of Belshazzar, and Urengur, who reigned here around 2400 BC.

On the other side of the Great Ziggurat we see an Iraqi air force base, yet the twin-boomed F-15 fighter that shoots over us out of the blue is all American. We are in one of the no-fly zones imposed on Iraq in 1991 and supervised by the UN.

Back in the Chevy, we follow a trail into the burning desert littered with the military detritus of that first Gulf War. Rocket cases, depleted uranium warheads, spent artillery shells – all bleached and strangely skeletal as if they were the bones of unclassified alien creatures. This bizarre track leads us slowly yet inexorably to Eridu. There is a hint of a 'tell' or raised mound indicating the remains of an ancient city. And there is the heat. Fifty degrees.

When we crunch up the sand-smothered remains of the

ziggurat, the soldiers ask their sergeant to ask me why I want to come here. There's nothing to see. It's very hot and dangerous, too. Stuart is amused to watch me stand on the summit of the hidden layers of this ancient ziggurat and to explain why I think it matters. They are conscripts and very young. I notice their patched and darned uniforms, their scored and pitted sub-machine guns. In the *Epic of Gilgamesh*, we learn that at a time when all the world was sea, the gods made Eridu; and only when they had done so did they create humankind. In the oldest Mesopotamian creation myth, written thousands of years before the books of the Bible, the city came before humans and no city came before Eridu. Mesopotamians equated humankind with civilization.

After the sea shifted and the land here dried up, and even when it had long been sidelined in terms of economic, military and civic power, Eridu was held to be special, a holy citadel. By scraping away sand and fossilized seashells, we uncover steps. If only we could walk down them and into Eridu as it would have been 5,000 and even 6,000 years ago. Isn't it strange? This has been perhaps the most haunting place I have ever been to – a city older than creationists believe the world to be – under an unforgiving sun in an unforgiving and unforgiven land, with precious little to see but a mound of sand and dunes and spent weaponry stretching into a horizon where land and sky dissolve into a dancing heat haze.

Back in Nasiriyah, I suggest we take the soldiers for a meal. It's 4 p.m. and they have had nothing to eat all day. They are thin. Their sergeant accepts cordially. In a time-warp restaurant – we could be in the 1930s – the soldiers slot their guns into old umbrella racks and go off to wash. I wonder who might have carried an umbrella here. A British civil servant, perhaps, or are these racks for parasols? No one knows. We eat mutton, rice and salad with fresh flatbreads. As I look around the table, I feel suddenly sad. I have been able to get to Eridu, a journey that has mattered so very much to me, with the help of soldiers of Saddam Hussein's army. When the Americans and British come here, these young men won't stand a chance. In a few months' time, they may all be dead.

I have been reading *Gilgamesh* these past few nights. This time, though, the ancient epic means so much more than it has done before. I wonder what these lines sounded like in Mesopotamian:

Do we build houses forever?
Does the river forever raise up and bring on floods?
The dragonfly leaves its shell
That its face might but glance the face of the sun.
Since the days of yore there has been no permanence;
The resting and the dead, how alike they are.

Strange, too, I can't help thinking, how British and Indian troops battled the Ottoman army here in July 1915. It's as if history will repeat itself through a distorting mirror, right outside the restaurant door. The reason the British fought in Nasiriyah in 1915 was to protect the port of Basra, which from the late 1920s played – as it still plays – a key role in the supply chain of oil from the Persian Gulf to countries around the world, including Britain and the United States. The Americans are angry with Saddam for nationalizing the Iraqi oil industry 30 years ago.

I'd really like to talk politics around the table over tea and *kanafeh*, a pastry pudding made of what looks like semolina and soft cheese, smothered in syrup and something else surprisingly delicate. 'Rose water,' says Kerim from across the table when I ask. But political talk, I know, is taboo. For all its shifting sands, I'm on safe ground with ancient history.

When we drive back north from Basra tomorrow, says Kerim with a wry smile, we'll take a different route and Stuart can photograph the site of the Garden of Eden. It's at Al-Qurnah.

'Is the Tree of Knowledge still there?' asks Stuart.

'I think so.'

If it is, perhaps we can take a seed from it and plant it in the gardens at Chequers.

*

We found the Tree of Knowledge in the dilapidated garden of an abandoned hotel facing the confluence of the Tigris and Euphrates near Al-Qurnah. The tree was very dead, but not that old. The rest of the Garden of Eden was desert. On the way north from there, on the main road running close to the Iranian border, we passed one mud fort complete with crenellations after another, manned by young Iraqi soldiers. I wondered how prepared they were to meet 63-ton US Army M1A1 Abrams battle tanks armed with 120mm guns.

Eridu continues to sleep its ancient sleep, unvisited and forgotten. Ur and Babylon were damaged during 'Operation Iraqi Freedom'. The Battle of Nasiriyah, 23rd March–2nd April 2003, witnessed the death of some 400 Iraqi and 32 American soldiers.

Iraq fell to coalition forces in a matter of weeks. There were no weapons of mass destruction. Saddam Hussein fled to a hole in the ground near a farmhouse in Ad-Dawr close to Tikrit, his hometown. He was hanged on 30th December 2006. By then, Iraq had descended into hell. It has yet to recover.

As of July 2019, the United Kingdom's Foreign Office advised against all travel north of Baghdad, and all but essential travel to the south of the country: 'The security situation throughout Iraq remains uncertain, and could deteriorate quickly. You should monitor media reporting and make sure you have robust contingency plans in place.' In 2002–03 Bush and Blair had no contingency plans in place. Out of chaos came Isil, sheer bloody terror around the world, and the wanton destruction of historic monuments in Iraq and elsewhere in the region. Nothing, however, has stood in the way of British railway enthusiasts, who have found and shipped a former Iraqi State Railways Stanier 8F 2-8-0 back to England for restoration to running order.

I do not know what happened to Kerim or Mohammed. My inquiries have been futile. Stuart Freedman is, as he has been since 1991, a terrific photographer. His work has been published extensively – *Life*, *GEO*, the *Guardian*, *Time*, *Newsweek*, *Paris Match*, the *Sunday Times Magazine* – covering stories from Afghanistan to the former Yugoslavia, via Mauretania, Rwanda, Haiti, India, Iraq and Pakistan.

In 2009, Tony Blair was awarded the Presidential Medal of Freedom by George Bush at a ceremony at the White House, in recognition of his work to 'improve the lives of citizens' and for promoting 'democracy, human rights and peace abroad'.

Courtesy of the Oriental Institute at the University of Chicago, I've read the archaeological adventures of James Henry Breasted, who travelled to Ur and Eridu in March 1920. He was tickled pink to change trains for Nasiriyah at Ur Junction – 'What do you think Abraham would say to that!' he exclaimed in a letter home to his 'dear little family'. Driving out to Ur in a Model-T pickup, he found 'none of the architectural grandeur of the Egyptian buildings' and, indeed, his excellent photographs show a heap of bricks rather than the proud ziggurat I climbed to the top of in 2002. At Eridu, however, he can be seen seated in a solar *topee* at the top of the ziggurat, which seems more complete than it is now. It would have been fun to have been able to join Breasted's party. Two months after his visit, Iraqis – Sunni and Shia together – rose up against the occupying British forces. Thousands of Iraqi lives were lost as the revolt was crushed, notably with the help of the fledgling RAF. The revolt cost the British government £40 million to subdue, or twice the annual budget for running Iraq. The following year, Faysal ibn Husayn – Lawrence of Arabia's former colleague in armed revolt – was crowned king, but the British were very much behind the scenes; as, from 1927, were British and American oil companies, until 1932 when Iraq became its own country. Or did it?

NINETEEN

Wolsztyn to Poznań: 0416 hours

9th January 2003

Toe German alarm clock that ticks away much of its strictly regimented life in the zip pocket of my travel bag bleeps. It's 3 a.m. I have one of those 'where am I?' moments. In a room in a guesthouse in Wolsztyn, a low-lying Polish town set among lakes and forests on the great Prussian plain between Poznań and the German border, that's where. Like some automaton, I wash and dress – in layers beginning with silk thermal underwear and finishing with a green Swedish army jacket and steel-toed boots – step into the hallway, stopping to stare at the thermometer, and head out onto a silent street.

Half past three. Well below zero. Icy pavements under fresh-fallen snow. A wind whipped up in Siberia howls across frozen lakes and songless birch woods, around the frosted onion dome of the Baroque parish church tower and through cobbled streets. What am I doing here? A sharp whistle and the compelling exhaust of a main-line steam locomotive are all the reminders I need. Fully awake now, I'm walking to Wolsztyn station – rebuilt in 1961, the 1886 original was destroyed by German bombing on 1st September 1939 – where, for a twenty-first-century spell that might be broken at any time, steam trains reign supreme.

Here, thanks to English brothers Howard and Trevor Jones, main-line steam trains, passenger and freight, fan out through forests to Poznań, Poland's second city; to Zbąszynek, an architect-designed town for railway workers founded as Neu Bentschen in the 1920s; and to Leszno, celebrated long ago for its printers and where Catholics, Protestants and Jews lived and worked together before Hitler, blitzkrieg and the Nazi bacillus *Einsatzgruppen*. Steam trains to these destinations – once Polish, then Prussian, then Polish again, then Nazi German, and Polish since the end of the Second World War – are not enthusiasts' specials, but scheduled trains owned and worked by the staff and crews of Polskie Koleje Państwowe (PKP), the Polish State Railway. They are the last of their kind.

Tired of running a travel business at home in England, Howard Jones emigrated to Poland to drive steam engines and find a way of ensuring he could continue to do so. On my arrival by train from Berlin a few days ago, Howard explained that money raised from enthusiasts drawn here from around the world through the Wolsztyn Experience – founded seven years ago to allow enthusiasts to ride, fire and even drive main-line steam locomotives – helps subsidize the costs PKP has to foot to maintain steam here when all else is diesel and electric.

Why Wolsztyn? The answer has been clear each morning I've walked from my guesthouse to the station of this one-time wool town and its railway yard. This is a time warp where muscular 1950s steam locomotives, the quarter roundhouse shed they rest in, the semaphore signals they obey, the drab olive-green and battleship-grey East German double-deck coaches they pull and the stations they serve are set forever, at the very latest, in 1961. This, though, is not some lovingly preserved railway, but the real workaday thing here and now in the twenty-first century. Howard and Trevor Jones are doing their best to keep Wolsztyn's railway scene this way – and, to date, PKP has allowed them to do so.

I meet Martin French, a local authority manager from Sutton, Surrey, outside the cold station. We've been teamed up this week to work the footplate of Ol49-69, a PKP two-cylinder 2-6-2, one of a class of 116 mixed-traffic locomotives built by Fablok of Chrzanów between 1951 and 1954, four of which were sent as gifts to North Korea. I wonder if they're still there. These are the equivalent, in British terms, of the contemporary and successful British Railways Standard class 5 mixed-traffic 4-6-0s, although the fireboxes of the Polish engines are much bigger than their British counterparts – the last of which were withdrawn from regular main-line service in 1968 – and their tractive effort slightly higher. They are game machines, packing a punch, especially when accelerating trains on tight schedules away from snow-encrusted stations. Resolutely functional maids of all work and clearly derived from German precedent, the Ol49s make much modern design and most Bauhaus architecture seem positively effete.

Martin and I are due to hook up with our locomotive at the station when the regular crew bring her down from the depot to meet her train, the 0416 fast-stopping train to Poznań, comprising a rake of four green VEB double-deck coaches. Dating from the early 1950s, each of these massively constructed vehicles seats 135 passengers.

While we wait, we eat hot sausages in warm rolls and drink coffee served from a stall by the station. Remarkably, despite this desperately early time of day, passengers are turning up for the train. We're sure there must be some hardcore steam enthusiasts among them, yet they seem like bona fide commuters to me. What time do they start work in Poznań, for heaven's sake? I hope they'll be on early trains back.

A sharp whistle signals the arrival of our locomotive. We scuttle down the underpass and climb up to the island platform to join her. Up on the spacious footplate, the warmth of the fire is a godsend. Andrzej the regular driver has stashed sausages, rolls and canteens of tea and coffee on a steel shelf above the firebox and between parades of valve wheels. Yesterday he showed me how to cook sausages, steak, eggs and toast on a fireman's shovel. The fireman hands his shovel to Martin, who'll be doing the hard work this morning: maintaining the fire and 16-bar (228-psi) boiler pressure, shovelling coal into the searing depths of a 40-square-foot grate and working the steam injectors to keep water – metamorphosed into wet steam – flowing from tender to boiler. Martin has fired steam locomotives in Britain often enough to make him master of his task. It's a skill he revels in.

Andrzej – a 'card' is the happily old-fashioned word that best describes him – ushers me theatrically to the driver's side of the footplate. A funny man, and something of a practical joker, Andrzej is a fine engineman with sharp eyes, practical hands and razor-sharp instincts. Like his equally friendly colleagues,

Andrzej seems to be – as far as I can work out from spirited engineman's-bar conversations, in bits and bobs of Polish, English, French, German and what-have-you – a Catholic communist trade unionist who is keen on individual freedom and steam locomotives and skilled at making and growing things at his proud family home. His job this morning is to leave me to drive as I see fit, while keeping a hawk eye on what I'm up to and, of course, on the road ahead. That iron road beyond the length of the locomotive's jet-black boiler is not all darkness, as Ol49-69 boasts three powerful headlamps that light the way – helped this morning by the brightness of snow on fields.

I drive from the right-hand side of the footplate, so Andrzej, looking down the platform from the fireman's side of the cab, gives me the 'right away' as the platform clocks point to 0416. Then the signals ahead are up and the guard's whistle blows and his lamp flashes. Clearing the locomotive's cylinders of condensation, winding her quickly into gear and opening the regulator, 0149-69 barks crisply and without a hint of a wheel slip into wind and flurries of snow, and along past the signal box where I remember to salute the signalman. I wind the reverser back from the 50 per cent cut-off needed for starting to 35 per cent and open up, the black and green 2-6-2 accelerating remarkably quickly, and so she needs to. Our schedule is based on a new diesel timetable, requiring us to work the engine hard between the 15 stations from here to Poznań, some 50 miles down the line.

But the line is largely on the level, so the trick is getting away from intermediate stations and up to 100 km/h as quickly as possible, running with a wide throttle opening and a short cut-off for speed and economy, and braking not late, of course, but without wasting precious seconds. The train's air brakes are powerful, so it would be easy to come to a halt all too quickly. I need to stop just in front of the signals at the platform ends of stations whose names I find hard to pronounce, one eye on my watch. When we stop – Rakoniewice, Rostarzewo, Grodzisk, Granowo, Stęszew and the rest – I lean from the cab and watch ever-more commuters pile on board. By Poznań, our train will be carrying more than 500 passengers.

Traces of early-morning light between stops reveal deer and hares running across fields, a heavy horse pulling a farm cart, sorties of crows, storks' nests on farmhouse chimneys, worn Soviet-era cars at clattering crossings, and a rural landscape innocent of executive and other horrid new housing and destructive developments. This is a truly rural ride.

I take it all in silently, Andrzej allowing me to concentrate, shouting 'Vissell!' only when I fail to sound Ol49-69's piercing alarm at the exact moment needed to alert stoats and weasels who may be thinking of making a dash across the tracks at distant farm crossings.

An hour and 40 minutes into the journey, we cross a chattering lattice bridge and sweep down to join the main electrified line leading to Poznań and on from there to Warsaw. We gallop along with electric trains at 100 km/h, observing colour-light signals gleaming green as far as I can see, and draw in to the busy, graffiti-smothered city station. Quietly pleased, I stop the train bang on time. That final spirited sprint along the main line made up for the two minutes I'd lost somewhere along the way.

Martin pokes around with the fire as Andrzej yells '*Piwo! Wódka!*' hinting at the evening celebration that lies ahead in the engineman's bar at Wolsztyn. Leaning from the cab again, I watch passengers streaming off the train and down the subway stairs. Not one casts a glance at the steam locomotive that has brought them to work, and why should they? This is a regular scheduled service. It might be the only service like it in Europe, but on this bitingly cold Thursday morning it's for getting to and from work, not for ogling.

*

The Wolsztyn Experience soldiers on, although foreign visitors may soon be unable to ride the footplates of main-line steam locomotive in Poland. To date, these have included jumbo jet pilots, bankers, undertakers, civil servants, photographers and journalists. The daily commuter trains between Wolsztyn and Poznań have not been steam-hauled for some years. Steam has been for weekends only. Steam, however, was in charge as late as 2018 on certain weekday runs to Leszno, 60 kilometres from Wolsztyn. Ol49-69, the locomotive I fired and drove, was still at work in 2019 and is expected to run special trains into the future. In 2018, she ran a 2,500-kilometre tour from Wolsztyn to Warsaw, Olsztyn and the Russian border and back. I had first seen her in steam when I came this way in 1997 with my friend and former *Independent* colleague Simon Calder. After an interesting trip that saw us on a pre-dawn five-hour bus ride from Gdańsk to Kętrzyn, a 90-minute walk from there to explore Hitler's East Prussian headquarters, *Wolfsschanze*, in the Masurian Forest, a 7½-mile trek in torrential rain from there to the Baroque Jesuit monastery of Święta Lipka, and then a long train ride to Wolsztyn, we slept in the engine shed before boarding the 0416 to

Poznań. When I tried to open a window, all the better to hear the fast-pounding exhaust of the 2-6-2 at the front of the train, I was berated in no uncertain terms by well-dressed ladies with smart hairdos. They were quite right, of course. The cold, the soot, the noise.

There were no such concerns on the footplate of Ol49-69 six years later. I remember my first footplate run on the 0416. My PKP driver, Andrzej, disappeared from view as I accelerated our train into the freezing dark, and there, all of a sudden, he was waving to me from behind the smokebox door. Poles, eh? Polish RAF pilots flying from Northolt during the Second World War were just as crazy, and very successful, too. Their spirit clearly lives on.

I wrote the story of my 2003 trip for the *Guardian* newspaper, whose travel editor, Andy Pietrasik, happens to be an English-born Pole. We went to drink vodka and eat at a fashionable Polish restaurant. I remember, despite the vodka, telling Andy that I wasn't sure whether I'd be happier working as an engine driver in Wolsztyn than as a journalist in London. He replied, 'You're lucky, you've been both.'

TWENTY

London to Helsinki via Travemünde: Jeep Cherokee and MV *Finnpartner*

15th–19th June 2005

Pedro was a first-class dog. Gracious, well mannered, handsome in an English Baroque manner and rarely less than very smart indeed in his year-round hunting outfit, he was a dog one could take anywhere. A well-travelled, long-legged bulldog, born on the Lancashire coast, he was known by a number of aliases. When young he might be the dashing El Pedro, when older the distinguished Don Pedro. Which immigration official studying his photograph ever knew that the imposing English gentleman they saw before them was also none other than Mr Beezer, Mr Okefenokee and Mr G. P. Gruntpig?

Away from the Lancashire litter, Pedro's first home was a flat in Holland Park where, from a wrought-iron balcony, he would watch the Queen on her way to Windsor Castle, her progress announced by police motorbike outriders blowing whistles as they approached junctions and traffic lights. I liked to think she saw him. During the week his daily walk was to studios in Westbourne Park. An averagely healthy human could manage this in 25 minutes. For Pedro, if he deigned to walk, this was an hour's stroll with a stop at the florist's on the way for a big stick or perhaps an exotic stem to carry, followed by a second break for a breakfast croissant. And not any croissant. Not the frozen-to-microwave type proffered by chain cafés, but a proper freshly baked French croissant. He turned his nose up at the former type, leaving them to hounds, mongrels, pigeons and terriers. His neat little tail had something of the look of a croissant about it, or was it a cinnamon roll? He liked cinnamon rolls, too, as he was to discover on a summer adventure to Finland.

If the weather was not to his liking, Pedro would turn right out of the house and wait for a taxi on the corner of the street. I'm sure he raised his paw one wet morning to hail a 'black fast'. Most cabbies were only too grateful for the custom because: (a) they loved the idea of bulldogs and Pedro was, by any standards, an exceptionally fine-looking member of his breed; and (b) their status among their own peer group could only be raised by driving such a distinguished canine gent around town. 'You'll never guess who I had in the back this morning...'

Pedro dined out frequently. He was a favourite guest of the Ladbroke Arms, a gregarious London pub that served him a steak on his birthdays. On weekends he ate his croissant at 202 Westbourne Grove, a fashionable café selling chic clothes and pretty gewgaws, where Stefano the waiter – all in white – was on hand to greet him and to ensure Pedro received nothing less than silver service.

He enjoyed constitutionals in Richmond Park, Holland Park and Regent's Park, where, one day and a stick's throw from Cumberland Terrace, he fell head over paws in love with Tiggy, a sportif boxer in an exotic short stripey coat. He took the occasional mud bath, coming home from Holland Park one Sunday afternoon as if impersonating a Victorian coal heaver. He enjoyed pruning trees. One Saturday morning he tackled the low-lying branch of a plane in Kensington Gardens. With some effort he severed a 6-foot-long section. Head and compact tail held high, he carried this proudly home.

He loved to watch birds, was a member of the Kennel Club, and when he moved from town to country he proved expert in the flattening, compacting and indeed wholesale destruction of cardboard boxes and packing cases. His party piece, however, was to jump up and get a firm hold with his jaws of a rope hanging from an oak tree in a hilly wood about a mile from his new home. He would set himself in motion like a spinning top, faster and ever faster. It was a sight to see. On trips to London he stayed at Miller's Residence, Westbourne Grove, where he was very much at home in Martin and Iona Miller's playfully Victorian B&B, its 40-foot breakfast and drawing room chock-a-block with antiques, books, brocades, pictures and amusing bric-a-brac. In the same spirit, rooms were named after English romantic poets.

And yet, for all his poetic soul, skills and exceptional intelligence, the world was closing in on dogs like Pedro, just as it was on hotels like Miller's Residence. Nickel by dime, a dog's freedom to dine and to travel was being taken away. Few twenty-first-century dogs have been able to see the world in the way Tintin's Snowy did. Whenever Tintin, a journalist who very rarely wrote, rushed to exotic parts of the world to solve a crime – with or without the questionable help of detectives

JONATHAN GLANCEY

Thomson and Thompson – Snowy would be at his side. To be precise, Snowy took seats and berths on international trains, ocean liners, airliners and in any number of Hergé's accurately depicted cars.

To travel as the fictional Snowy and Tintin did became increasingly tricky in the non-fiction world of the early 2000s. Even on trips to France, where dogs were welcome in many and perhaps most restaurants and hotels, things were changing. For some undisclosed reason they were banned from Eurostar trains, meaning dogs were forced to take to the roads, while ferries would accept them only if they were locked up in cars or claustrophobic cells somewhere below their Plimsoll lines.

Even so, we managed a long summer drive together from London to a seaside village near Port-Vendres using *routes nationales*, not least because these were often shady and the Jeep's air con, rarely used, decided to pack up before Chartres. We stopped for the night at a gloriously romantic château to the east of Poitiers. The owners were away. There were no other guests. We were put up in a coach house renovated in the 1920s, where we had an enormous room and an almost equally big bathroom with open windows and view of the château's turrets and gables.

Asked if I'd like to eat, I explained that Pedro and I would eat together. Outside, of course, they said. A table was prepared. Pressed and darned linen showing traces of just one or two antique wine stains that had never quite come out in the wash. Worn and polished early-nineteenth-century silver. A 1930s decanter, wine and water glasses perhaps twenty years its senior, and mid-nineteenth-century crockery adorned with

364

summery patterns, their glazes showing signs of enjoyable use in decades gone by.

Dinner itself was fetched from the château kitchen on a trolley with wobbly wheels. And when – *'Le voilà!'* – the venerable cloches were raised in theatrical manner, there was a big dish of succulent ham and scrambled eggs for Pedro. How did they know that this was one of his favourite treats? The staff were clearly enjoying themselves, playing while the family was away, and yet I still wonder if I would have been treated quite so regally if Pedro had not been with me. Pedro said thank you for his meal and fell fast asleep. This was France at its best, comfortable in its skin, formal and informal at one and the same time – a way of being that few people around the world seem to understand today.

So when I read this note on a Finnish website – 'All Finnlines ferries allow pets on board' – I was quietly excited. Could we enjoy a proper Tintin-esque journey across Europe all the way to the Finnish lakes without Pedro being humiliated by the witlessness of bureaucrats, the intolerance of 'you can't bring that dog here' jobsworths, and assorted killjoys and 'haters'? On board, good. But where on board? A phone call set my mind at rest. If Mr Pedro wished to sail to Finland from Germany, he would stay with humans in a proper cabin and with access to a dog deck commanding bracing views of the Baltic and with the necessary offices. This was encouraging news.

The ship sailed from Travemünde, north of Lübeck, 670 miles from Holland Park. To get there, Pedro was chauffeured in my old Jeep Cherokee, looking out of the window for much of the way, from early-morning London via the Eurotunnel train to Calais, and up the coast to Dunkirk – where we explored some of the German concrete gun emplacements built by the Todt Organization that appear to have set the look for British Brutalist architecture of the 1960s and '70s – before crossing the Belgian border and stopping for lunch at De Panne.

Here, the wholly unpretentious 5 Voor Twaalf brasserie served excellent food to humans and charming canines alike. Pedro ate a delicious steak, as the patron, chef and waiters looked on adoringly. He washed down his meal with a polite sip of local water. Pedro tended to drink once a day, a large bowl at six in the evening. But he was on holiday here, and not unwilling to bend a rule. He was never impolite.

From De Panne we followed the frequent coastal trams to stop briefly at De Normandie, the hotel and restaurant built in 1936 by Jean Van Den Burgh in homage to the magnificent new French transatlantic ocean liner SS *Normandie*, which was launched the previous year. Designed by the architects Laurent and Willy Bruggeman, De Normandie was undergoing restoration at the time of our visit. It made me think of what fun it would have been to have strolled the decks of the sublime SS *Normandie* with my bulldog, whose natural gait was always like that of a rolling sailor.

At Knokke-Heist, Pedro did something he had never done before. Out of the car, he bolted across the beach to the sea. He couldn't swim, but loved to paddle. He was also fond of rock-pooling and exploring sea caves. On the drive along the Flanders coast he had smelled sea air. So off he went pell-mell to meet the North Sea as soon as the invitation was made. I had never seen him move so quickly.

Pedro liked Knokke-Heist, with its haute-bourgeois streets smelling of good food and – after a comfortable night in the Art Nouveau Hotel Villa Verdi – the promise of a perfectly shaped and baked croissant. After breakfast, supposedly fast roads around Antwerp were anything but. Pedro dozed off as the Jeep rolled slowly east, until the motorway opened up across the Dutch border. Loping towards the Rhine and its industrial cities, we remembered to exit the autobahn before it became busy. We cantered north-east through Geldern, Alpen, Wesel, Schermdeck, Haltern am See and Dülmen to the hem of Münster.

A thunderstorm was rolling in from the south, bringing purple electric skies over Schloss Wilkinghege, a handsome *Wasserschloss* – it was surrounded by a moat – built in 1719 by the architect Gottfried Laurenz Pictorius to replace an earlier house. The *schloss* suited Pedro to a B. B, that is, for Baroque – as he was. We ate outside in chatty company, as the storm circled us yet gallantly held back rain. This was a friendly place, the owners keen on dogs and Pedro much admired. The schloss offered rooms, gained from the top of a very grand staircase, filled with antiques, Pedro's like an art gallery. He was happy to share it. In the morning, a breakfast fit for a kaiser was on generous display in a vaulted and whitewashed undercroft.

As peacocks made that piercing call no one seems able to find the exact word for, Pedro motored through the gates of the *schloss* and up fast, easy roads skirting Osnabrück, Bremen and Hamburg before Lübeck heaved into surprisingly medieval view. It was time for a walk.

The RAF hit Hamburg very hard indeed during the Second World War, but although it bombed Lübeck, too, the old city was sufficiently intact to get a feel of what it might have been like before the Second World War. Its veteran brick buildings are lovely things, functional yet poetic – and, here and there, even playful. Travemünde proved to be well preserved, too, although the one unmissable building here is the Maritim, a skyscraper hotel opened in 1972. I wondered how far guests could see from its 35th-storey restaurant.

Along Skandinavienkai, our green and white ship, MV *Finnpartner*, sat waiting for Pedro's arrival. One of four 35,534-ton Hansa class roll-on, roll-off ferries built in 1994–5 by Stocznia Gdynia at Gdansk, she carried 600 cars, 200 lorries and coaches, and 270 passengers in 182 cabins on two decks. I had read this when I booked our tickets. To me, at least, *Finnpartner*'s statistics were interesting. Where, for example, Viking Line ferries like *Mariella*, plying between Stockholm and Helsinki today, have room for 2,500 passengers, *Finnpartner* carried ten times fewer. It felt spacious and relaxed.

The crew was easy-going, if efficient. *Finnpartner* felt a happy ship, especially perhaps because it had nothing to prove. Here was a workaday ferry, a seagoing 'pantechnicon', free of frills and matter-of-fact. No disco. No floorshow. No entertainment except for the sight of the sea, decent food, a TV if you had to and drinks from the bar. Her pace was like Pedro's, a steady amble, with big Sulzer diesels snoring somewhere deep below deck. She took two nights to cross the Baltic. Pedro sat out whenever he could, and watched the waves and the coastlines of Denmark, Sweden, Poland, Lithuania, Latvia and Estonia slide slowly by.

A part of the joy of living with dogs comes from wanting to share their evident ability to live life in the present, as it comes. Of course they have memories, and yet these are rarely restraints on their ability to seize the day and enjoy the moment. I wondered what Pedro was thinking as *Finnpartner* slipped anchor at Travemünde and steamed – or, more accurately, dieselled – her way into a becalmed Baltic. For me, the Baltic, so placid today, was a sea of ghosts.

I looked across to Neustadt and could almost see and hear RAF Typhoons diving towards the docks there, unleashing rockets and cannons against the former transatlantic ocean liners SS *Deutschland* and SS *Cap Arcona*, the freighter *Thielbek* and a smaller vessel. This attack happened on 3rd May 1945. Unbeknown to the British, *Deutschland* was being converted into a hospital ship, although she bore no sign of this, while *Cap Arcona* and *Thielbek* were jam-packed between them with some 7,500 concentration camp inmates. Representing 30 nationalities, these prisoners were – or so the Germans claimed – about to be shipped to Sweden. According to Graf von Bassewitz-Behr, commander of the Hamburg Gestapo, the SS had other plans. The ships were to be scuttled so no Jew, Gypsy, political suspect or Soviet soldier – sealed without food or water in their holds – would find freedom on the other side of the Baltic.

The SS weren't needed. Unwittingly, the RAF did the Nazis' job for them. Typhoon pilots even shot up survivors in the water with 20mm cannons, assuming them to be SS. Those who made it to shore from the wrecks of the *Thielbek*, *Cap Arcona* and *Deutschland* were machine-gunned or bludgeoned to death by the Germans. Bodies continued to wash up on these shores for several years.

My mind drifted towards an earlier SS *Deutschland*, and its floundering in a snowstorm on the Kentish Knock on a passage from nearby Bremerhaven to New York in December 1875, inspiring a magnificent poem that freed the imagination of Gerard Manley Hopkins.

It was time to eat. Sadly, dogs were barred from the dining room, although I think Pedro would have disapproved of the studious rush by humans to the buffet. Mostly Finns and Germans, passengers were prompt to the second for meals. Unlike their British counterparts on board continental ferries, however, they neither pushed nor piled their plates mountain-high with as much food as they could possibly carry, and surely more than they could possibly eat, as if this were 1945 and ration books ruled the larder and dinner table at home.

Pedro relished the next day and night at sea. We sailed into Helsinki exactly on time, where an enormous cruise ship was being built in a dock close to the city centre, as if city and sea were one and the same enterprise. Saluted by a charmed purser, Pedro the confident sea dog rolled his way below decks. Off we drove along half-deserted breakfast streets, heading north to summer lakes, boats, sauna, salmon and forests. But, as all dog stories must surely end, that is another tale.

*

Pedro was eight and a half when he died. His heart gave way. He collapsed in front of the Duchy of Cornwall offices on St Mary's, on a walk back to the Star Castle Hotel. I fell to my knees and kissed him on his big head. He was gone in an instant.

He had enjoyed his trip to the Scilly Isles. While his new companions, a pair of Basset Hound ladies, had been seasick on board RMV *Scillonian III* – a flat-bottomed mail boat built in Appledore in 1977 – as she rolled at 15 knots through a Jolly Rogered sea from Penzance, before negotiating the azure shallows of the Cornish archipelago, Pedro sat on deck in a manner that lived up to the meaning of his name: Rock. He was spellbound on boat rides between St Mary's, St Agnes and St Martin's. He toyed with seaweed and fetched big tubers found on beaches. He ate his meals as neatly as ever. He did two things, though, that made me wonder about him. He sat very close to me on shores and beaches – normally he preferred some space of his own – and he stared into distances, as if there were some land over the horizon wanting his attention.

He is buried – John the gardener did most of the digging – wrapped in a favourite tartan blanket in the gardens of Star Castle Hotel. The owners could not have been kinder. Bernard Johnson carved a Cornish slate to place over his grave. It reads 'Don Pedro'. Perhaps a child coming this way might still ask, 'Who was Don Pedro?' To which the answer is an English legend and the greatest of sea dogs.

RMV *Scillonian III* still plies to and from Penzance and St Mary's between spring and autumn. MV *Finnpartner,* refitted in Gdańsk in 2007 when she was repainted blue and white, works the Malmö to Helsinki route. Since 2012, the Travemünde service has been operated by one of four 45,923-ton Star class cruise-ferries, built by Fincantieri in Ancona on the Adriatic coast. These carry up to 554 passengers and make the trip in 27 hours, with just the one night on board. They offer live music and shows. I think the following statement, of fact and intent, says all that needs to be said concerning the new style of crossing the Baltic from Germany to Finland: 'The ship has a total of 4 suites. Passenger suite deals are inclusive of dining packages, 1 bottle of sparkling wine, 1 box of chocolate-covered marshmallows, minibar beverages, 1 drink coupon pp [per person], skincare products.' Star class ferries, however, do still accept dogs in certain cabins.

Miller's Residence has long gone, and in December 2013 the unforgettable Martin Miller was gone, too. As fast-breeding humans expand their territory – slashing and burning forests; sending hordes of people on 'environmentally friendly' cruises to polar regions; building wilfully bad housing at a feverish rate while disseminating hatred, greed and intolerance – animals are finding it hard to maintain a claw-hold on their world. My rock and fount of wisdom, Pedro, may have known this, but he was too well mannered to tell. I miss him.

Glossary

A-pillars: metal pillars holding a car windscreen in place.

articulated coaches: carriages sharing bogies to reduce weight.

Atlantic: name for locomotives with 4-4-2 wheel arrangement derived from early use of the type by the Atlantic Coast Line Railroad and the Philadelphia and Reading Railway which ran 4-4-2s to and from Atlantic City, New Jersey.

Bagutta: Milanese trattoria opened in 1927 and a meeting place for generations of artists, journalists, lawyers, playwrights, architects and designers, its walls graced with hundreds of signed works of art of those who ate here. Closed in 2016.

Baltic: European name for locomotives with 4-6-4 wheel arrangement derived from Nord railway 4-6-4s of 1911 designed to work Paris to St Petersburg expresses – from the Seine to the Baltic.

Beaux Arts: a style of French neo-classical architecture taught at the École des Beaux-Arts, Paris from the 1830s until the First World War and popular with US architects who studied at the school.

Bofinger: much-loved Parisian brasserie close to the Place de la Bastille, first opened in 1864 by the Alsatian refugee Frédéric Bofinger.

bogies: known as trucks in the US, bogies are the pivoting assemblies underneath railway vehicles supporting axles, bearings and wheels.

booster engine: auxiliary two-cylinder engine mounted under the cab of large steam locomotives connected to trailing truck axles or the lead truck of tenders. Having helped to get heavy trains on the move, the booster cut out at speeds of between 20 and 35mph.

brake third/brake first: railway carriage incorporating guard's or brake compartment, also used for carrying luggage, parcels, animals and bicycles.

Brooks's: gentleman's club, St James's Street, London, founded in 1764 by members of the Whig aristocracy.

Brunswick green: a deep-green paint colour using copper compounds developed in England from the mid eighteenth century and used extensively by the Great Western Railway and British Railways. The Pennsylvania Railroad version of the colour appeared more black than green.

burra **peg**: double whisky, from *burra* (Hindi for big) and *peg* (English for drink).

catenary: overhead wires and supporting lineside structures of electric railways.

Checker cab: stylish American taxicabs operated most notably in New York and Chicago and manufactured in Kalamazoo, Michigan, in the 1930s by companies owned by Russian-born Chicagoan Morris Markin. Checker cabs, last made in 1982, were a familiar sight in US city streets until the 1990s.

chup suey: alternative period spelling for chop suey, a hugely popular Chinese dish of meat, eggs and vegetables bound in a starch-thickened sauce. Of unknown origin, some say it was invented by Chinese Americans working on the construction of the transcontinental railroad, completed in 1859.

Claud Butler: highly successful London-based bicycle manufacturer, at its peak in the 1930s.

compound: system using steam twice in high and then low pressures, increasing the work done by expanded steam. Compound locomotives were often highly efficient. Steam ships employed triple and even quadruple expansion compound engines, optimizing the use of steam for a given amount of fuel.

congested districts (Donegal): districts designated in 1891 by Act of Parliament along the Atlantic coast in which too many people were observed to be scratching a living from unyielding soil, bogs and mountainous territory.

coupé: car with two doors and sloping fixed roof, or compartment in a railway carriage without rear-facing seats.

Crittall window: steel-framed windows synonymous with 1930s British architecture, made from 1889 by the Crittall Manufacturing Company of Witham, Essex.

Curragh, The: premier Irish racecourse in County Kildare.

cylinder cocks: these blow condensation at pressure from a steam locomotive's cylinders before it moves.

Dabai/Dubai: former pearl diving village on south-east coast of the Persian Gulf. Deeply depressed in the 1930s. Radically transformed by discovery of oil in 1966.

de Havilland Propellers: a subsidiary of the de Havilland Aircraft Company founded in 1935 to manufacture variable pitch propellers. In later years, it specialized in missiles.

duralumin: a hard, light alloy of aluminium with copper and other elements developed from 1903 by the German metallurgist Alfred Wilm at Dürener Metallwerke AG. Widely used in German, British and American airships as well as fixed-wing aircraft.

ETR: *Elettro Treno Rapido*; a sequence of high-speed electric trains developed from 1936 for the Italian State Railways. This included *Il Settebello*.

footplate: cab of steam locomotive.

Gill Sans: sans-serif typeface of 1928, closely related to Johnston, designed by Eric Gill for Monotype. Gill had assisted Edward Johnston. Gill Sans was adopted by the London and North Eastern Railway and, from 1948, by the state-owned British Railways.

gondola: airship cabin mounted below the fuselage.

griddle car: café-bar-style carriage serving simple hot meals of the egg, bacon, sausage variety, notably on British Railways' main-line services of the 1950s and 60s where the provision of a full restaurant car service was deemed unjustified.

Hudson: American name for locomotives with 4-6-4 wheel arrangement. The first US 4-6-4s were built in 1927 for the New York Central Railroad and ran along the Hudson Valley.

indicated horsepower: power developed in the cylinders of locomotives.

Johnston script: hugely influential, elegant and characterful modern sans-serif display type commissioned from the Arts & Crafts calligrapher Edward Johnston by Frank Pick of the (London) Underground Electric Railways in 1913. Based on Roman lettering on Trajan's Column, it became the official script of the London Passenger Transport Board in 1933.

Kulak: originally prosperous Russian peasants or smallholding farmers. Lenin and Stalin labelled any peasant with a few acres and a few cows a 'Kulak', calling them 'bloodsuckers, vampires, plunderers of the people and profiteers who fatten on famine'. In collectivizing farms for the greater glory of Soviet Communism, the Kulaks were to be 'liquidated'. More than a million were executed. Without them, many more peasants starved to death.

landaulette: car body style derived from horse-drawn carriages with the driver separated from passengers by a division (usually a glass screen) and passenger cabin covered by a convertible top.

Louis Who-ey: uncertain historical French styling.

Mallet: type of locomotive with two sets of engines mounted on bogie frames below a single boiler. Invented by the Swiss engineer, Anatole Mallet in 1884. Often of great length and power, they were designed to negotiate tight bends and were ideal for mountainous routes.

nacelle: streamlined casing housing an aircraft or airship engine.

Nuremberg Laws: Nazi race laws of September 1935 depriving German Jews of their rights as citizens.

open third: third-class carriage with central gangway and without compartments.

overdrive: a secondary gearbox, normally operated by a switch, allowing speed at lower engine revs beyond or 'over' direct drive (usually fourth gear in cars of the 1950s and 60s), and spelling relaxed high-speed touring and lowered fuel consumption. Replaced by fifth gear.

Pacific: name for locomotives with 4-6-2 wheel arrangement. In 1901, a batch of Q class 4-6-2 locomotives built by Baldwin Locomotive Works, Philadelphia, and the first of their kind, were shipped to New Zealand across the Pacific. The name stuck.

Piano, Renzo: globally acclaimed Genovese architect (b. 1937) who made his name co-designing the Pompidou Centre, Paris, with Richard Rogers.

propylaeum: monumental ancient Greek gateway.

quarter lights: small pivoting triangular windows in the front and, sometimes, also in the back windows of classic saloon cars.

reverser/cut-off: the reverser, operated through a screw gear or ratchet lever on the footplate, allows steam locomotive drivers to cut-off steam from entering cylinders at particular percentages. When starting, the driver will work the locomotive at a high percentage cut-off to maximize the flow of steam in the cylinders, reducing this as the locomotive gets into its stride.

RKO: one of the big five studios of Hollywood's 'Golden Age'.

Rogano: opened in 1935, its interior based on that of the RMS *Queen Mary*, this carefully preserved Glaswegian restaurant, remains an Art Deco and culinary delight.

Rührei mit Spargelspitzen: asparagus with scrambled eggs.

St Mary Axe: street in the City of London once dominated by the Baltic Exchange of 1903. Badly damaged by an IRA bomb in 1992, which killed three people and wounded 91, the site of the once opulent Edwardian building is occupied today by 30 St Mary Axe, or the 'Gherkin' (2004), a 591-ft office tower designed by Foster and Partners in what appears to be the guise of a vertically mounted airship.

Scullin discs: lighter and stronger than conventional spoked wheels, these disc wheels manufactured by the Scullin Steel Company of St Louis, Missouri, looked just the ticket for resolutely modern-looking streamlined locomotives.

semi-fast: limited-stop fast main-line passenger train serving more intermediate stations than an express.

shaft horsepower: power delivered to a propeller or turbine shaft, a measurement common to ships and turbo-prop aircraft.

shooting brake: estate car.

sky bully: insensitive and pushy on-board airline employee who despises mere passengers and treats them accordingly.

Spartacist: member of Spartacist League, a Marxist German revolutionary movement founded during the First World War by Karl Liebknecht and Rosa Luxemburg. Renamed the Communist Party of Germany and crushed during Spartacist Revolt of 1919.

Speed Graphic: classic large-format press camera made, until 1973, by Graflex of Rochester, New York. Although not speedy to use, it boasted a shutter speed of 1/1000 sec, which is how it justified its name.

steam turbo-electric: electric power generated by steam turbines for ships and locomotives.

stupa: hemispherical mound-like structure usually containing a sacred Buddhist relic.

tuppenny: something buyable for two pre-decimal British pennies.

Upperby: locomotive depot, Carlisle, closed 1968.

valve gear: mechanism that operates the inlet and exhaust valves of a steam locomotive to admit steam into the cylinder and allow exhaust steam to escape.

Vestibule First Diner: first-class dining car with central gangway and without compartments.

Walschaerts valve gear: form of steam locomotive valve gear patented by Belgian engineer Egide Walschaerts in 1844. Popular, reliable and easy to maintain, it was adopted worldwide (see **valve gear**).

Acknowledgements

The author would like to thank the following for their kind support and help with historical, technical and geographic detail: Laurie Akehurst, Mark Allatt, Roger Bell, Tim Benton, Tim Brittain-Catlin, George Carpenter, Stuart Freedman (http://www.stuartfreedman.com), David Gladstone, Oliver Green, Dan Grossman, Michael Harrison, Harry Jack, Ian Jack, Howard Jones, Josephine Kelly (Cashelnagore Station, Donegal https://cashelnagore-railway-station.business.site/), Angus MacKinnon, Chris Nettleton, Matthias Sauerbruch, Bill Simpson, Edward Talbot, Caroline Warhurst (London Transport Museum). He would also like to thank James Nightingale and James Pulford of Atlantic Books, his copy editor Gemma Wain, Stephen Millership for the design of the dust jacket and Sarah Chalfant, his special agent.

Illustration Credits

New York Central System's *20th Century Limited, c.* 1938 *(Ivan Dmitri/ Michael Ochs Archives/Getty Images)*

Passengers in the observation car of New York Central System's *20th Century Limited, c.* 1938 *(Ivan Dmitri/Michael Ochs Archives/Getty Images)*

Section two

Poster depicting a *Hiawatha* train, 1939

London Transport RT3781 back at work on Route 11, November 2014 *(Au Morandarte/WikiCommons)*

Bristol 405 at the 1955 Paris Motor Show *(ullstein bild via Getty Images)*

A Bristol Superfreighter at the new Ferryfield Airport, Lydd, Kent, 1955 *(Peter Rogers/BIPs/Getty Images)*

Fiat Littorina railcar, Eritrea *(Courtesy of Daniel Simon)*

Steam train at Massawa docks, Eritrea *(Courtesy of Daniel Simon)*

A Midland Red CM5T at Victoria Coach Station, November 1959 *(Keystone Press/Alamy Stock Photo)*

'Il Settebello' at Milan Centrale, 1950s *(Allan Cash Picture Library/ Alamy Stock Photo)*

Jaguar Mk 2 3.8 *(Courtesy of the author)*

Interior of the 1964 Jaguar Mk 2 3.8 *(National Motor Museum/ Heritage Images/Getty Images)*

A Chinese QJ class 2-10-2 accelerates away from Daban, March 2001 *(Courtesy of John West)*

A QJ train on the Jinpeng Pass, February 2005 *(Courtesy of John West)*

A Chevrolet Suburban heads off road in Iraq *(Mohammed al Dulaimy/ MCT/MCT via Getty Images)*

A Polish State Railways Ol class 2-6-2 near Wolsztyn, Poland *(Glyn Fletcher/Alamy Stock Photo)*

Pedro the sea dog *(Courtesy of the author)*

Index

NYC Niagara class locomotives, 192–3
Nystrom, Karl, 199

O'Donnell, Declan, 95–6, 101
O'Donnell's Hotel, Burtonport, 34
O'Leary, Michael, 3–4
O'Rorke, Brian, 159
Old Black Lion, Hay-on-Wye, 287,
    294–5
Operation Chastise, 294
Oriental Hotel, Bangkok, 172, 176
Orion, RMS, 159
Ottaway, Eric, 230–32, 261
Owain Glyndwr (locomotive), 292, 301
Owencarrow Viaduct, 32, 34
Oxford, 54, 55

P2 Steam Locomotive Company, 148
P&O, 36
Pacific locomotives, 12–13, 111, 114,
    125, 128, 191, 196, 202, 276, 343
  Britannia Pacifics, 225, 245
  Mallard, 93, 138–9, 143, 147–8, 202
Pagano, Giuseppe, 272, 281
Pan American Airways 152, 155
Paris, France, 220–22
  Metro, 221, 222
Pelley, William Dudley, 201
Pennsylvania Railroad, 182, 191–2
Petacci, Claretta, 280
Pevsner, Nikolaus, 228
Piacentini, Marcello, 281
Piano, Renzo, 278, 281, 283
Piccadilly Circus station, London, 245
Pick, Frank, 58, 99, 228–31, 236, 238,
    240–42, 245
Pioneer Zephyr (train), 189
PKP class Ol49 (locomotive), 355–8, 360
Poelzig, Hans, 65
Poland, 353–60
Polglase, Van Nest, 43
Polskie Koleje Państwowe (PKP), 354
Pomezia, Italy, 282, 283
Ponti, Gio, 268, 275
Poore, Dennis, 214
Powell, Griffith 'Taffy', 216
Poznań, Poland, 353–54, 358–9
Prince of Wales (locomotive), 148
Princess Coronation Class Pacifics, 114,
    128, 202

Princess Royal Class Pacifics, 113–14,
    128, 130, 135
Princess Alexandra (locomotive), 121
Princess Alice (locomotive), 121
Princess Elizabeth (locomotive), 113–14
Princess Margaret (ferry), 14–15, 36
Pullman Car Co., Illinois, 41

QJ Class 2-10-2 locomotives, 319,
    322–31
Quainton Road, Buckinghamshire,
    50–51, 58, 59
Quant, Mary, 237, 243
Queen Elizabeth (locomotive), 121
Queen Mary (locomotive), 120–25
Queen Mary, RMS, 97, 98, 104–5, 108
Quicksilver (locomotive), 135–6, 142–5

Raedwald of East Anglia (locomotive), 7
Raffles Hotel, Singapore, 174, 176
railmotors, 47–8
Rails to the Rising Sun (Small), 256
Railway Magazine, The, 112, 119
Rangoon, Myanmar, 172
Raphoe (locomotive), 22–4, 35
Recife, Brazil, 86–7, 90
Red Arrow express train, 142
Reith, John, 1st Baron Reith, 237–8
Restaurante Primavera, Massawa, 249,
    258
Reynolds, Quentin, 218
Rhein-Main airfield, 65, 67
von Ribbentrop, Joachim, 116, 138, 148
Richard, Cliff, 244
Richards, James Maude, 129
Richmond, Vincent Crane, 212–13
Ricketts, Charles Spencer, 56
Riddles, Robert 'Robin', 305–6
Rio de Janeiro, Brazil, 66, 72, 74–5, 79,
    88, 94
Ritter, Karl, 72, 75, 83, 91
Riverside bus garage, Hammersmith,
    240, 243
Robert Stephenson and Hawthorns Ltd,
    343
Robeson, Paul, 140–41
Robinson, John, 58
Rogers, Hugh, 305
Rome, Italy, 280–81
Rosapenna Hotel, Co. Donegal, 20, 34

Rothschild family, 52, 54, 56, 65
Routemasters, *see* London Transport:
   RM buses
Royal Anglian Regiment (locomotive), 7
Royal Highlander (train), 303, 312–13,
   315
Royal Scot locomotives, 12–13
Royal Ulster Riflemen (locomotive),
   12–13
Rudyard Kipling (locomotive), 225
Rumsfeld, Donald, 335
Russia, 318–19
Ryanair, 3

de Saint-Exupéry, Antoine, 79
St Mary the Blessed Virgin, Sompting,
   214
St Paul, Minnesota, 196, 202–203
St Paul's Cathedral, London, 233, 244
samba, 73, 82, 91
Sandys, Duncan, 116, 130
Sänger, Dr Eugen, 81, 92–3
Santa Maria Novella station, Florence,
   278
Santos-Dumont, Alberto, 88–9
Sarah Siddons (locomotive), 60
Schleger, Hans, 240
Schloss Wilkinghege, Germany, 367
Scillonian III, RMV, 371
Scotland, 127, 306–9, 311–13
Scott, C. W. A., 65–6
Seaman, Richard, 145, 148, 165
Searle, Frank, 231
Sempill, Lord, *see* Forbes-Sempill,
   William, 19th Lord Sempill
'September 1913' (Yeats), 29–30
Serco, 316
Settebello (train), 267–83
Settrington, Freddie, *see* Gordon-
   Lennox, Frederick, 9th Duke of
   Richmond
Shanahan, Michael, 18
Shap Fell, Cumbria, 9, 112, 124, 129
Sheeler, Charles, 189
Shelley, Percy Bysshe, 289–90
Shinkansen bullet train, 256, 278
Shire, Loftus Wyndham, 261
Shoreham Airport, 214
Short Brothers Seaplane Works,
   Rochester, 159–61, 177

Short Empire 42C class flying boats,
   157–9, 171, 174–5
Short Sunderland flying boat, 170–71,
   175
Silbervogel rocket plane, 92
Silver City Airways, 216, 223
Silver Fox (locomotive), 147
Silver Jubilee (train), 135, 146
Silver Link (locomotive), 135
Sinclair, Donald McIntyre, 261
Singapore, 151–4, 174, 175
Sir John Betjeman (locomotive), 6
Sir Nigel Gresley (locomotive), 147
Small, Charles R., 6, 247–8, 256
Smith, Andreas Whittam, 304
Soane, Sir John, 53, 54, 60
South Western Hotel, Southampton,
   155, 176
Southampton Terminus station, 155
Southern Railway (SR), 152–3, 213
Soviet Union, 141–2, 239
Spanish Civil War (1936–39), 91
Sparrow Hawk (locomotive), 147
'Speedliners', 199
Speer, Albert, 73, 93, 118
Spitfire (aircraft), 115, 122, 139
Stacchini, Ulisse, 268
Stamp, Sir Josiah, 116, 128
Stanier, Sir William, 112–13, 115, 259
Stanier Class 8F, 343, 350
Stansby, J. B., 118
Stephenson, Robert, 139, 262
Stokenchurch Gap, 285, 289, 301
Strabane, Northern Ireland, 22–3
Stranraer, Scotland, 12, 13, 15, 36
Supermarine, 27, 115, 122, 157, 159
   S.6B (seaplane), 27
Symphony of the Seas, MS, 108–9
Szlumper, James Weeks, 293

Talisman express train, 146–7
Tatler magazine, 298
Taurus Express (train), 343
Termini station, Rome, 279–80
Thielbek (freighter), 369
Thomas, Edward, 213
Tiberias, Lake, 165–6, 176
Titanic, RMS, 155
Togo, Heihachiro, 156
Tone, Wolfe, 29–30

THE JOURNEY MATTERS